From Early Warning Systems to Asset Managers' Behavior: Evidence for Mature and Emerging Markets

STUDIEN ZU INTERNATIONALEN WIRTSCHAFTSBEZIEHUNGEN

Herausgegeben von Prof. Dr. Michael Frenkel

Band 12

PETER LANG

Frankfurt am Main · Berlin · Bern · Bruxelles · New York · Oxford · Wien

Daniela Beckmann

From Early Warning Systems to Asset Managers' Behavior: Evidence for Mature and Emerging Markets

PETER LANG
Internationaler Verlag der Wissenschaften

Bibliographic Information published by the Deutsche Nationalbibliothek
The Deutsche Nationalbibliothek lists this publication in the Deutsche Nationalbibliografie; detailed bibliographic data is available in the internet at <http://www.d-nb.de>.

Zugl.: Hannover, Univ., Diss., 2007

D 89
ISSN 1618-503X
ISBN 978-3-631-56955-9

www.peterlang.de

Preface

Asset managers have clearly become relevant on international financial markets during recent years. Any understanding of these markets, either in order to improve theoretical modeling or to implement good policies, must be based on a thorough understanding of its core actors, i.e. asset managers. Daniela Beckmann's dissertation provides important empirical contributions to improve our understanding of the role and the behavior of asset managers.

In the first set of papers, the author deals with early warning systems (EWS) of currency crises as they are used by banks, asset managers and macro policy institutions. The experience of the last decade has dramatically shown that currency crises, such as the Asian crisis in 1997/98, can destroy the progress that years of growth have brought to an economy within weeks. It thus seems rational to try to forecast currency crises while aiming to avoid or at least to weaken them in the future.

Beckmann contributes in two steps. First, recent advances made in this line of studies are surveyed (*chapter 2*) and, second, robust lessons are derived from an extensive empirical treatment. Both steps are useful as the flood of papers makes it necessary to take stock and to distinguish between more and less promising approaches suggested. The author's own empirical work (*chapter 3*) extends earlier studies by a considerable margin. Several lessons for practical EWSs are derived which hopefully support future research and application in this field. These lessons include some more obvious results, such as better fit on smaller samples, but also seem to demonstrate that some studies have been on the way towards an overfitting of the model as results are not very promising when the model is applied out of the original sample.

Beckmann's further papers deal with information from survey studies to which asset managers from various countries in three continents have contributed. *Chapter 4* of this book asks whether asset managers from Thailand and Indonesia – the emerging countries covered in this series – may behave more biased than managers from developed markets, here approximated by managers from Germany. This kind of comparison is to the best of my knowledge new to the literature. The focus is on determinants of herding behavior and home bias. Seen from a German perspective it is fair to treat the two emerging markets largely as one group, indicating already that they may be different from mature markets. Moreover, their home bias is clearly larger than in Germany which might be interpreted as more biased behavior. However, even though the respective questionnaire items ask hypothetical questions, the room for international asset allocation is narrow, and often non-existent due to national regulation, which has probably also influenced responses.

Another paper, *chapter 5*, analyzes Italian asset managers, also in comparison with their German colleagues. The analysis serves two purposes: first, it informs about differences between the Italian and the German market, thus indicating in which respect national peculiarities still matter in asset management. Second, this paper provides information about gender-related differences, finding that female asset managers tend to respond as expected from the general psychological literature on differences between men and women.

The last two chapters in this dissertation do not focus on in-depth country studies but analyze the cross-section of several countries. *Chapter 6* examines the possible influence of cultural differences on asset managers' behavior. Taking the well-known framework of Hofstede to characterize country-specific cultures, this study indeed shows that and in which way culture still co-determines behavior. This finding fits into a recent literature which is interested in identifying the role of culture in global financial markets, which do not seem to leave any room for national differences.

Chapter 7 is also related to this issue as one might neither really expect relevant gender differences in international financial markets. However, there is much research on the impact of gender on behavior in general, and there is a clear result that gender makes a difference. At the same time there seem to be influences that reduce the gender effect, such as experience with certain situations (obviously reflecting learning) and also the presentation of more concrete choices in financial terms (instead of abstract lotteries); these influences are both highly relevant in asset management and thus motivate this research as an interesting extension of earlier work. In asset management one may state a third influence, i.e. the very strong incentives to render performance – this incentive should work as a mechanism to homogenize behavior in the sense that asset managers try to learn efficient behavior from others. Interestingly, the present study in this book finds that female asset managers in the four countries covered still behave different from their male colleagues and the difference is exactly like the one expected from general gender studies. Nevertheless, one can recognize the homogenizing impact in this field as the differences are not too large, they do not apply to every questionnaire item and they cannot be related to differences in performance. An intuitive example in the latter respect is risk aversion: female asset managers seem to be more risk averse than men but the gap is small and what counts in asset management is only risk-adjusted performance.

Overall, this study generates lessons of academic interest and provides useful material that can help asset managers to improve their behavior and thus their performance. I would therefore wish this research the attention it deserves in both areas: academia as well as asset management.

Hannover, 13.7.2007 *Prof. Dr. Lukas Menkhoff*

Acknowledgements

This dissertation has evolved during my time as research and teaching assistant at the Gottfried Wilhelm Leibniz Universität Hannover. While working at the Chair for Money and International Finance of Prof. Dr. Lukas Menkhoff, I received substantial support of various people and institutions. Some of them, I would like to thank here in particular:

First of all, I am deeply grateful to my supervisor, Prof. Dr. Lukas Menkhoff. He did not only steadily encourage and challenge my research interests and efforts, but also strongly promoted international conference participation, fruitful exchanges, and practical experiences, while offering indispensable professional and personal guidance to me at any time.

Moreover, I would like to thank Prof. Dr. Ulrich Schmidt (Christian-Albrechts-Universität zu Kiel) for his outright disposition to undertake the second review of my dissertation as well as for his helpful comments, and Prof. Dr. Hermann Waibel (Gottfried Wilhelm Leibniz Universität Hannover) for warmly chairing my oral exam.

This research would not have been possible without the financial market professionals who supported it: I am very thankful to all asset managers who cotributed as oral interview partners and / or participated in the written survey. In addition, I very much benefited from organizational support by the investment associations and partner institutions in the respective countries. Financial support by the VolkswagenStiftung that allowed conducting the surveys in different parts of the world is also gratefully acknowledged.

Furthermore, I would like to express my warmest thanks to all my colleagues – both at the Chair for Money and International Finance and beyond – who made the four years at the University breezy. A familiar working atmosphere allowed sometimes technical, sometimes personal advice, and I am very grateful to all my colleagues' valuable feedback and constructive input to my work.

Last but surely not least, I am heavily indebted to my family and friends for their great and continued encouragement. Above all, my true-hearted thanks go to my partner Michael Schwarz, who spread humor, patience and faith whenever I needed it, and to my parents, Renate und Dieter Beckmann. They have always fostered my ideas and ambitions, allowed me great latitude and kept me grounded. This dissertation is thus dedicated to them.

Hannover, July 2007 *Daniela Beckmann*

Table of Contents

Part II: Financial Markets from a Behavioral Perspective – the Role of Asset Managers' Behavioral Biases, Cultural Background and Gender

Evidence from Country Studies

Cross-Country Evidence

1 Introduction

1.1 Motivation and contribution of this dissertation

Institutional investors, such as mutual funds, have often been seen as key drivers behind financial globalization (cf. Kaminsky et al., 2001). As the latter also implies an increasing integration of emerging financial markets, investors' expectations of higher yields and additional diversification advantages are often confronted with new investment opportunities in a less transparent environment and implied potential risks of financial crashes like those experienced in the 1990s and at the beginning of this century. Far from surprising, mutual funds have been both praised as leaders of global financial integration and blamed as originators or at least intensifiers of financial crises (cf. Aitken, 1998, Kaminsky et al., 2004).

As a first direct response to the cumulative appearance of financial turbulences during the last decade, the World Bank (2001) announced the question of efficient regulation of financial intermediaries, i.e. banks and institutional investors, especially in emerging markets to be of key importance. This, however, demands detailed knowledge about the institutions and professional players acting in these markets. While analyses of U.S. mutual funds are numerous, evidence for emerging market funds is – except for empirical work on U.S. funds investing in emerging markets[1] – pretty scarce. Moreover, many studies concentrate on funds' behavior at the aggregate level, while neglecting to directly focus on professional decision makers.[2] However, individual asset managers[3] could underlie a broad range of behavioral biases for which the approach of behavioral finance offers several insights and explanations (cf. Barberis and Thaler, 2003, for a survey). Taken in combination with the profession's fiduciary character, the industry's incentive structure as well as the huge volumes under management by mutual funds worldwide[4], the industry and its actors surely deserve a closer look.

As a second trend in light of the financial crises of the 1990s, the development and steady advancement of early warning systems, aiming to predict and

---

1 Cf. for example Borensztein and Gelos (2003) or Ong and Sy (2004).

2 Exceptions are provided by e.g. Chevalier and Ellison (1999, 1999a) or Niessen and Ruenzi (2006).

3 The terms asset manager, (mutual) fund manager and investment manager are used synonymously in the following.

4 According to the Investment Company Institute (www.ici.org) assets under management by mutual fund investment companies sum up globally to US$ 19.41 trillion by the end of the second quarter in 2006.

thus to prevent currency crises[5], received strong research emphasis by economists around the globe and in the international organizations, such as the IMF (cf. Berg et al., 2005). This is not difficult to understand when taking into account that e.g. the Asian twin crisis in 1997 came unexpected for most parts of the international community. Moreover, it caused, like other financial crises before, especially in the short to medium run[6] devastating economic consequences for the affected economies (cf. e.g. Mishkin, 2001): with the outbreak of the crisis, countries like Thailand or South Korea, previously considered as "growth miracles", experienced massive reserve losses, a breakdown of their pegged currency as well as huge capital reversals from international investors that quickly lamed economic activity in the affected countries.

While in internationally integrated financial markets, financial crises – and currency crises among them – will continue to occur in different forms and dimensions, Tornell (1999), for example, reinforces that experienced crises neither hit nor spread across single countries in a merely random manner. In fact, it is widely agreed that affected crises countries shared at least some common characteristics and vulnerabilities: appreciated real exchange rates in fixed exchange rate regimes, excessive money supply, a cutback in exports, or e.g. previous lending booms in fragile banking systems are some of the fundamental developments which researchers have identified as first indications of upcoming currency and banking crises, and which they have thus integrated as indicators into designed early warning systems (cf. e.g. Kaminsky, 1998, Goldstein et al., 2000). So far, the array of approaches, models and claimed innovative contributions in this field is wide. Therefore, it seems firstly important to review what has been done so far. Secondly, the deduction of robust lessons from existing approaches could contribute to a better understanding of the causes of financial crises and of what early warning systems can predict and what they cannot.

One most interesting aspect in financial crises, apart from economic similarities between affected countries or e.g. regional proximity as evidenced in the Asian twin crises, is the role of tight financial linkages. The latter have been

---

5 Early warning systems presented in this dissertation explicitly concentrate on currency crises, while so-called twin crises (cf. Kaminsky and Reinhart, 1999) as a combination of banking and currency crises are only selectively addressed. A still small, recently developing strand of literature discusses a new type of twin crises, derived from the combination of debt and currency crises (cf. e.g. Reinhart, 2002, Bauer et al., 2003). Ciarlone and Trebeschi (2005) are among the first to design an early warning system for debt crises while applying similar techniques as presented in the remainder of this dissertation for currency crises prediction.

6 Barro (2001) shows that combined currency and banking crises typically reduce economic growth by 2% per year over a five-year period. The Asian financial crisis even cut growth short by 3% per year. Barro does not, however, find evidence for persistence of growth effects beyond the five-year period. Revealing an even shorter typical recovery period of three years, Hong and Tornell (2005) generally confirm these findings.

considered as a transmission channel for financial contagion, i.e. the risk of one country to be affected by a crisis in another country (cf. Fratzscher, 2003, for an overview). In case of financial distress in one country, global investors are assumed to quickly adjust their portfolio allocation, and, if done by many investors in the same way, this could create a wave of large capital reversals. So-called sudden stop financial crises are caused in this way (cf. Kaminsky, 2006). Simulations based on equity market data and country ratings by Calvo and Mendoza (2000), for example, show that herd behavior of this kind can indeed induce large outflows of capital from emerging markets. Broner et al. (2006) are among the first to empirically analyze the portfolio reallocation of several emerging market mutual funds. In their analysis, they explicitly consider investors' risk aversion, taken portfolio decisions and reveal the non-negligible role of the latter in the transmission of shocks across countries. Although a direct integration of mutual fund behavior into practical predictions of financial crises is still some way ahead, more detailed knowledge on both issues is highly desirable and would contribute to a deeper understanding necessary to preclude or at least mediate future crises.

So, on the one hand, what do we learn from research conducted on early warning systems and underlying fundamentals? Does contagion matter and has it yet been integrated into early warning systems? Can we derive robust lessons when carefully comparing and assessing different approaches? On the other hand, how do professional investors in both emerging and more mature markets act in their professional investment decisions? What can we learn about their risk aversion and related behavioral biases? Does the market environment, offered incentives or country specific factors like the asset manager's cultural background influence asset manager's behavior? Which impact do personal asset manager's characteristics have?

This dissertation intends to answer these questions. For this purpose, it comprises two parts with two completely different kinds of data sets: On the one hand, different models of early warning systems are reviewed, replicated and tested with the help of fundamental macro level time series data from the IMF International Financial Statistics data base. Relying on data for 20 countries and 25 years of monthly observations for in-sample predictions as well as another seven years covering data set for out-of-sample forecasts, many crises of the last 35 years in several developing and emerging markets can be covered. On the other hand, individual asset managers' views, perceptions and behavioral biases are analyzed with the help of micro level data, generated in an international written questionnaire survey project with mutual fund managers[7].

7 I am highly thankful for the possibility to also use data for the following analyses which have been collected by colleagues and research partners within our international research project on "Behavioral patterns and its determinants in the investment process of institutional investors", namely and above all Lukas Menkhoff and Torben Luetje, Luca

In detail, these asset managers were virtually questioned all around the world, i.e.

- in Thailand and Indonesia, representing the two emerging markets in the sample,
- in Germany, which we consider our home market and a well-suiting reference in the following selected country studies,
- in Italy, the second European country in the sample and a market of comparable size to the German one,
- in Japan, to cover another Asian but more advanced market,
- and, last but not least, in the United States, the world's biggest and most developed market and asset management industry.

All questions in the questionnaire were carefully designed to provide information on hypotheses derived from either theoretical behavioral finance models or interesting former empirical findings – e.g. on risk taking or competition behavior –, with the help of asset manager studies and private investor data, in household surveys or experimental frameworks. In detail, we questioned professional market players about their perception of the market, asked for self-assessments and surveyed their personal risk taking and investment behavior. In addition, regarding asset manager's personal characteristics, survey studies have the advantage of allowing to easily generate a whole set of control variables. This appears very useful as personal characteristics like e.g. the asset managers' age, experience or gender have been found to significantly influence investment behavior (cf. e.g. Menkhoff et al., 2006).

Altogether, we generated a sample of 1,165 questionnaires[8] between spring 2003 and spring 2005. The single country samples are representative for covered countries' mutual fund industries and offer interesting insights into the latter. Especially in this regard, we owe particular thanks to the countries' respective investment management associations for their organizational support and indispensable reference letters as well as to all participating asset managers: the latter did not only spend their valuable time to fill in the questionnaire but also acted as multipliers by forwarding blank questionnaires to colleagues and team members while convincing them to participate as well. Finally, several asset managers highly contributed by sharing ideas and comments in previous oral interviews all around the globe that helped to assure comprehensibility as well as country specific fit of posed questions, and thus secured the usefulness of the generated survey data.

Rebeggiani, as well as Megumi Suto. In addition, financial support by the Volkswagen-Stiftung is very gratefully acknowledged.

8 This number is considerably large in comparison to former survey studies on institutional investors: While the early analysis of Shiller and Pound (1989) is based on 71 questionnaires, Arnswald (2001) uses 275 valid responses from German equity fund managers while e.g. Menkhoff et al. (2006) rely on 117 questionnaires.

1.2 Outline

This dissertation is split into two parts: Part I addresses evidence from early warning systems and the role of fundamentals, Part II turns the attention to financial markets from a behavioral perspective. In particular, the role of professional asset managers' behavioral biases, risk taking, culture, and gender are addressed by both selected country studies as well as the provision of cross-country evidence.

The remainder of this dissertation is thus organized as follows: following these introductory remarks, Chapter 2 provides a survey of new approaches of early warning systems. While the number of financial crises and currency crises among them has increased over the last two decades, early warning systems have been designed as an instrument for trying to avoid currency crises. Crises, however, seem to change their characteristics over time. Reviewing recent academic work on early warning systems, Chapter 2 therefore first provides a framework to assess new contributions since 1998. While the application of new methods in extracting information from fundamentals is assessed, at the same time the review also reveals differences in approaches regarding explanatory power as well as potential weak points in proposals made. Having the variety of work in mind, finally, a set of core fundamentals in establishing an early warning system is found to be remarkably stable.

Chapter 3 ties up with these findings when aiming to derive robust lessons about practical early warning systems. Taking into account that early warning systems are subject to restrictions that apply to exchange rates in general – i.e. fundamentals matter, but their influence is small and unstable over time –, different approaches are put to the acid test by using a limited number of core fundamental variables. Despite obvious limitations on the predictability of exchange rate movements, and financial crises in particular, four major lessons are derived: First, early warning systems have robust forecasting power and thus help policy-makers to prevent crises. Second, policy-makers have to decide about critical early warning system elements. In first place, they have to choose the exact definition of what they consider a crisis: different definitions do not only draw different pictures regarding crisis dates and history for a chosen country sample but might also demand different measures to be taken. Besides, the sensitivity of the forecasts is another aspect that critically depends on policy-makers preferences. Third, early warning systems' performance is increased by taking a logit model, shorter samples and a regional approach. Fourth, the finding of contagion may motivate policy to shield its economy against inefficient international financial markets.

Changing to the behavioral perspective on financial markets in the following, Chapter 4 starts the analysis of professional asset managers' behavior with the help of generated survey data. As a first country study, we test whether asset managers in an emerging market environment behave differently, i.e. possibly more biased, from their more mature market counterparts. Survey evidence from asset managers in the two emerging markets, Thailand and Indonesia, as well as Germany, as a more mature reference market, is therefore presented. Being able to control for asset managers' risk behavior as well as personal characteristics, our work contributes to the literature by analyzing two highly discussed behavioral patterns, i.e. herd behavior and a home-biased asset allocation, in diverging market surroundings. Compared to the German market professionals, we detect a higher risk propensity among asset managers from Thailand and Indonesia. Notwithstanding, risk biases are confirmed to significantly matter for herding behavior – both for the German market and in the two emerging ones. Indeed, revealing particularly risk and loss averse asset managers to follow the trend, we shed light on herd behavior as a possible, from the individual perspective even rational response to both incentives and negative career menaces. Furthermore, the analysis of home bias confirms the role of professionals' risk biases also for asset allocation decisions. Moreover, particularly in the two emerging markets, comparably strong regulatory influence as well as personal characteristics are found to matter in addition.

A second selected country study is provided in Chapter 5. This time, broad new insights into the Italian mutual fund industry are offered. While this chapter is the only one that does not explicitly include emerging markets data, findings on overconfidence, risk taking and gender dissimilarities in a mature market environment offer valuable motivation for later also presented cross-country analysis. Surveying Italian professionals, Chapter 5 does not only reveal typical gender differences among Italian asset managers but also detects divergence in behavior compared to also surveyed German counterparts. While disclosing Italian professionals' overly positive self-assessment in general by directly asking them about their own performance and achievements in asset management, evidence for male overconfidence is primarily discovered. Yet, these findings are not accompanied by overconfidence in forms of an excessive control illusion of the own information level – neither for Italian asset managers in general nor for Italian male or female asset managers in particular. In contrast, asset managers' risk taking reveals further differences: Italian female professionals do not only assess themselves as more risk averse than their male colleagues, they also prefer a more passive portfolio management compared to the level they are allowed to. Moreover, in a tournament scenario near the end of the investment period female asset managers do not try to become the ultimate top performer when they have outperformed their peer group so far. However, in case of underperformance, the risk of deviating from the benchmark makes especially female professionals willing to seize a chance of catching up. Overall, compared to their German counterparts, Italian asset managers are found to be slightly more risk averse. Matching former results on Italian mutual funds, the impact of derived findings at the individual asset managers' level on trading activity, management style and performance are discussed.

The last two studies finally provide cross-country evidence on the influence of culture on asset managers' behavior on the one hand, and for the question of possibly existing gender differences examined as a struggle between nature and incentives in professional asset management on the other hand. Research in Chapter 6 relies on Hofstede's four cultural dimensions while presenting comparative survey evidence on asset managers' views and behavior in the United States, Germany, Japan and Thailand. Indeed, cultural differences are found to be most helpful in understanding country differences which cannot be explained by pure economic reasoning. In short, controlling for various determinants, the dimension of more Individualism predicts less herding behavior, more Power Distance leads to older and comparatively less experienced managers in the upper hierarchy, Masculinity brings men into top positions and to higher volumes of assets under personal responsibility, and Uncertainty Avoidance is related to higher safety margins against the tracking error allowed and relatively more research effort. These consequences, i.e. the culturally different importance of herding, age, experience, gender, tracking error and research effort, clearly affect investment behavior, although in a complex way.

Lastly, Chapter 7 re-addresses the question of a gender difference in asset managers' behavior. In particular, we question if women will be women in the sense of whether incentives can dominate nature in the asset management industry. In order to test this question, gender-related behavior is analyzed in an environment of strong incentives, i.e. in fund management, by the help of 649 surveyed professionals from four countries. Indeed, female asset managers are found to behave as expected from gender studies: they are more risk averse and shy away from competition, although the degree of overconfidence is not related to sexes. Regarding country patterns, no gender difference for the United States, a small but obvious one for Germany, a bigger one for Italy and the largest one for Thailand are revealed. Possibly, high incentives – like in the U.S. – are considered to be strong enough to completely erase the natural gender difference.

1.3 Conclusions and outlook

All in all, this dissertation shows that while searching for early indications of financial distress and trying to combine meaningful indicators in sophisticated models, one should keep in mind that early warning systems face a heavily difficult task: predicting currency crises implies the forecast of exchange rate movements which ever since the work of Meese and Rogoff (1983) remains challenging for economists until today. Indeed, our analysis shows that fundamentals matter and early warning systems reveal at least to some degree robust forecasting power. However, we also disclose how policy makers and researchers might be tempted to fine-tune their models in order to improve forecast results – even without necessarily also understanding financial crises better. Besides, already simple measures of contagion are found to advance results, leaving the field surely open for future research.

Analyzing professional asset managers' behavior offers further valuable insights: investment managers indeed seem to underlie several biases which both confirm behavioral finance theory and former empirical results but also disclose some unexpected findings: individual risk and loss aversion, for example, do not only influence comparatively inexperienced investors but also matter among professionals. The same is found for a home-biased asset allocation. Revealed herd behavior fits psychological influences and obvious trend behavior in the market which amends fundamental developments. Moreover, it is interesting to learn about individual asset managers' perceptions and overly positive self-assessments as well obvious internalization lying behind behavioral patterns and biases (cf. e.g. the analysis addressing overconfidence, risk and competition behavior in Chapter 5 or the one of cultural factors in Chapter 6). Finally, revealed gender differences leave room in addition for a deeper discussion of mutual fund managers' behavior; deriving trading, performance, and price impacts; as well as possible consequences regarding the industry's development and incentive structure. I hope this dissertation contributes by offering interesting stimulus in this respect.

Part I:
Early Warning Systems and the Role of Fundamentals

2 Early Warning Systems: A Survey of New Approaches[9]

2.1 Motivation

While the number of financial crises and currency crises among them has increased over the last two decades, nobody would claim that they have become less severe. Indeed, whenever a crisis occurs, there is a heavy toll to pay for the respective economy and its population. The motivation for crisis prevention thus seems quite obvious. Particulary after the Asian crises in 1997, early warning systems have been suggested as one instrument for trying to avoid financial crises or at least for trying to reduce unwanted side-effects of financial crises (cf. Eichengreen, 1999, Frenkel and Menkhoff, 2000). However, crises appear to behave like a hydra: whenever something is learned from experience, new characteristics of a subsequent crisis emerge (cf. Kaminsky, 2006). It is therefore of the highest importance to keep one's knowledge about financial crisis analyses up to date when aiming to advance research in the field. We want to contribute to this goal by reviewing lessons from recent academic work on early warning systems.

As Kaminsky, Lizondo and Reinhart (1998) – in short KLR; Kaminsky et al. in the following – give a tabulated review of earlier work, this analysis is limited to literature after 1998. We are thus similar to Abiad (2003) and Berg et al. (2005) in respect to the time period covered. The approach is different, however, regarding its focus: whereas Abiad (2003) surveys 30 papers in short (in the style of KLR) and Berg et al. (2005) mainly compare three private sector models with two IMF models, i.e. the ones by KLR and by the Developing Country Studies Devision, we restrict ourselves to what we regard as major steps in the discussion and thus review five contributions in more detail. Two out of these five are new in comparison to Abiad (2003). One is Bussiere and Fratzscher (2006), the other one is an assessment of Abiad's approach itself (2003).

The remainder is organized as follows. Chapter 2.2 suggests an analytical framework in order to discuss new approaches systematically. This kind of discussion is provided in Chapter 2.3, where we first describe the widely recognized contribution of Kaminsky et al. (1998) as the benchmark against which we discuss more recent approaches. Chapters 2.3.2 to 2.3.5 basically analyze the contributions of Berg and Pattillo (1999), emphasizing the value of a probit model, Edison (2003), considering extensive robustness checks, Bussiere and

9 I would like to thank my co-author of an earlier version of this paper Lukas Menkhoff. This chapter represents an updated version of the article entitled "Early Warning Systems: Lessons from New Approaches", published in Frenkel et al. (Eds.) (2004), *Sovereign Risk and Financial Crises*, Berlin et al.

Fratzscher (2006), proposing a multinomial logit model and Abiad (2003), favoring a Markov-switching approach. Additional literature is subordinated to the themes emphasized in Chapter 2.3.2 to 2.3.5. Chapter 2.4 concludes with an outlook for future research.

2.2 A framework to analyze early warning systems

The general objective of early warning systems (EWSs) should be to inform about unwanted developments as early as possible. In the field of international finance, however, the meaning of an EWS is much more narrow. In essence, EWSs are by and large instruments to warn about sudden exchange rate deviations. They are thus focused on currency crises only and do not discuss what has been termed debt crises and banking crises. Even though all of these kinds of financial crises are different, they are related to some degree. Regarding banking and currency crises, Kaminsky and Reinhart (1999) have coined the term of a "twin crisis", as both kinds of crises often occur at a similar time and place. A banking crisis often, but not always, precedes a currency crisis. Consequently, indicators of financial sector fragility may be useful as input in EWSs. Regarding debt and currency crises, the empirical work on interrelations is more recent (cf. e.g. Reinhart, 2002, Sy, 2004 or Dreher et al., 2006). Theoretically, one would expect that debt crises reflect solvency aspects of countries, whereas EWSs rather aim to predict severe liquidity crises of countries, too. One might thus consider integrating indicators of a possible debt crisis as input in an EWS.

Early warning systems (EWSs) are widely used among international financial institutions (IFIs) as well as in the private financial sector. Whoever takes a position in the international arena has a natural interest in forecasting sudden changes in the economic environment. EWSs represent a guide to IFIs for successful policy making in many countries and warn them in due time to change their policy stance. EWSs are helpful for the private sector to generate profits from appropriate position taking. Thus, both groups apply EWSs although they have very different motivations.

In order to construct an EWS several decisions have to be made regarding five basic elements (see Figure 2.1 for an overview):

- Firstly, an appropriate crisis definition has to be found. Some conventions have been developed regarding this element but they are of course not binding and we will see in Chapter 2.3.3, how certain studies differ with in this respect.
- Secondly, the set of explanatory variables considered has to be decided. Variables mostly include a lagged development of the exchange rate, several variables describing the state of the economy's external situation and variables of the financial sector.

- Thirdly, a certain function type needs to be selected in order to get as much relevant information from the variables as possible. From our point of view, the most significant contributions have been made in this area, as can be seen from the selection of studies in Chapter 3.
- Fourthly, the time period for the backward testing of the EWS has to be decided in advance. Long periods are warranted from a statistical point of view. In light of the above mentioned instability, however, shorter time periods may bring better results.
- Fifthly, which group of countries may be of interest? The major decision regarding this element refers to considering either emerging countries only or also including industrialized countries in the EWS. In the case of private sector EWSs, users may restrict themselves to the countries of commercial interest to them.

Figure 2.1 A basic framework for an EWS

1. crisis definition	=	3. function of	2. explanatory variables

over 4. a certain period

and 5. a group of countries

This framework of five elements helps to systematically discuss different contributions made in the literature. It is also, however, an instrument to reflect how EWSs function and what one might expect from them. It seems plausible to suppose that developers of an EWS aim for two private objectives: in order to demonstrate a rationale for their work, they have an incentive to provide a different "product", and in order to impress their audience, they have an incentive to present an EWS which produces measurable success. The five elements introduced above help to discuss consequences from this private agenda on the kind of new EWS approaches. Regarding product originality, one would expect that the approaches differ in several respects and are less often a clear development of earlier work. Regarding performance measures, each of the five elements can be used to improve figures: selecting a more homogeneous crisis definition, taking many diverse variables, using a complex functional relationship, evaluating a short period and choosing a homogeneous sample of countries. Finally, just optimizing the "forecasting power" of such an EWS.

The last point is of particular interest when reflecting the basic goal of an EWS. Forecasting exchange rates is an extremely ambitious exercise as there is no fundamental model that would be able to explain a set of exchange rates over a longer period of time, not to mention forecasting (cf. Frankel and Rose, 1996, Sarno and Taylor, 2002). Even recently developed models that rely on quite complex econometric methods in order to extract systematic information from fundamentals too often seem to be dependent on very specific circumstances (cf. Faust et al., 2003). From this perspective, one will be rather pessimistic about assessing the true value of any EWS.

Fortunately, there is a more optimistic perspective, too. Consider the existence of empirical work demonstrating that exchange rates are related to fundamentals – loosely and not very reliably but there are indisputable linkages. In particular the literature on purchasing power parity shows very clearly that exchange rates react to large deviations from PPP (cf. Rogoff, 1996). The downside of this literature is the long horizons needed for this linkage to become effective. However, techniques of non-linear exchange rate modeling may be able to extract information even on horizons of one year only (cf. MacDonald, 1999, Clarida et al., 2003). The most important thing for our purpose is, however, a gradual and possibly decisive difference between exchange rate forecasting and EWSs. The latter are only interested in very large changes in exchange rates and thus in rather rough relations between fundamentals and exchange rates. This difference may possibly be of a substantial nature and enough to bring about better results than could be expected from "normal" exchange rate forecasting. Nevertheless, the affinity to exchange rate modeling should make users, developers and discussants of EWSs cautious. This caution will influence our discussion of new approaches in the next chapter.

2.3 A discussion of new approaches

The Mexican crisis of 1995 and even more the Asian crisis of 1997 stimulated all branches of crisis literature. The political impetus came from the significant world-wide impact of these crises, whereas the academic one was rather motivated by the unexpected character of these crises. Thus, it seems advisable to include insights from the major crises of the last decade and to cover the discussion from the late 1990s. Moreover, this period witnessed the emergence of more systematic studies of EWSs. Eichengreen et al. (1995, 1996) and Frankel and Rose (1996) comprehensively address currency crises in industrialized and developing countries each, whereas Kaminsky and Reinhart (1999), examine banking and balance-of-payments crises. This is how the overall approach had been developed until 1996 but it is the work of Kaminsky et al. (henceforth KLR, 1998) that surveyed earlier studies, covered most indicators and relied on monthly data – this, therefore, serves as our benchmark.

2.3.1 The leading indicator approach of KLR

The KLR leading indicator approach is based on the idea of monitoring the evolution of a large number of different macroeconomic and financial variables exhibiting an abnormal behavior in periods preceding a crisis. When an indicator variable exceeds a formerly designed threshold value, a warning signal about an upcoming crisis in the following months is issued. This is why the KLR idea is also widely known as the signal approach.

Financial crises are generally understood as a synonym for speculative attacks and/or extreme pressure on the exchange rate. Therefore, concerning the crisis definition, KLR use an index of exchange market pressure which is constructed as a weighted average of monthly percentage changes in the nominal exchange rate and in gross international reserves. These two components are weighted in such a way that they have the same conditional variance. Reflecting the pressure on the currency as an increase of the index, either due to a currency's depreciation or to a loss of international reserves, a crisis is considered a period in which the index is more than three sample standard deviations above its sample mean.

Their review of former studies discloses a large variety of possible explanatory variables. Mainly due to theoretical assumptions and the availability on a monthly basis, KLR finally choose 15 macroeconomic and financial variables. These range from the real exchange rate, reserves and trade variables to variables reflecting money supply, lending and the equity index. Most of them are defined as the percentage change in the level of the variable with respect to its level a year before, ensuring the setting off of seasonal effects.

In order to extract information from these variables KLR choose a univariate approach. They consider one indicator variable after another, evaluating its individual performance in terms of predictive power as well as the lead time and persistence of their signals. The period within which indicators are expected to be able to anticipate a crisis is called the signaling horizon. KLR favor a relatively long 24-month window. This approach is finally applied on a dataset of 20 countries, including 15 developing and 5 industrialized countries, over the sample period of 1970-1995. They proceed in the following manner:

Firstly, the threshold levels have to be calculated, taking into account the need to balance the risk of having false signals on the one hand and not issuing a warning and therefore missing a crisis on the other hand. The thresholds are not country- but indicator-specific when using the same percentiles of the distribution of observations per indicator for each country. KLR define the optimal threshold for each indicator by minimizing its so-called noise-to-signal-ratio, which is the ratio of false signals to good ones. In addition to the noise-to-signal-ratio, they propose different performance measures, used for the identification of core fundamentals in further studies as well.

Secondly, KLR take a closer look at the average number of months between the first signal issued and the occurrence of a crisis. They discover that all indicators issue the first signal between 18 months and a year before the outbreak of the crisis.

Thirdly, they complete their analysis by measuring the persistence of the signals. Comparing pre-crisis periods to tranquil ones, they examine the average number of signals per period. Except for the real exchange rate with signals being five times more persistent in the 24-month window leading to a crisis, for the majority of indicators, signals seem to be twice as persistent in pre-crisis times.

To summarize findings, KLR rank the indicators according to their forecasting ability, signal lead time and persistence of the signal. Those indicators performing best in the KLR study include industrial production, exports, deviations of the real exchange rate from the trend, equity prices, as well as the ratio of broad money to gross international reserves. KLR recommend including a broad range of indicators in order to recognize the widely spread symptoms as early as possible.

Moreover, they regard a treatment of different indicators in the form of a composite indicator as an indispensable, natural extension of their study. Work in this direction is, among others, presented in Kaminsky (1998) and Goldstein et al. (2000), with convincing in- and out-of-sample results.

2.3.2 The probit approach of Berg and Pattillo

The basically univariate leading indicator approach of KLR and, even more, its extension via composite indicators, call for a classical multivariate technique. Berg and Pattillo (1999) carefully craft this design in two steps: firstly, they reproduce KLR and then, secondly, compare the power of the leading indicator approach with several variants of their probit approach.

Berg and Pattillo thus logically consider the same framework as KLR, including the above presented crisis definition, indicator choice, function type and sample. As their results broadly resemble those of the KLR study, Berg and Pattillo arrange some further modifications: concerning the time period, they re-estimate the model only through data from April 1995, aiming to mirror the situation an analyst would have been in before the Asian crisis. In order to adjust the analysis to "crises in emerging markets", they change the country coverage by removing the industrialized countries and augmenting the number of considered emerging markets up to 23. Subsequently, they add two indicators to the analysis expecting them to be informative as well. Finally, after having examined all indicators separately, Berg and Pattillo construct a composite indicator according to Kaminsky (1998).

When testing this composite indicator, Berg and Pattillo illustrate the trade-off between missing crises on the one hand and having false alarms on the other hand. Though attesting the KLR approach to perform better than guesswork and considering it therefore a helpful contribution, they point to the very high number of both missed crises and false alarms.

That is why they apply a probit regression technique to the same data and crisis definition. The dependent variable takes a value of one in the case of an upcoming crisis and zero otherwise. Berg and Pattillo discuss three advantages: firstly, they question the usefulness of the threshold idea for each individual indicator. Secondly, they are able to consider possible correlations among the indicators. Thirdly, the probit approach is easier to test for statistical significance and coefficient constancy over time and countries.

In the following, they propose three different probit models. The first one uses the indicator form of the variables, with indicators equaling one above a threshold and zero otherwise (as in the KLR approach). The second model is characterized by variables entering linearly, whereas the third one is based on sample splits and assumed piecewise-linear trends.

Comparing the performance of these three probit models with one another and with the one of KLR and Berg and Pattillo, we find that the probit approach tends to outperform KLR-based probabilities. The direct comparison of the KLR approach and the first probit model especially shows the latter to be better in terms of scores and goodness-of-fit. Ranking the three probit models turns out to be difficult though, as their relative performance is ambiguous.

After having assessed the in-sample performance, Berg and Pattillo answer the question whether the Asian crisis could have been predicted by the KLR model or by one of their proposed probit-based ones. To this end, they select four Asian crisis countries as well as one Asian and three Latin American non-crisis countries and examine the performance of each KLR indicator individually in 1996. To their surprise not a single indicator issues a signal in all of the crisis countries. Combining thereupon the single indicator information in a composite measure of crisis probabilities somewhat improves the result. Overall, however, the explanatory power is not stunning.

In order to assess their probit based models, Berg and Pattillo use the same in-sample data as for the KLR approach. Again, both in terms of predicted probabilities and ranking correlation, the probit based alternatives generally perform better than the weighted-sum composite indicator created of the KLR approach. Among the three different probit based models, especially the linear specification seems to outperform all other alternatives.

These results reveal the relative advantage of the probit approach in comparison to the leading indicator approach when applied in competition with each other. Moreover, it is the standard probit form where explanatory variables enter in unmodified form that performs best. Based on these findings it may be no surprise that probit models have become the workhorse in the EWS literature (cf. e.g. later studies of Kamin et al., 2001, Kumar et al., 2002, and Komulainen and Lukkarila, 2003). Concerning the core right-hand variables, however, the outcomes are broadly consistent with former studies, especially KLR.

2.3.3 The robustness checks of Edison

The main contribution of Edison (2003) is – in contrast to most other papers – not to present an "innovation" but to thoroughly test the robustness of earlier findings. During her work she reveals a fact that deserves attention in future research: the application of an unchanged crisis definition – according to the standard method – identifies different crises due to a change in the sample period.

Edison starts her analysis with a reproduction of the KLR results. In the course of her study, however, she implies a certain number of deviations from the original EWS framework in order to improve its performance. These modifications include expansions of the country coverage, the dataset and the variables. Moreover, selecting the case of Mexico, Edison concentrates her analysis on an individual country and introduces a simple threshold calculation attempt that does not depend on the pooled information of all sample countries but on country-specific data. Furthermore, she considers regional differences and the above mentioned changes in the crisis definitions.

Regarding the five basic elements of an EWS, Edison draws upon the following framework: As in previous work, a crisis is understood "as a period of extreme pressure in the foreign exchange market" (Edison, 2003). Relying therefore also on the above presented exchange market pressure index, Edison considers a crisis to occur when the index exceeds 2.5 standard deviations of its sample mean. Concerning the variables, she originally uses the same ones as KLR plus an extension of seven other indicators. The situation is similar for the time and country coverage. Edison takes the KLR approved crisis window of 24 months and firstly uses the sample of monthly data from 1970 to 1995 for twenty countries, before, in a second step, expanding the dataset to 1998 and 28 emerging markets.

Except for little discrepancies in the performance related ranking of some indicators that she, also in reference to the reproduction attempt of Berg and Pattillo, ascribes to data inconsistencies, her reproduction results broadly meet those of the KLR study. That is why, in the following, Edison tries to improve the performance of the existing model with the help of several modifications: considering in- and out-of-sample performance, using two different composite indicators for the latter and assessing estimated probabilities under regional focus and for the overall country sample at different points in time, Edison tellingly shows how much even small variations imply changes in the results.

In further sensitivity analyses, based on the noise-to-signal ratio as well as the share of crises called, she firstly not only identifies regional performance differences among the indicators but also attests a generally better performance for the Latin American countries. Secondly, addressing the drawbacks of the commonly used sample-dependent crisis definition, she discovers changes in the dating of crises for the Asian countries due to a sample expansion. Thirdly, when recalculating the results with the help of the sample-independent method of Frankel and Rose (1996), Edison shows that the performance of the indicators, however, seems invariant to the dating method.

To sum up, Edison assesses a comprehensive amount of possible expansions and deviations from the original KLR framework as well as a thorough conduction of sensitivity analyses. In the end, she identifies very similar important leading indicators as former studies and calls for statistical perfection. The next approach presents progress in the latter respect.

2.3.4 The multinomial logit approach of Bussiere and Fratzscher

Bussiere and Fratzscher (2006) discuss a questionable aspect of the earlier literature, i.e. the distinction of only two states of the world that have to be explained: crisis or tranquil periods. They show convincingly that the post-crisis period is a distinct time, too, and that consideration of three states leads to improved forecasting results. In order to distinguish three states they remove the binomial probit model used earlier and instead propose a multinomial logit approach.

Concerning the exchange market pressure index, Bussiere and Fratzscher slightly deviate from those presented above. They take not only changes of the real effective exchange rate instead of the nominal exchange rate into account, but also include changes in the interest rate in the index. It was especially the interest rate which was often excluded by former work due to difficulties with market dates (for exception cf. Eichengreen et al., 1996). Bussiere and Fratzscher define a currency crisis as an event when the pressure index is at least two standard deviations above its country average.

As regards variables, they test the conventional universe with one exception, i.e. two contagion variables. Their paper is not the first to address this issue, as Eichengreen et al. (1996) already focused on contagion. However, Bussiere and Fratzscher are among the first to include contagion variables in a careful mainstream probit-kind approach (cf. also Caramazza et al., 2000, Fratzscher, 2003 or Kaminsky and Reinhart, 2000).

Their sample comprises a monthly data set from December 1993 to September 2001 for 31 Latin American, Asian and Eastern European countries and South Africa. The multinomial approach is conducted on a reduced sample of 20 countries only. So sample size and time period are smaller than in many other studies.

The main finding is that the multinomial approach clearly outperforms a binomial approach in-sample as well as out-of-sample. Moreover, they try to compare their approach to performance measures of earlier publicized EWSs and claim superiority. However, these latter kinds of comparisons necessarily lack a level playing field as e.g. deviations in crisis definition or sample shortness which might improve results cannot be denied. In summary, there is convincing evidence that a binary dependent variable is inferior to distinguishing three states.

A related line of studies argues that the differences in states of the world may not only justify the forecasting of crises but also the forecasting of calm periods. A particular reason for this approach is given in the theoretical so-called generation II models of currency crises which emphasize the existence of multiple equilibriums. This implies that very similar fundamentals may sometimes lead to a crisis but sometimes do not, which may help to understand the poor predictive power of EWSs. Osband and Van Rijckeghem (2000) provide such an "inverse" EWS. However, it covers less than 50% of all months and is thus of limited help for practical purposes.

2.3.5 The Markov-switching approach of Abiad

The approach of Abiad (2003) can surely be seen as the most distinct among presented models. Instead of requiring an a priori crisis dating, Abiad estimates a Markov-switching model that concentrates on the endogenous identification and characterization of crises periods. Furthermore, this avoids the loss of information accompanying a transformation of the different indicators into a one-zero binary crisis variable (as e.g. in the KLR approach).

How is the Markov-switching model implemented? One assumption is the fact that there are two states – periods of tranquility and of speculative attacks – which cannot be observed directly. The crisis variable can thus be seen as latent. There are, however, directly observable variables whose behavior changes depending on the value of the crisis variable. Given a current state, either a tranquil or a crisis period, there exists a certain probability of moving to the other or staying in the former state. In the chosen model, the probability of moving from one state to another depends on the individual country's fundamentals and is considered to change over time.

Abiad's work does not represent the first empirical application of a Markov-switching model for crisis assessment (cf. e.g. Cerra and Saxena, 2002, and Martinez-Peria, 2002) but to our knowledge it is the first to look at several emerging markets and a wide set of indicators. The underlying framework can be summarized as follows: Abiad examines 22 variables, combining standard indicators with newly proposed variables to describe capital flows and financial sector sensitivity. His analyses are based on monthly data from January 1972 to December 1999 for five Asian countries. Regarding the time window, he differs distinctly from the norm, being mostly between one year and 18 months, as his Markov model provides just one-month ahead forecasts. These can be made comparable to other work only with the help of far-reaching assumptions (cf. Abiad, 2003, p. 28).

Abiad starts his analyses with the coefficient estimation and the identification of the most predictive variables, running his model with each of the 22 indicators for each single country. Discovering the real overvaluation indicator to be the only one significant across the whole sample, he finds that the indicator performance varies between the different countries.

In the following, the final model with selected indicators is estimated in a country-by-county approach. Two states can generally be identified: State 0 as a low-mean and low-volatility regime and State 1 as both a high-mean and high-volatility regime. Receiving high average standard deviations in crises periods and low ones in tranquil times, volatility can be seen as a major differentiation characteristic. A closer examination of the country-specific results allows one to identify crises episodes as well as the models' anticipation performance.

In order to better evaluate the in- and out-of-sample forecasting performance, Abiad summarizes his results using a yes-no-matrix of signals and crises. He also calculates goodness of fit measures and compares his results in-sample to those of KLR and Berg and Pattillo. Especially in terms of correctly called crises, the Markov model seems to outperform the other approaches. Nevertheless, results have to be taken with caution as they lack comparability. Turning to out-of-sample performance, Abiad lets his country models forecast probabilities and send signals for the period of January 2000 to July 2001. While three countries remain calm, for two of the five countries the model extracts higher vulnerabilities in both 2000 and 2001. A deeper analysis of the underlying fundamentals delivers satisfying explanations.

Despite the impressive advantage gained by relying on the Markov switching model, there remain two lines of doubt. Edison (2003), as well as others, breaks a general EWS effectively into several more specific EWSs, e.g. for regions. Abiad (2003) takes another step along this way by explaining country-specific crises, which has the consequence of losing a general explanation. Another concern refers to the endogenous crisis definition: what sounds attractive at first sight may be dangerous from another viewpoint – what do we really want to explain? Are there certain crises to be explained or do we leave it to an algorithm to define the dependent variable? Which algorithm do we prefer as there are competing approaches (cf. also Pozo and Amuedo-Dorantes, 2003)? Or to overstate the argument: do we “explain” that which we can explain best?

2.4 Conclusions

What can we learn from the approaches presented? Do we now better understand the predictable causes of currency crises than we did five years ago? Three aspects seem to be worth considering: firstly, EWSs are a difficult field as they require in the last instance the forecast of exchange rates. Secondly, there are hardly any systematic and rigorous comparisons between different approaches for EWSs. Thirdly, the second "aspect" just mentioned establishes the problem of identifying unanimous lessons learned. We thus give our impression of useful progress having been made since the KLR study.

The difficulty of forecasting currency crises on a truly ex ante basis is shown by Berg and Pattillo (1999a), who apply three EWSs proposed before 1997 to the Asian crisis. Berg and Pattillo compare the leading indicator approach presented by KLR with the probit based annual panel data model of currency crashes of Frankel and Rose (1996) and the approach of Sachs et al. (1996), which rests upon a cross-sectional regression analysis of 20 emerging markets in 1995. Berg and Pattillo reconstruct the original models, then make some adjustments concerning sample and variables. Their results are disappointing, as only the KLR approach seems to provide a useful, though not overwhelming, forecast performance. Seen from a different perspective, there is something that can be learned from an EWS (for an example cf. Goldfajn and Valdés, 1998).

A closer look at the analysis of Berg and Pattillo (1999a) exemplarily supports our second "aspect" from above, as there are severe problems in drawing conclusions: the chosen models differ critically not only in terms of the aim they were originally created for, but also regarding their basic elements. Neither crisis definition, nor sample size, data structure or forecast horizon coincide in the three models – a fact that should be taken into account when comparing and judging performance. Concerning identified crisis indicators, however, the three models compared point in the same direction: an overvalued real exchange rate, high domestic credit growth or a high ratio of broad money to gross international reserves increase the probability of a currency crisis. Pretty similar results emerge from a closer look at our major studies surveyed (see Table 2.1). Especially deviations of the real exchange rate from the trend as well as changes in the ratio of M2 to international reserves show up again. Recalling the underlying crisis definitions just reveals considerable momentum in worsening fundamentals: the best prediction of a currency crisis is an overvalued exchange rate.

With these caveats in mind we, thirdly, discuss what we regard as progress in the field by drawing on the major studies presented in Chapters 2.3.2 to 2.3.5. Kaminsky et al. (1998) built on earlier work (in particular Eichengreen et al., 1995, and Frankel and Rose, 1996), and confirm that there are indeed changes in economic fundamentals before the outbreak of crises. However, these changes can be of quite complex nature so that no single indicator or small group of indicators would reliably inform about future crises. Berg and Pattillo (1999) extend KLR mainly by showing the advantage from extracting information with the help of a multivariate approach, here a probit model.

Bussiere and Fratzscher (2006) mark the next step as they demonstrate further advantages of a multinomial logit model. Abiad (2003) finally proposes a

Markov switching approach which is the most advanced from a technical point of view although not necessarily the best instrument for an EWS.

Table 2.1 Considered variables and identified core indicators in major studies

Study	Considered variable groups and no. of indicators examined	Core indicators / star performers[a]
KLR (1998)	• Current account (3) • Capital account (3) • Real sector (2) • Financial indicators (6)	• Deviations of the real exchange rate from trend • Exports (growth) • M2 / int. reserves (growth) • Index of output • Index of equity prices
Berg and Pattillo (1999)	Reproduction of KLR + 2 additional variables: • M2 / reserves (level) • Current account / GDP (growth)	• Deviations of the real exchange rate from trend • Exports (growth) • M2 / int. reserves (growth) • Int. reserves (growth) • M2 / reserves (level) • Current account / GDP (growth)
Edison (2003)	Reproduction of KLR + 7 additional, mainly global real sector variables and financial indicators	• Deviations of the real exchange rate from trend • Exports (growth) • M2 / int. reserves (growth) • Int. reserves (growth) • Index of equity prices • Short-term debt / int. Reserves (growth)
Bussiere and Fratzscher (2006)	• External competitiveness (5) • External exposure (6) • Domestic real & public sector (6) • Domestic financial sector (4) • Global factors (4) • Contagion (2)	• Deviations of the real exchange rate from trend • Current account (%GDP) • Short-term debt / int. reserves • Real GDP (growth) • Domestic credit to private and government sector (level, growth) • Financial interdependence
Abiad (2003)	• Macroeconomic (11) • Capital flows (5) • Financial fragility (6)	• Deviations of the real exchange rate from trend • M2 / int. reserves (level) • Bank deposits / M2 (growth)

a Our rating of a variable as a star performer emerges from the overall results of the respective study, including extensions and sensitivity analyses or country-specific considerations as in the case of Abiad (2003). The core variables of Bussiere and Fratzscher (2006) listed here represent those chosen in their final model.

In summary, we doubt that the many contributions to this literature – Abiad (2003) reviews about 30 over a four-year period – really fulfill what they promise, i.e. to improve EWSs. Authors have strong incentives to present an improved EWS but there are only few studies which really care to systematically show why and where their own contribution brings progress in comparison to earlier empirical work. Even in our sample of thorough studies, one may question whether the often specific crisis definitions, small country samples or short time periods are driving forces behind the "success" claimed. It is thus Edison (2003) who stands out in her effort to test for robustness of findings. Her results indeed reveal an enormous amount of heterogeneity in approaches but also stability in fundamentals that help to understand and possibly forecast currency crises. So, is it only the "right" set of fundamentals that matters, or do the new approaches presented here also help – as we think – in improving EWSs?

3 Robust Lessons about Practical Early Warning Systems[10]

3.1 Motivation

Financial crises have not declined in number, frequency or severity over the last two decades, rather the contrary (Bordo et al., 2001). Each crisis causes enormous costs in the countries concerned. Even if many crises may help to promote overdue structural change, they are costly and it is a worthwhile objective to realize adjustments without this heavy toll. Thus, international financial institutions invest in researching early warning systems (EWS).[11] There is now a wide range of studies available, however, without real converging results: studies vary in coverage of countries and time, they apply different methods and they may even define crises quite differently. So are there any robust findings that might help policy makers? This paper does not add another EWS to the existing body of literature but systematically analyzes the robustness of main approaches and aims at contributing to the actual policy discussion. It is shown that, indeed, most findings critically depend on their empirical design. EWSs are a somewhat dubious subject from this perspective. However, there also emerge robust lessons that help us to better understand and implement EWSs.

The modern approaches to understanding determinants of currency crises started in the early 1990s. The largely unexpected shake-up of the European Monetary System in 1992/93 motivated Eichengreen, Rose and Wyplosz (1995,

---

10 I would like to thank my co-authors Lukas Menkhoff and Katja Sawischlewski. This paper was originally published under the title "Robust lessons about practical early warning systems", in *Journal of Policy Modeling* 28:2, 2006, 163-193, and is reproduced by kind permission of Elsevier Inc., Amsterdam. Helpful comments by Marcel Fratzscher, Torben Lütje, Stefan Niermann and Hans-Herrmann Steinbeck as well as an anonymous referee are gratefully acknowledged. Moreover, we highly appreciate all comments and advices received by participants of the 12th Annual Conference on Pacific Basin Finance, Economics, Accounting, and Business in Bangkok/Thailand, the Research Seminar at the Gottfried Wilhelm Leibniz Universität Hannover/Germany, the Göttinger Workshop Internationale Wirtschaftsbeziehungen 2005 in Göttingen/Germany, the Annual Conference Research Committee Development Economics 2005, Verein für Socialpolitik at the Institute for World Economics in Kiel/Germany, the 20th Annual Congress of the European Economic Association (EEA) in Amsterdam/Netherlands, the 14th World Congress of the International Economic Association (IEA) in Marrakech/Morocco, as well as the critical study and discussion by students of the Master programme in Economics 2004/2005 at University of Minho in Braga/Portugal.

11 See for example Berg et al. (2000) as well as the many studies conducted by IMF staff (e.g. Kaminsky, Lizondo and Reinhart, 1998, Berg and Pattillo, 1999, 1999a, Edison, 2003, Abiad, 2003, and Sy, 2004). Furthermore, see Kamin, Schindler and Samuel (2001), representing research by the Federal Reserve Board. Bussiere and Fratzscher (2002) provide an example of ECB work on this topic.

1996). Thereafter, attention focused more on developing countries (Frankel and Rose, 1996), spurred by the Mexican crisis (e.g. Sachs, Tornell and Velasco, 1996) and, above all, by the Asian crisis (e.g. Kaminsky, 1998, Kaminsky, Lizondo and Reinhart, 1998, Berg and Pattillo, 1999a). More currency crises followed, e.g. major ones in Russia and Argentina, stimulating ongoing research in common factors and an optimal EWS design. In the beginning, efforts were directed into analyzing an increasing set of variables, collecting larger samples and introducing multivariate techniques. Recent trends in this field point towards further modifications in method, such as applying a multinomial logit approach (Bussiere and Fratzscher, 2002), a Markov Switching approach (Martinez-Peria, 2002, Abiad, 2003) and extreme value theory to identify crises (Pozo and Amuedo-Dorantes, 2003). Another trend is towards focusing on regional studies, such as Esquivel and Larrain (1999), Brueggemann and Linne (2002) or Pasternak (2003).

The universe of proposed EWSs thus stretches over five dimensions: variables, sample period, sample countries, crisis definition and method applied. Each EWS is a combination regarding these five dimensions, so that – due to focus and product differentiation – usually results cannot be compared to each other. Moreover, most studies do not present extensive robustness checks, so it is not clear which improvement claimed will last under different conditions. There is thus an obvious need to make results comparable in order to derive useful policy lessons. It is, however, also obvious that due to the complexity involved, analytical restrictions are needed. Fortunately, several earlier studies have carefully analyzed the usefulness of variables and found that variables often point in the same direction, in particular in a multivariate approach. As, moreover, all variables are rather more able to give a warning signal of a possible upcoming crisis than predict the timing and exact occurrence of the latter, a selection of few meaningful fundamental indicators will work (Salvatore, 1999). In this respect we follow the suggestion of Berg and Pattillo (1999a, p. 573 et sqq.) to rely on their handful of variables only.

Regarding the issue of robustness, Edison (2003) is the most complete study published. She basically extends the leading indicator work of Kaminsky, Lizondo and Reinhart (1998) – in short: KLR – in four of the five dimensions mentioned above, although with different intensity. Our study also departs from KLR, who presented the broadest approach at that time and has thus been a benchmark study until today. Going beyond Edison (2003), we systematically apply several methods to generate warning signals, we analyze the influence of crisis definition more thoroughly and we consider some recent proposals to improve forecasting power of EWSs.

We find, as did Berg and Pattillo (1999a) and Edison (2003), that it becomes more difficult over time to replicate earlier crisis dates. So the dependent variable may change from study to study even if all parameters are kept the same. Fortunately, this haziness in data does not seem to influence results too much.

Berg and Pattillo (1999a) show that a logit approach can improve results of EWSs. To some extent, this holds for our extensions, too. We test their logit model with variables given as number as well as with variables given in a reduced 0-1-form. The two approaches do not differ that much although the reduced form yields somewhat better results. One surprise is, however, the implementation of the multinomial logit proposed by Bussiere and Fratzscher (2002). This technique does not provide the expected useful forecasting results when applied out-of-sample but seems to depend decisively on the underlying data.

Regarding the crisis definition, it is found that the choice between the several definitions offered by the literature is non-trivial. Comparing the KLR approach with the narrower Frankel and Rose (1996) – in short: FR – proposal and the broader Bussiere and Fratzscher (2002) – in short BF – measure indicates: It is the KLR measure which seems most practical.

Further examinations on EWS parameters in order to improve forecasting ability reveal that there are indeed options available: we find that the recent trend in the literature towards focusing on regional EWS has some justification in the sense that it helps to improve forecasts. Finally, due to instability over time, shorter samples also tend to provide better forecasts. One should be aware, however, that regional EWSs as well as shorter samples tend to homogenize the problem: explanations are thus "better" because they are easier and not necessarily because one would understand better.

In summary, our understanding of EWSs – which basically aim at predicting larger exchange rate changes – may be guided by core insights from the empirical exchange rate literature: fundamentals matter but their influence is small and unstable (Frankel and Rose, 1995, Sarno and Taylor, 2002). Keeping these limitations in mind, there emerge four major lessons on the elements of robust EWS and on appropriate policy design: First, EWSs have robust forecasting power. Changes in core fundamentals signal future problems and thus help policy-makers to prevent crises. Second, policy makers must decide about pros and cons of competing crisis definitions as well as about the calibration of EWS (false alarms vs. missed crises). Third, EWSs' performance is increased by taking a logit model to condense information from various fundamental variables and by taking shorter samples and regional EWSs to address instability over time and countries. Fourth, the robust forecasting contribution of a regional contagion dummy indicates that international financial markets do not function always efficiently. Policy has to take this into account and may want to have instruments at hand to partly disintegrate its economy from detrimental shocks.

The remainder of this paper is organized as follows: Chapter 3.2 presents our extension of the KLR approach over time and countries. Chapter 3.3 examines the advantageousness of several logit approaches compared to the composite indicator. The pros and cons of various crisis definitions are analyzed in Chapter 3.4. Further approaches to improve forecasts are discussed in Chapter 3.5. Chapter 3.6 concludes by shedding light on the design of robust EWSs on the one hand and resulting policy conclusions on the other.

3.2 KLR extensions over time and countries

3.2.1 Reproducing the KLR approach

In order to tie up to previous research and assure data consistency, we begin our robustness analyses with a replication effort of the benchmark KLR approach. Starting with the crisis definition, KLR use an index of exchange market pressure (in short: EMPI) for each country that is constructed as a weighted average of monthly percentage changes in the nominal exchange rate (NER) and in gross international reserves (RES). These two components are weighted in such a way that they have the same conditional variance. Reflecting the pressure on the currency as an increase of the index, either due to a currency's depreciation or due to a loss of international reserves, a crisis (C) is considered a period in which the EMPI is more than three standard deviations above its country-specific mean.

$$EMPI_t^i = \frac{NER_t^i - NER_{t-1}^i}{NER_{t-1}^i} - \frac{\sigma_{\Delta NER}^i}{\sigma_{\Delta RES}^i} \cdot \frac{RES_t^i - RES_{t-1}^i}{RES_{t-1}^i};$$

$$C_t^i = \begin{cases} 1, & if \quad EMP_t^i > \overline{EMP^i} + 3\sigma_{EMP^i}^i \\ 0, & otherwise \end{cases}$$

Periods of hyperinflation, with price level increases of more than 150% in the previous six months, are treated separately, forming sub-samples with extra EMPI and crisis calculations for each country. The chosen sample contains 20 countries including 15 developing and 5 industrialized countries over the sample period from January 1970 to April 1995. The first four columns of Annex 3.1 give an overview of identified crises by KLR and Edison (2003) as well as the results of our own replications.[12]

12 All data used derive from the IMF international financial statistics (IFS). When trying to reproduce the crises, 2.5 standard deviations instead of 3 above the EMPI mean appear to be most applicable. Our proceedings align with Edison (2003, p. 11). Nevertheless, the results are quite astonishing: KLR identify 75 crises, Edison finds 70 in the same sample, but only 47 of them match exactly with the ones of KLR. Our replication identifies 79 crisis, 36 of them correspond exactly to the original ones, 45 to the replication by Edison. Berg and Pattillo (1999, p. 565), who replicate the KLR benchmark as well, assign these discrepancies to differences in the raw data resulting from data revisions and individual data "cleaning". Taking into account that the latter fail to match 14 out of the 75 KLR cri-

After determining the crisis dates, the next step consists of choosing meaningful indicators to give a warning signal when crossing a formerly designed threshold value. KLR identify 13 out of 16 tested variables to be appropriate with the help of the so-called (adjusted) noise-to-signal ratio. This ratio contains the number of false signals as a share of possible false signals (B/B+D), divided by the number of good signals as a proportion of cases in which good signals could have been issued (A/A+C). Good and bad signals are distinguished according to the following matrix.

	Crisis (within next 24 months)	No crisis (within next 24 months)
Crisis signal	A	B
No crisis signal	C	D

With A: Number of months in which the indicator issued a good signal; B: Number of months in which the indicator issued a false alarm or "noise", and thus a bad signal; C: Number of months in which the indicator failed to issue a signal (which would have been a good one); D: Number of months in which the indicator desisted from issuing a signal (which would have been a bad one).

In order to create an easy-to-handle model we choose the set of 6 variables proposed and statistically verified by Berg and Pattillo (1999a), namely deviation of real exchange rate from trend, growth of international reserves, of exports, and of M2 to international reserves, as well as current account to GDP and M2 to international reserves in levels (for details about the construction of the variables, see Annex 3.2).

Following Eichengreen, Rose and Wyplosz (1995), Figure 3.1 sheds light on the average movements of the chosen indicators in a 48-month event window around the identified crisis dates and their average course in tranquil periods respectively. All indicators exhibit clearly perceptible patterns showing that their course is different before and after the crisis.

Figure 3.1 Movements of different variables in crisis times[a]

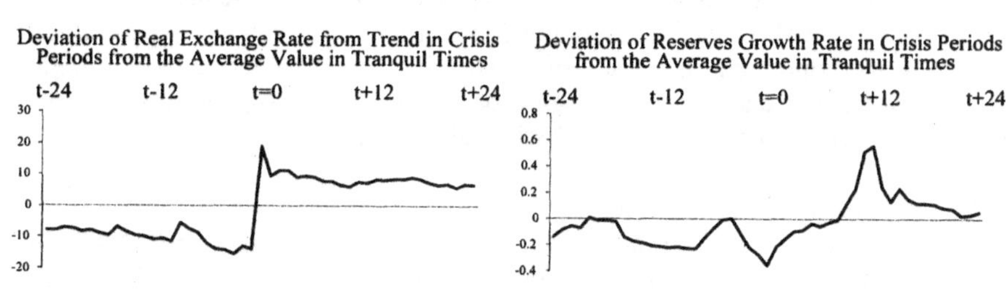

ses only one year later while Edison misses 28 three years afterwards, our results five years later appear reasonable.

Figure 3.1 Movements of different variables in crisis times[a] (continued)

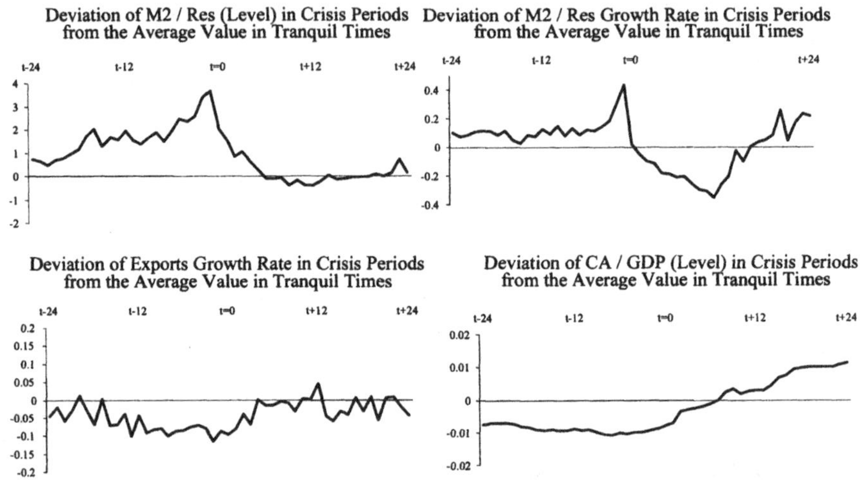

a The graphs show the deviation in course of the respective variable in a 24-months window before and after the crisis from its average value in calm periods. Results are calculated concentrating on the original KLR sample, but they are similar when enlarging the sample to 28 countries as presented later on (see 2.3). Except for M2 / reserves (level) and CA / GDP (level) as well as the real exchange rate, the variables indicate growth rates in reference to the same month of the previous year. The real exchange rate is expressed as deviation of its deterministic trend.

Table 3.1 (columns 1-2) presents information on the individual indicator's performance of our replication. For all six variables we reproduce noise-to-signal ratios smaller than one and thus consider all variables to contribute meaningfully to an EWS. The real exchange rate variable clearly performs best. Our results are in line with KLR and former replications. In order to assess the meaning of an indicator's signal better, we also calculate the so-called conditional probability (A/A+B) that indicates the probability of the occurrence of a crisis within a 24-month window after the respective indicator has issued a signal. Again, the real exchange rate variable proves to be the top performer with a conditional crisis probability of 67% when signaling.

3.2.2 Extending KLR over time

We then extend the KLR sample to a period from January 1970 to December 2002. This has different implications: First, the EMPI is highly sample-dependent. An extension changes not only the country-specific mean but also the calculated standard deviation. As a consequence, we identify slightly differrent crisis periods than before (see Annex 3.1, column 5).[13] Taking a closer look at the countries concerned, a further conclusion emerges: As countries hit by the Asian financial crisis in 1997/1998 seem to be especially affected by shifts in crisis periods, one might suppose that heavy crises influence mean and standard deviation in a way that weaker crisis signals are no longer identified (e.g. in Malaysia). Thus, the identification of a currency crisis with the help of the KLR definition depends critically on the country's historical experiences and the considered time period respectively.

Table 3.1 In-sample[a] performance of univariate indicators: KLR definition and sample variations

Sample	Original KLR sample 1970-4/1995		Time extension 1970-2002 original KLR sample		Country extension max. sample[b] original 1970-4/1995		Time + country extension 1970-2002 max. sample[b]	
Variable[c]	Noise / signal[d]	P(crisis | signal)[e]	Noise / signal[d]	P(crisis | signal)[e]	Noise / signal[d]	P(crisis | signal)[e]	Noise / signal[d]	P(crisis | signal)[e]
Real exchange rate	0.18	0.67	0.17	0.65	0.25	0.56	0.23	0.55
Exports	0.59	0.38	0.66	0.31	0.65	0.33	0.73	0.28
Reserves	0.50	0.41	0.46	0.39	0.48	0.40	0.49	0.36
M2 / reserves	0.56	0.38	0.50	0.37	0.58	0.35	0.55	0.33
M2 / reserves (level)	0.55	0.39	0.53	0.35	0.57	0.34	0.58	0.32
CA / GDP (level)	0.51	0.45	0.49	0.37	0.47	0.43	0.43	0.39

a The sample compromises the original KLR sample, i.e. data from 20 countries for the period from January 1970 to April 1995.

b The extended sample contains Argentina, Bolivia, Brazil, Chile, Denmark, Finland, Greece, India, Indonesia, Israel, Colombia, Korea, Malaysia, Mexico, Norway, Pakistan, Peru, Philippines, Portugal, Sweden, Singapore, Spain, Sri Lanka, South Africa, Thailand, Turkey, Uruguay and Venezuela.

c Except for M2 / reserves (level) and CA / GDP (level) as well as the real exchange rate, the variables indicate growth rates in reference to the same month of the previous year. The real exchange rate is expressed as deviation of its deterministic trend.

d The noise-to-signal ratio shows the number of bad signals as a share of possible bad signals, divided by the number of good signals as a share of possible good signals.

e The conditional probability indicates the probability of a crisis in a 24 months window after the respective indicator issued a signal.

Second, all six indicators keep their forecasting power with a noise-to-signal ratio smaller than one (see Table 3.1, columns 1-3). Furthermore, indicators

13 Adding up to 93 crisis periods, 13 of the old ones can no longer be detected. Instead, 26 new crises are identified, but only 18 of them can be ascribed to the additional months considered.

mainly keep their performance relative to each other with the real exchange rate variable staying the best performer.

3.2.3 Expanding KLR over countries

Following Edison (2003), we also consider 8 additional countries which experienced at least one currency crisis. Differently from extensions in a time dimension, additional countries have no influence on the crisis identification as the respective EMPI and standard deviations are calculated separately for each country. Annex 3.1 shows the identified crisis periods for the expanded sample: 104 for the shorter period (1970-1995) and 126 for the extended period (1970-2002).

Table 3.1 (columns 4-5) sheds light on the indicators' performance after also including additional countries. Again, to a great extent, all indicators keep both a noise-to-signal ratio smaller than one as well as their performance order. The worse results for the four variables, real exchange rate, exports, M2 / reserves and M2 / reserves (level), support the idea that the more (heterogeneous) countries are examined, the more difficult it gets to achieve meaningful signals. Nevertheless, all chosen variables seem to be adequate.

3.2.4 Forecasting out-of-sample

Up to now, we have only considered the performance of univariate indicators in-sample. However, in order to assess the applicability of our variables to form an EWS, we should assess two further aspects. First, it seems reasonable to analyze the indicators' information jointly, as currency crises are often the result of simultaneously appearing weaknesses. Second, reliability out-of-sample is most important when aiming for a forecast.

Therefore, in a first step, we define crises for the whole period from 1970 to 2002, but rely on the period from 1970 to 1995 for crisis identification as well as for the design of the single indicator thresholds. The remaining 92 months from May 1995 to December 2002 represent the out-of-sample test period.

In a second step, we follow the idea of Kaminsky (1998, p. 14 et sqq.). Having looked at each indicator separately so far, we combine the information provided by all variables to a composite indicator:

$$I_t = \sum_{j=1}^{n} S_t^j / \omega^j$$

Accordingly, the different indicator signals are summed up (ΣS) and weighted with their inverse noise-to-signal ratio ($1/\omega$) each). Depending on the number of variables signaling, the composite indicator can take different values. As pure values of the composite indicator do not say anything about the crisis probability, the associated (conditional) probabilities have to be calculated.

In a third step, finally, the in- and out-of-sample performance can be assessed. When comparing the composite indicator with the best univariate indicator, the real exchange rate, two aspects emerge: First, in general, results out-of-sample are (as expected) worse in comparison to the in-sample consideration. Second, the composite indicator clearly outperforms the univariate benchmark, especially out-of-sample. As presumed, it is thus worthwhile to continue to work with the combined information of different indicators. Our results align with those of Goldstein, Kaminsky, and Reinhart (2000, p. 64 et sqq.), and are hence not explicitly displayed here.

3.3 From composite indicators to logit models

In this chapter, we go beyond the univariate KLR indicator approach and the composite indicator as a step towards a multivariate framework. We analyze whether multivariate logit models outperform former approaches and which among them might be most appropriate for practical purposes.

3.3.1 Two logit model alternatives

Describing the crisis probability as a non-linear function of different variables, logit and probit models feature the possibility of analyzing their statistical significance in a multivariate approach. Following Berg and Pattillo (1999a; in short BP), we consider the 6 BP variables over the original KLR time and country sample. The variables enter the logit model in both the binary signal 0-1-form and with continuous values, alternatively. So far, we have considered a crisis window of 24 months, i.e. a signal is considered to be a good one if an indicator issues a signal and a crisis follows within the following 24 months. For the logit approach we thus have to transpose the dependent crisis variable (see also Bussiere and Fratzscher 2002, p. 10):

$$Y_t^i = \begin{cases} 1 & \text{if a crisis follows within 24 months} \\ 0 & \text{otherwise} \end{cases}$$

Table 3.2 shows the two estimated logit models. In both models, the same four variables are significant at the 1% level and their coefficients show the expected and correct signs.[14] The odds ratio also displayed permits us to draw conclusions with regard to the conditional probability. If in the binomial logit model

14 M2 / reserves as well as CA / GDP are excluded from the logit models due to their lack of significance. In the model with variables entering as binary signals, positive coefficients imply a rising crisis probability whenever the indicators cross their formerly designed thresholds and issue crisis signals. In the model with continuous values, coefficients' signs vary according to the definition of the respective variable. A positive coefficient for the ratio of M2 / reserves (level) e.g. implies a rising crisis probability whenever the ratio heightens. By contrast, expressed by the negative coefficient, decreasing reserves growth heightens the crisis probability.

with binary signals, e.g. the exports variable emits a signal, the crisis probability is about 62.1 % higher than without the signal. Again, the real exchange rate variable shows the highest conditional probability.

Table 3.2 Two logit model alternatives relying on the KLR sample

	Binomial logit model with variables entering in form of binary 0-1 signals			Binomial logit model with variables entering in form of their continuous values		
Variable[a]	Coefficient	Odds ratio e^{β}	Significance	Coefficient	Odds ratio e^{β}	Significance
Real exchange rate	1.976	7.213	0.000	-0.019	0.981	0.000
Exports	0.483	1.621	0.000	-0.408	0.665	0.001
Reserves	0.685	1.983	0.000	-0.368	0.692	0.000
M2 / reserves (level)	0.474	1.606	0.000	0.038	1.039	0.000
No. of observations		5065			5065	
Pseudo-R^2		0.14			0.09	

a Exports and reserves are expressed as growth rates in reference to the respective month of the previous year, whereas M2 / reserves is a level consideration. The real exchange rate is expressed as deviation of its deterministic trend.

As before, we are not only interested in in-sample, but also in out-of-sample results: Our performance assessment both in- and out-of-sample of the two logit alternatives in comparison to the composite indicator can be found in Table 3.3. In order to assure comparability, we reduce the latter to exactly the same four variables entering the binomial logit models. Following Berg and Pattillo (1999a), we take the two alternative cut-off probabilities of 25% and 50% to issue a signal. As the objective of an EWS consists in properly forecasting upcoming crises, the percentage of crises called correctly can probably be considered the most important criterion. However, without taking into account the number of false alarms as well, a performance assessment is only half-hearted.

At first sight, the trade-off between correctly called crises and false alarms becomes obvious and can be seen as valid over all different approaches. Hence we also return to this issue in our policy-related conclusions. At this point in time, let us take a closer look at the in-sample performance of the binary logit with variables e.g. entering in the form of binary signals: using the 50% cut-off, the last model provides an obviously better performance compared to the other two models as far as correctly signaled crises as well as false alarms are concerned. Bringing the cut-off probability down to 25%, the number of correctly called crisis periods is augmented to 53% – but at the cost of more false alarms. The models are thus difficult to compare. Out-of-sample, performance results

Table 3.3 In- and out-of-sample[a] performance of two logit model alternatives and a composite indicator benchmark

	In-sample			Out-of-sample		
	Composite indicator[b]	Binomial logit model with variables in form of binary 0-1 signals	Binomial logit model with variables in form of continuous values	Composite indicator[b]	Binomial logit model with variables in form of binary 0-1 signals	Binomial logit model with variables in form of continuous values
	Goodness-of-fit (50% cut-off)					
Percent of crisis periods correctly called[c]	23	27	10	24	20	2
False alarms as percent of total alarms[d]	40	34	23	76	76	90
Percent of tranquil periods correctly called[e]	94	95	99	83	79	94
Percent of observations correctly called	70	77	75	73	64	71
	Goodness-of-fit (25% cut-off)					
Percent of crisis periods correctly called[c]	30	53	75	25	39	70
False alarms as percent of total alarms[d]	45	56	63	77	72	72
Percent of tranquil periods correctly called[e]	92	76	53	82	67	38
Percent of observations correctly called	76	70	59	72	60	46

a The period from January 1970 to April 1995 is considered as in-sample. The out-of-sample period ranges from May 1995 to December 2002.

b In order to assure comparability, the composite Indicator contains the same 4 variables that enter the logit models.

c A crisis signal is considered as correct, if the estimated crisis probability is above the cut-off probability, and a crisis is coming up in the next 24 months.

d A false alarm is an observation where the estimated crisis probability is above the cut-off probability, but no crisis is coming up in the next 24 months.

e A signal for a tranquil period is considered as correct, if the estimated crisis probability is underneath the cut-off probability, and no crisis is coming up in the next 24 months.

once again worsen compared to in-sample estimations. Furthermore, with a 50% cut-off, the composite indicator shows the best performance. However, applying a 25% cut-off, it is the binomial logit model with signals which shows a higher percentage of correctly called crises as well as less false alarms. So taking the four cases considered in Table 3.3 as the benchmark, each of the three models is best in one case but only the binary logit model is never the worst. Though performance results are not unambiguous, the binary logit model seems to perform most robustly.

3.3.2 The multinomial logit

So far, the dependent variable could either take a value of 1, representing a crisis period, or 0 for tranquil times. We thus assumed variables to behave differently in crisis and non-crisis times. However, reality is more complex. Variables seem not only to deviate from their normal level before but also noticeably after a crisis (see Figure 3.1). Accordingly, instead of comparing only two states (crisis and non-crisis times), an EWS could also address what can be called a "post-crisis bias".

To our knowledge, Bussiere and Fratzscher (2002) represent the pioneering work in this direction and thus form our reference. Instead of a binomial logit model they estimate a multinomial one with the following three different states:

$$CC_t^i = \begin{cases} 1 & \text{if a crisis is upcoming in the next 24 months ([pre-]crisis period)} \\ 2 & \text{crisis and the further 24 months after a crisis (recovery period)} \\ 0 & \text{otherwise (tranquil period)} \end{cases}$$

Taking three states into account would presuppose that a mean value comparison of the possible three states displays significant differences. The results of our analyses for the six indicators shown in Table 3.4 confirm this.

Table 3.4 Mean value comparison of key indicators (24-months windows)[a]

Variable[b]	Average all periods	Average tranquil periods	Average crisis periods	Average post-crisis / recovery periods	Significance in differences? (ANOVA)
Real Exchange Rate	1.221	2.028	-7.654	10.608	Yes / 0.000
Exports	0.153	0.176	0.110	0.150	Yes / 0.000
Reserves	0.290	0.313	0.176	0.373	Yes / 0.000
M2 / reserves	0.082	0.064	0.196	-.0173	Yes / 0.000
M2 / reserves (level)	3.067	2.570	4.363	2.775	Yes / 0.000
CA / GDP (level)	-0.022	-0.020	-0.029	-0.018	Yes / 0.000

a The mean value comparison comprises data of the original KLR sample. We consider 24 months before and after a crisis, respectively. Alternative shortenings of the time window to two times 12 months unveils similar results.

b Analogous to Table 3.1, Note c.

Considering, for example, the real exchange rate variable 24 months before and after a crisis respectively, a significant difference in mean values becomes obvious. Whereas the average value in crisis times is -7.654 and thus implies a negative deviation from the trend, representing an overvalued local currency, the mean value for the crisis itself and the 24 months after the crisis is 10.608. Alternatively, the time window is shortened to two times 12 months, but results stay consistent over all variables (and are thus not presented here).

Aiming to assess whether a multinomial logit can really improve crisis recognition and forecast, Table 3.5 sheds light on both in- and out-of-sample performance of the different types of logit models. In order to make results comparable, we use the same four variables for the multinomial as for the binomial logit model.[15]

Table 3.5 In- and out-of-sample[a] performance: A binomial and a multinomial logit model in comparison

	In-sample		Out-of-sample	
	Binomial logit model[b]	Multinomial logit model[b] (24 months[c])	Binomial logit model[b]	Multinomial logit model[b] (24 months[c])
	Goodness-of-fit (50% cut-off)			
Percent of crisis periods correctly called[d]	27	27	20	21
False alarms as percent of total alarms[e]	34	33	76	75
Percent of tranquil periods correctly called[f]	95	94	79	75
Percent of observations correctly called	77	71	64	59
	Goodness-of-fit (25% cut-off)			
Percent of crisis periods correctly called[d]	53	30	39	21
False alarms as percent of total alarms[e]	56	38	72	75
Percent of tranquil periods correctly called[f]	76	92	67	75
Percent of observations correctly called	70	71	83	59

a As in Table 3.3.
b The independent variables enter the binomial and the multinomial logit model in binary 0-1 form. Calculations with independent variables entering in form of continuous values reveal weaker results and are thus not explicitly considered here.
c Shortening the considered time windows to 12 months before and after the crisis, respectively, disclose similar, though even slightly worse results that are not shown here.
d-f Analogous to Table 3.3, Notes c-e.

15 For the construction of the multinomial logit model, we rely on Bussiere and Fratzscher (2002, p. 19 et sqq.). Like them, we choose the tranquil regime as the base regime. We estimate the probabilities of being rather in the tranquil period or in a (pre-)crisis or a recovery period according to changes in the independent variables. Each observation can be assigned to the state with the highest probability. However, in order to take different cut-off probabilities into account, we also include different cut-off thresholds for signalling a pre-crisis state. In Table 3.5, the performance results of our estimated multinomial logit model are thus compared with those of the binomial logit model using a 25% and a 50% cut-off probability respectively.

Three aspects emerge when comparing the multinomial logit model with the binomial one: First of all, considering both the 25% and 50% cut-off probabilities in sample, it is worth doubting whether a multinomial logit model generally improves forecasting performance. Different from Bussiere and Fratzscher (2002), we do not find superior performance results in comparison to our binomial logit model. Second, out-of-sample using a 50% cut-off, the multinomial model seems slightly better than the binomial model regarding crisis periods correctly called and false alarms. However, results are not at all convincing when considering the 25% cut-off probability. Third, a binomial logit model is easier to implement as an EWS and we thus decide to continue our work relying on the binomial logit with variables entering in binary form to be the best performing method. We now explicitly consider different crisis definitions presented in the literature.

3.4 The impact of different crisis definitions

Obviously, the robustness question also applies to the kind of crisis definition used. Though this part of an EWS can be considered as a more philosophical issue as either someone believes something is a crisis or not, there can be at least three different kinds of crisis definitions found in the literature, which comprise between one and three variables. Moreover, the interpretation of concrete values to be reached before a crisis is called, differ from study to study. We compare and analyze the proposals of Frankel and Rose (FR, 1996) and Bussiere and Fratzscher (BF, 2002) with KLR concerning robustness and stability.

FR concentrate explicitly on currency crashes. In contrast to KLR, who include both international reserves and the exchange rate – and thus account for averted as well as successful attacks on the domestic currency, FR focus on the latter. According to their definition, a crisis is considered a period of a nominal exchange rate (NER) devaluation of at least 25%. Additionally, in order to take hyperinflation into account, at the same time this has to comply an exceeding of the previous year's change in the exchange rate by at least 10%.[16]

16 FR admit that their cut-off points are somewhat arbitrary but sensitivity analyses support the settings. The idea of adding a second criterion is supported by Esquivel and Larrain (1999, p. 8) who also try to ensure in their work that only meaningful currency devaluations (in the sense of those effecting the purchasing power parity) are considered as crises. When applying the FR definition, due to our use of monthly instead of annual data, we adjusted crisis definition and the proposed 3-year windowing by FR (1996, p. 358) to monthly reference. The transformation from yearly to monthly data is again arbitrary. Godfjan and Valdés (1998) e.g. take a 2-month window when reproducing FR.

$$Crisis=\begin{cases}1 \text{ if } \frac{NER_t^i - NER_{t-1}^i}{NER_{t-1}^i} > 0.25 \cup \frac{NER_t^i - NER_{t-1}^i}{NER_{t-1}^i} - \frac{NER_{t-1}^i - NER_{t-2}^i}{NER_{t-2}^i} > 0.1 \\ 0 \text{ otherwise}\end{cases}$$

Whereas FR reduce the KLR definition to the exchange rate focus, BF enlarge it by additionally considering interest rate changes. They base their decision on the idea that a central bank has mainly three options to respond to speculative attacks: In order to stabilize the exchange rate the bank can either augment the interest rate or sell international reserves. A third option would be to let market forces work and thus the currency devaluate. All three components are included in the EMPI of BF.

$$EMPI_t^i = \frac{1}{\sigma_{REER}^2}\left(\frac{REER_t^i - REER_{t-1}^i}{REER_{t-1}^i}\right) + \frac{1}{\sigma_r^2}\left(r_t^i - r_{t-1}^i\right) - \frac{1}{\sigma_{RES}^2}\left(\frac{RES_t^i - RES_{t-1}^i}{RES_{t-1}^i}\right)$$

Aiming to avoid sample splits due to hyperinflation periods, they concentrate on the real effective instead of the nominal exchange rates (REER). Accordingly, they consider real interest rates (r). The single components are weighted with their inverse sample variance over all countries for the whole period: the higher the variance, the smaller their weight. Originally, a crisis is considered a period when the EMPI is at least two standard deviations above its country average.[17]

Annex 3.1 (columns 6 to 10) shows the results of applying both the FR and the BF definition to the original KLR sample and its variations. The respective results of our binomial logit models are displayed in Table 3.6.

The in-sample FR performance results are convincing, whereas out-of-sample the FR logit model is beaten by the KLR model. Moreover, two aspects should be considered most skeptically: The performance tests for FR are based on a small sample of quite homogenous countries. Neither the EMS nor the Asian crisis is largely identified and thus a considerable number of countries that did not experience any crisis had to be dropped from the analysis. We doubt that an exclusive concentration on currency crashes is warranted for a practical EWS covering a wide set of heterogeneous countries.

In contrast, the BF definition shows a high stability over time and country variations. Admittedly, as EMPI variances are calculated over the whole sample period, the crisis definition seems less sensitive to country specific characteristics. Performance results, however, especially the percent of crises correctly called, are not fully convincing. Furthermore, restricted data availability and the

---

17 For our reconstruction we slightly modify the definition by taking real exchange rates. Furthermore, when trying to reproduce the results of BF, we find a 2.5 standard deviation to be most appropriate.

lack of consistency in the interest rate data should be taken into account when choosing the BF definition.

Table 3.6 In- and out-of-sample[a] performance of binomial logit models: Different crisis definitions and KLR sample

	In-sample		Out-of-sample	
	FR definition	BF definition	FR definition	BF Definition
	Goodness-of-fit (50% cut-off)			
Percent of crisis periods correctly called[b]	35	4	17	3
False alarms as percent of total alarms[c]	33	30	89	50
Percent of tranquil periods correctly called[d]	93	100	70	99
Percent of observations correctly called	75	81	61	84
	Goodness-of-fit (25% cut-off)			
Percent of crisis periods correctly called[b]	54	37	29	16
False alarms as percent of total alarms[c]	49	64	86	89
Percent of tranquil periods correctly called[d]	78	84	63	76
Percent of observations correctly called	71	75	57	67

a The sample only comprises countries which experienced a crisis. Applying the FR definition, these are Argentina, Bolivia, Brazil, Chile Indonesia, Israel, Colombia, Mexico, Peru, Philippines, Turkey, Uruguay and Venezuela of the (small) original KLR sample, plus Pakistan, Sri Lanka and South Africa, being part of the expanded one. In-sample analyses refer to the period from January 1970 to April 1995. The preceding 92 months till December 2002 are considered as out-of-sample.

b-d Analogous to Table 3.3, Notes c-e.

In summary, the choice of a crisis definition is in the last instance a policy decision. Under many circumstances, however, the KLR definition seems to be most practical.

3.5 Further lessons for improving forecasts

So far, we have analyzed different methodological approaches as well as three crisis definitions over different sample periods and countries. Three further aspects emerge: There can be observed a recent trend to downsize analyzed samples by focusing on selected regions when scrutinizing EWSs (see Esquivel and Larrain, 1999, Brueggemann and Linne, 2002). Others apply different approaches to one country (see e.g. Alvarez-Plata and Schrooten, 2003, 2004) or choose single examples of few countries to assess the proposed technique (see Abiad, 2003, for example). It seems interesting to examine what happens if the sample is split up into regional sub-samples. Furthermore, we want to assess whether shortening samples could improve results. The third aspect addresses another growing body of empirical literature: the danger of contagion.

3.5.1 Regional sample splits

The KLR sample comprises a very heterogeneous set of countries. Applying the FR definition has shown that different types of crisis seem to be attributable to different countries. We thus analyze the robustness of former results with the help of the KLR crisis definition and the expanded sample across three different regions: Latin America, Asia and Europe.

As before, we focus exclusively on the multivariate approach.[18] The outcome is shown in Table 3.7. Latin American results, in- and out-of-sample, outper-

Table 3.7 In- und out-of-sample[a] performance of a binomial logit model after sample split up[b], KLR definition and KLR sample

	In-sample			Out-of-sample		
	Latin America	Asia	Europe	Latin America	Asia	Europe
	Goodness-of-fit (50% cut-off)					
Percent of crisis periods correctly called[c]	40	5	20	37	0	0
False alarms as percent of total alarms[d]	39	26	33	79	0	100
Percent of tranquil periods correctly called[e]	92	100	96	65	100	99
Percent of observations correctly called	80	80	74	59	69	79
	Goodness-of-fit (25% cut-off)					
Percent of crisis periods correctly called[c]	60	39	89	41	27	92
False alarms as percent of total alarms[d]	53	60	70	79	48	80
Percent of tranquil periods correctly called[e]	78	85	18	61	89	8
Percent of observations correctly called	74	75	38	57	69	25

a As in Table 3.3.
b The expanded KLR sample is split into three regional sub samples. "Latin America" covers Argentina, Bolivia, Brazil, Chile, Colombia, Mexico, Peru, Uruguay and Venezuela, "Asia" contains India, Indonesia, Korea, Malaysia, Philippines, Thailand, Pakistan, Sri Lanka as well as Singapore, and Denmark, Finland, Greece, Norway, Portugal, Sweden, Spain and Turkey are considered separately as "Europe". Israel and South Africa are dropped from consideration.
c-e As in Table 3.3.

18 Regional performance results of the individual indicators are not explicitly displayed here but can be resumed briefly. All three regions have the top indicator in common: It is once more the exchange rate variable. All the same, differences across the regions become also evident with one aspect which is worth mentioning: all Latin American variables display consistently better noise-to-signal ratios than in Europe and Asia. These results are in line with Edison (2003) who assesses differences between Asia and Latin America and also gets clearly better performance results for the latter.

form those of the other two regions. Especially out-of-sample, an explicit application of the presented model on Asia or Europe does not seem to make sense as crisis periods are no longer recognized and in Europe even false alarms skyrocket. Taking into account that the FR crisis definition, relying exclusively on the exchange rate, recognizes more Latin American crises than the other two definitions, and the real exchange rate variable proves its star performer quality one more time, results are not surprising.

To conclude, deviations between different regions exist. In order to improve an EWS' forecasting performance while still relying on a broad set of countries considered, some of the regional commonality might also be brought to an EWS by adding a regional dummy variable.

3.5.2 Shortening the sample

We continue our robustness analyses with a split in time dimension. Based on Choueiri and Kaminsky (1999), who find supporting evidence for a change in the nature of crises over time, the hitherto considered sample period of 25 years (1970 to 1995) might appear too long for reliable coefficients over time. Supposing shorter sample periods to reveal somewhat better results due to higher crisis homogeneity, we divide the extended sample period from 1970 to 2002 into three sub-periods: the first one ranging from 1970 to 1980, the second from 1981 to 1990 and the third from 1991 to 2002.

Table 3.8 displays the multivariate in-sample performance with the help of well-known binomial logit models. We take the logit model for the period from

Table 3.8 In-sample[a] performance of a binomial logit model: Shortening samples to ten year periods

	1970-1995	1970-2002[b]	1970-1980	1981-1990	1991-2002[b]
	Goodness-of-fit (50% cut-off)				
Percent of crisis periods correctly called[c]	27	25	44	22	3
False alarms as percent of total alarms[d]	34	47	34	42	52
Percent of tranquil periods correctly called[e]	95	90	94	93	99
Percent of observations correctly called	77	69	83	71	68
	Goodness-of-fit (25% cut-off)				
Percent of crisis periods correctly called[c]	53	40	54	52	98
False alarms as percent of total alarms[d]	56	57	40	54	67
Percent of tranquil periods correctly called[e]	76	84	90	73	4
Percent of observations correctly called	70	73	82	67	35

a The in-sample period comprises each indicated range.
b Crises are calculated according to the KLR crisis definition for the sample from January 1970 to April 1995. For the period from May 1995 to December 2002, thresholds of the original crisis definition are used.
c-e Analogous to Table 3.3, Notes c-e.

1970 to 1995 as a benchmark to compare it with the full sample (1970-2002) and with distinctively shorter samples. The assumption that shorter samples might improve performance can be confirmed, especially for a 25% cut-off probability. Nevertheless, performance results vary clearly with the periods considered. The overall most convincing performance is reached for the 1970s. Independently of the chosen cut-off-probability the logit model for the period between 1970 and 1980 outperforms the other ones. For the two other periods, between 1981 and 1990 as well as the 1990s up to 2002, results once again face the problem of setting the right threshold and balancing correctly called crises and false alarms.

3.5.3 Grasping contagion

The idea of capturing the risk of one country being affected by another country's crisis – either due to regional proximity (like the experience of the Asian crisis of 1997 has shown) or because of similar characteristics that seem to overcome regional distance (e.g. the affection of Russia by the Tequila crisis in 1994) – is one of the subjects given the most emphasis in current research on financial crisis. Efforts to characterize, to prove and to analyze financial contagion are numerous (for a survey, see Moser, 2003, Karolyi, 2003 or Kaminsky, Reinhart and Vegh, 2003). Mainly three channels of transmission can be identified in the literature: Firstly, effects can spill over due to bilateral or multilateral trade linkages (see Eichengreen, Rose and Wyplosz, 1996, Glick and Rose, 1999). Secondly, those countries either exposed to the same environmental conditions and shocks (see Masson, 1999, Moreno and Trehan, 2000), or having economic and political similarities (see Sachs, Tonell, Velasco, 1996, Hartmann, Straetmans and de Vries, 2004) are more likely to experience a crisis with one another. The third channel consists in tight financial linkages, arguing e.g. that investors might adjust their portfolio allocation in case of a financial crisis in one country. Having the same major creditors in common with the crisis country could thus lead to higher vulnerability in the respective country as well (see Kaminsky and Reinhart, 2000, Van Rijckeghem and Weder, 2001, or Caramazza, Ricci and Salgado, 2004). A thorough assessment of how to measure and include contagion in EWSs is offered by Fratzscher (2003).

In order to assess possible effects on performance results, we add two contagion variables to our analyses, one for capturing global, the other for regional linkage. In contrast to other studies, however, which consider quite complex measures of financial and real contagion, we decide to lighten the gathering of contagion. We therefore rely on Eichengreen, Rose and Wyplosz (1996) and construct the new variables in the following manner:

Global contagion

$$D_t^{G,j} = \begin{cases} 1, & if \sum_{i=1}^{n} C_t^i > 0, \text{ with } i \neq j \\ 0, & \text{otherwise} \end{cases}$$

Regional contagion

$$D_t^{R,j} = \begin{cases} 1, & \text{if } C_t^i = 1 \text{ for } i \neq j \text{ but } i, j \in \textit{same} \text{ region} \\ 0, & \text{otherwise} \end{cases}$$

The contagion variable takes the value of one, if in another country of the sample or another country of the region, respectively, a currency crisis occurs; otherwise it takes the value of 0.

Table 3.9 shows the results of our logit model estimation including contagion. Only the regional contagion variable is significant at the 1 % level and its inclusion seems to improve the estimated logit model slightly.

Table 3.9 Binomial logit model[a] including contagion

Variable	Coefficient	Odds Ratio e^{B}	Significance
Real exchange rate	1.962	7.115	0.000
Reserves	0.426	1.531	0.000
Exports	0.661	1.937	0.000
M2 / reserves (level)	0.624	1.866	0.000
Regional contagion	0.397	1.488	0.002
No. of observations	4761		
Pseudo-R^2	0.15		

a The variables enter the logit model in the binary 0-1 form.

Table 3.10 confirms this assumption. Taking a look at the in- and out-of-sample performance of two logit alternatives with and without contagion, the trade-off between a slightly higher percentage of correctly called crises at the cost of slightly more false alarms is often recognizable. In one out of our cases, however, there is an unequivocal improvement.

We conclude that the inclusion of a simple contagion dummy based on geographic proximity can capture some country linkages and induced contagion risks to improve model performance. Therefore, the possibility of grasping contagion should not be ignored when constructing an EWS.

Table 3.10 In- and out-of-sample[a] performance of logit model alternatives with and without contagion

	In-sample		Out-of-sample	
	Logit without contagion	Logit with regional contagion dummy	Logit without contagion	Logit with regional contagion dummy
	Goodness-of-fit (50% cut-off)			
Percent of crisis periods correctly called[b]	27	28	20	21
False alarms as percent of total alarms[c]	34	35	76	74
Percent of tranquil periods correctly called[d]	95	95	79	79
Percent of observations correctly called	77	77	64	64
	Goodness-of-fit (25% cut-off)			
Percent of crisis periods correctly called[a]	53	47	39	33
False alarms as percent of total alarms[b]	56	53	72	70
Percent of tranquil periods correctly called[c]	76	81	67	73
Percent of observations correctly called	70	73	60	62

a-d Analogous to Table 3.3, Notes a and c-e.

3.6 Conclusions

Financial crises are among the most unwanted manifestations of the present international financial markets. Thus, much emphasis has been given to the development of EWSs in order to understand sources of crises or even better to avoid their outbreak. This research has been so fruitful that there are nowadays plenty of approaches available. Which approach, however, is most appropriate? Or to be less ambitious: what can we learn of this work, what should policy-makers do in this respect?

3.6.1 Elements of practical early warning systems

This paper addresses exactly the above raised questions by conducting robustness tests that go beyond earlier tests of such kind. In a nutshell, we find that reliable progress of new approaches is much smaller than usually claimed. A plausible explanation for this fact may be that findings are quite sensitive to their exact empirical specification: depending on the sample, the time period, the crisis definition, the method of variable aggregation and the variables chosen, there is always a different model at the top. In other words: there is no single best performing model for all circumstances. So, what can users of an EWS do?

We assess the appropriateness of competing approaches by taking the viewpoint of a user who has two requirements which seem to be self-evident: Any

EWS applied should be robust and the approach has to be practical. Under these conditions we come to five insights: First, EWSs are useful as they help to identify and even forecast fundamental origins of currency crises. Second, the crisis definition should not be too narrow and not too complicated, which is why we favor the KLR definition. Third, multivariate methods underlying EWSs do not differ too much regarding their performance, but a binary logit model seems slightly superior to others and at the same time easy to handle. Fourth, there is contagion in international financial markets and a practical way to roughly capture this effect is adding a regional contagion variable to the set of fundamental variables. Fifth, instability in fundamental relations can be addressed by downsizing samples, for example, by the application of regional or time period restrictions. This will help to get somewhat better results.

3.6.2 Policy discussion

Having these elements of practical EWSs in mind, what can economic policy do or should avoid doing? In the following we discuss four policy lessons:

First, the forecasting power of EWSs reveals that core macroeconomic fundamentals weaken before a crisis emerges (see Figure 3.1). Thus, macroeconomic policy should take information from these variables seriously and act in time. Real exchange rate appreciation, (relatively) declining reserves and (increasing) current account deficits indicate clearly that the economy may come into troubled waters.

Second, as shown, available EWSs seem to be – despite some existing forecasting power – too unreliable in their performance that international financial institutions, such as the IMF, should publish their signals. It has to be expected that such signals serve as a coordination device, similar to downgradings of rating agencies, and thus create a self-fulfilling prophecy. The potential damage due to false signals can hardly be compensated by the benefits. Nevertheless, there are good reasons to publish the information underlying EWSs as early as possible and to implement EWSs at the national or private institutions level as a monitoring instrument.

Third, any EWS involves a calibration issue regarding the identification of false alarms versus missed crises (longer in Bussiere and Fratzscher, 2002). Each institution implementing an EWS must thus make a decision on this issue. A more sensitive calibration, leading to more false alarms, seems appropriate if it is used to possibly identify fundamental weaknesses, whereas a very cautious calibration seems advisable if results would be made public (in order to avoid unjustified crises).

The research on EWSs demonstrates moreover that international financial markets do not show textbook-like behavior. Instead, the robust contagion dummy indicates, that sometimes countries fall into a crisis without respective developments of the fundamentals. This finding of inefficient international financial markets is corroborated by recent experimental (e.g. Hey and Morone, 2004) as well as institutional evidence (e.g. Gehrig and Menkhoff, 2005). We know that even professional actors in financial markets often behave short-term oriented and decide in a herding manner. So signals from markets may be wrong and policy should not "believe" in them. Instead, economic policy may want to realize some room for maneuver, keeping signals from international financial markets at bay, for example by disintegrating the economy to some degree from unwanted shocks of the global market.

Overall, it may be thus useful to put the research on EWSs into a broader perspective: EWSs try to forecast larger exchange rate changes by applying a fundamental model. Empirical exchange rate research has shown, however, that rewards to this task can only be meager, as there are no reliable exchange rate models for horizons up to a year or even longer (Sarno and Taylor, 2002). Seen from this perspective, the performance of EWSs is surprisingly good. An intuitive explanation may understand this as an analogy to the finding that fundamentals matter for exchange rates as well in the case of a huge inflation differential between countries (Frankel and Rose, 1996a). This analogy, however, indicates a reverse side to the coin: the impact of fundamental influences is mostly complex, i.e. exchange rates do not always adjust immediately to even huge inflation differentials.

Consequently, the forecasting power of any EWS must be quite limited, as is the case with its robustness, too. One may be tempted to fine-tune EWSs more and more but our results provide evidence against high expectations in this respect. Instead, it seems advisable to be aware of the structural instability in this field – partly reflecting instability of the international financial markets – and to practice the robust and practical insights that can be gained from earlier work.

Annex 3.1 Overview of different identified crises[a]

Source	Original KLR	Replications by Edison	Own replications	Own calculations	Own calculations	Own calculations		Own calculations	
Crisis definition	KLR	KLR	KLR	KLR	FR	BF		BF	
Period	1970-1995	1970-1995	1970-1995	1970-2002	1970-2002	1970-1995	1970-2002	1970-1995	1970-2002
Country sample	Small	Expanded	Expanded	Expanded	Expanded	Small	Small	Expanded	Expanded
Argentina	Jun 70 Jun 75 Feb 81 Jul 82 Sep 86 Apr 89 Feb 90	Mar 75 Jul 82 Apr 89 Dec 89	Mar 75 Jun 75 Nov 76 Jul 82 Dec 83 Apr 89 Feb 90	Mar 75 Jun 75 Nov 76 Jul 82 Dec 83 Apr 89 Feb 90	Mar 75 Jun 75 Nov 75 Mar 76 Nov 76 Apr 81 Jan 82 Jul 82 Oct 87 Apr 89 Jul 89 Dec 89 Jan 91 Jan 02	Jun 75 Dec 83 Apr 89 Dec 89	Jun 75 Dec 83 Apr 89 Dec 89	Jun 75 Jul 82 Apr 89 Dec 89	Jun 75 Jul 82 Apr 89 Dec 89
Bolivia	Nov 82 Nov 83 Sep 85	Nov 82 Nov 83 Sep 85	Nov 82 Sep 85	Nov 82 Apr 84 Aug 84 Nov 84 Sep 85	Oct 72 Feb 82 Nov 82 Nov 83 Apr 84 Aug 84 Nov 84 Feb 85 May 85 Sep 85	Nov 82 Feb 85 Sep 85	Nov 82 Feb 85 Sep 85	Nov 82 Apr 84 Feb 85 Sep 85	Nov 82 Apr 84 Feb 85 Sep 85

Source	Original KLR	Replications by Edison	Own replications	Own calculations	Own calculations	Own calculations		Own calculations	
Crisis definition	KLR	KLR	KLR	KLR	FR	BF		BF	
Period	1970-1995	1970-1995	1970-1995	1970-2002	1970-2002	1970-1995	1970-2002	1970-1995	1970-2002
Country sample	Small	Expanded	Expanded	Expanded	Expanded	Small	Small	Expanded	Expanded
Brazil	Feb 83 Nov 86 Jul 89 Nov 90 Oct 91	Sep 82 Mar 90 Nov 90 Oct 91	Sep 82 Nov 89 Nov 90	Sep 82 Nov 89 Feb 90 Nov 90 Jan 99	Dec 79 Feb 83 May 87 Jun 89 Dec 89 Oct 91 Jan 99 Sep 02	Sep 82 Jan 83 Jan 87 Jan 90 Nov 90	Sep 82 Jan 83 Jan 87 Nov 89 Feb 90 Nov 90 Sep 98 Jan 99 Apr 00	Sep 82 Nov 89 Nov 90	Sep 82 Nov 89 Nov 90 Sep 98 Jan 99
Chile	Dec 71 Aug 72 Oct 83 Dec 74 Jan 76 Aug 82 Sep 84	Jul 71 Sep 72 May 73 Dec 74 Jul 85	Jul 71 May 73 Oct 73 Jul 85	Jul 71 May 73 Oct 73 Jul 85	Jul 71 Sep 72 May 73 Oct 73 Dec 74 Mar 75 Jul 85	Jul 71 Dec 74	Jul 71 Dec 74	Jul 71 May 73 Dec 74	Jul 71 May 73 Dec 74
Colombia	Mar 83 Feb 85	Jan 85	Jan 85 Apr 85	Jan 85 Apr 85 Aug 95 Sep 98 Aug 99 Jul 02		Jan 84 Apr 84 Jan 85	Sep 74 Jan 84 Apr 84 Jan 85	Jan 84 Apr 84 Jan 85	Jan 84 Apr 84 Jan 85
Denmark	May 71 Jun 73 Nov 79 Aug 93	Jun 73 Nov 79 Aug 93	Mar 80 Mar 91	Jul 75 Nov 78 Mar 80 Mar 91		Jul 76 Dec 84	Jul 76 Dec 84 Jan 93	Jul 76 Dec 84	Jul 76 Dec 84

Source	Original KLR	Replications by Edison	Own replications	Own calculations	Own calculations	Own calculations		Own calculations	
Crisis definition	KLR	KLR	KLR	KLR	FR	BF		BF	
Period	1970-1995	1970-1995	1970-1995	1970-2002	1970-2002	1970-1995	1970-2002	1970-1995	1970-2002
Country sample	Small	Expanded	Expanded	Expanded	Expanded	Small	Small	Expanded	Expanded
Finland	Jun 73 Oct 82 Nov 91 Sep 92	Jun 73 Apr 77 Oct 82 Sep 92	Nov 78 Oct 82 May 86 Mar 91 Oct 91 Sep 92 Feb 93	Nov 78 Oct 82 May 86 Mar 91 Oct 91 Sep 92 Feb 93		Aug 86 Oct 91	Aug 86 Oct 91	Aug 86 Oct 91	Aug 86 Oct 91
Greece		Jan 83 Oct 85	Jan 83 Sep 84 Oct 85 May 89	Jan 83 Sep 84 Oct 85 May 89 Jan 01				Mar 90 Apr 91	Mar 90 Jan 01
India		Jul 91 Mar 93	Apr 91 Jul 91 Mar 93	Apr 91 Jul 91 Mar 93				Dec 90	Dec 90 Apr 91
Indonesia	Nov 78 Apr 83 Sep 86	Nov 78 Apr 83 Sep 86	Apr 70 Nov 78 Apr 83 Sep 86	Nov 78 Sep 86 Dec 97 May 98	Nov 78 Apr 83 Sep 86 Dec 97 May 98	May 75 Mar 83	Mar 75 Mar 83 Jan 98	May 75 Mar 83	May 75 Mar 83
Israel	Nov 74 Nov 77 Oct 83 Jul 84	Nov 74 Nov 77 Oct 83 Jul 84	Aug 71 Nov 74 Sep 75 Nov 77 Aug 83 Dec 88	Aug 71 Nov 74 Sep 75 Nov 77 Aug 83 Dec 88	Nov 74 Nov 77 Oct 83	Jul 84	Jul 84 Dec 88	Nov 77 Oct 83 Jul 84	Nov 77 Oct 83 Jul 84

Source	Original KLR	Replications by Edison	Own replications	Own calculations	Own calculations	Own calculations		Own calculations	
Crisis definition	KLR	KLR	KLR	KLR	FR	BF		BF	
Period	1970-1995	1970-1995	1970-1995	1970-2002	1970-2002	1970-1995	1970-2002	1970-1995	1970-2002
Country sample	Small	Expanded	Expanded	Expanded	Expanded	Small	Small	Expanded	Expanded
Korea		Jun 71 Dec 74 Jan 80	Jun 71 Dec 74 Jan 80	Jun 71 Jan 80 Nov 97	Dec 97			Dec 71 Jul 74 Oct 74 Jan 86 Dec 87	Dec 71 Jul 74 Oct 74 Jan 86 Dec 87 Nov 97
Malaysia	Jul 75	Nov 73 Nov 78 Mar 80 Feb 85 Dec 92	Nov 73 Jul 75 Nov 78 Mar 80 Feb 85 Dec 92	Jul 97 Dec 97		Dec 94	Feb 82 Dec 92 Dec 94 Jul 97	Dec 92 Dec 94	Dec 92 Dec 94 Jul 97 Jan 98
Mexico	Sep 76 Feb 82 Dec 82 Dec 94	Sep 76 Feb 82 Dec 82 Dec 94	Sep 76 Feb 82 Dec 82 Dec 87 Dec 94	Sep 76 Feb 82 Dec 82 Dec 87 Dec 94	Sep 76 Feb 82 Dec 82 Dec 87 Dec 94	Sep 76 Jun 82 Dec 94	Sep 76 Feb 82 Jun 82 Mar 90 Dec 94	Sep 76 Feb 82 Jul 82 Dec 82 Dec 94	Sep 76 Feb 82 Jul 82 Dec 82 Dec 94
Norway	Jun 73 Feb 78 May 86 Dec 92	Jun 73 Feb 78 May 86 Nov 92	Nov 78 Jan 81 May 86 Mar 91 Nov 92	Nov 78 May 86 Mar 91 Nov 92 Dec 97 Dec 01		Nov 77 Nov 92	Nov 77 Nov 92 Dec 96 Dec 97 Jun 99 Oct 00 Jul 01 Dec 01	Nov 77 Nov 78 Nov 92	Nov 77 Nov 78 Nov 92 Dec 96 Dec 97 Jun 99 Oct 00 Jul 01 Dec 01
Pakistan		May 72	May 72	May 72	May 72			May 72 Oct 90	May 72 Oct 90

Source	Original KLR	Replications by Edison	Own replications	Own calculations	Own calculations	Own calculations		Own calculations	
Crisis definition	KLR	KLR	KLR	KLR	FR	BF		BF	
Period	1970-1995	1970-1995	1970-1995	1970-2002	1970-2002	1970-1995	1970-2002	1970-1995	1970-2002
Country sample	Small	Expanded	Expanded	Expanded	Expanded	Small	Small	Expanded	Expanded
Peru	Jun 76 Oct 83	Jun 76 Oct 83	Sep 88	Sep 88	Jun 76 Oct 77 Oct 87 Sep 88 Jan 89 Aug 90	Sep 88 Aug 90	Sep 88 Aug 90	Sep 88 Aug 90	Sep 88 Aug 90
Philippines	Feb 70 Oct 83 Jun 84	Oct 83 Jun 84 Feb 86	Feb 70 Oct 83 Jun 84 Feb 86	Feb 70 Oct 83 Jun 84 Feb 86 Dec 97	Feb 70 Oct 83 Jun 84	Sep 83 Jan 90	Sep 83 Feb 85 Jan 90	Sep 83 Jan 90	Sep 83 Jun 84 Jan 90
Portugal		Mar 76 Feb 77 Jun 82 Jun 83	Feb 77 Jun 82 Jun 83 Mar 91	Feb 77 Jun 82 Jun 83 Mar 91 Oct 92					
Singapore		Dec 70 Jul 75 Nov 78 Mar 80	Dec 70 Jul 75 Nov 78 Mar 80	Dec 70 Jul 75 Mar 80 Dec 97 May 98				Dec 70 Jul 75 Mar 80	Dec 70 Jul 75 Mar 80 Oct 97 Jan 98 May 98

Source	Original KLR	Replications by Edison	Own replications	Own calculations	Own calculations	Own calculations		Own calculations	
Crisis definition	KLR	KLR	KLR	KLR	FR	BF		BF	
Period	1970-1995	1970-1995	1970-1995	1970-2002	1970-2002	1970-1995	1970-2002	1970-1995	1970-2002
Country sample	Small	Expanded	Expanded	Expanded	Expanded	Small	Small	Expanded	Expanded
South Afrika		Sep 76 Jul 84 Aug 85 May 86	Sep 75 Jul 84 Oct 84 Aug 85 May 86	Sep 75 Jul 84 Oct 84 Aug 85 May 86 Apr 96 Jun 98 Dec 01	Aug 85				
Spain	Feb 76 Jul 77 Dec 82 Sep 92 May 93	Jun 73 Feb 76 Jul 77 Mar 83 Sep 92 Mar 95	Mar 80 Mar 83 Mar 91 Sep 92	Mar 80 Mar 83 Mar 91 Sep 92 Jul 93		Jun 77 Oct 82 Mar 83 Sep 92	Jun 77 Oct 82 Mar 83 Sep 92 Dec 98	Jun 72 Oct 82 Mar 83 Sep 92	Jun 72 Oct 82 Mar 83 Sep 92 Dec 98
Sweden	Aug 77 Sep 81 Oct 82 Nov 92	Aug 77 Sep 81 Oct 82 Nov 92	Aug 77 Mar 91 Nov 92 Feb 93	Aug 77 Mar 91 Nov 92 Feb 93		Oct 76 Feb 85 Aug 92 Nov 92	Oct 76 Feb 85 Aug 92 Nov 92 Nov 96	Oct 76 Feb 85 Aug 92 Nov 92	Oct 76 Feb 85 Aug 92 Nov 92 Nov 96
Sri Lanka		Nov 77	Nov 77	Nov 77 Jul 98	Nov 77			Apr 75 Nov 77	Apr 75 Nov 77 Jul 90
Thailand	Nov 78 Jul 81 Nov 84	Nov 78 Jul 81 Nov 84	Nov 78 Jul 81 Nov 84 Feb 85	Nov 78 Jul 81 Jul 97 Nov 97		Nov 78 Oct 79 Oct 80 Apr 81	Nov 78 Oct 79 Oct 80 Apr 81 Jul 97 Nov 97	Nov 78 Oct 79 Oct 80 Apr 81	Nov 78 Oct 79 Oct 80 Apr 81 Jul 97 Nov 97

Source	Original KLR	Replications by Edison	Own replications	Own calculations	Own calculations	Own calculations		Own calculation	
Crisis definition	KLR	KLR	KLR	KLR	FR	BF		BF	
Period	1970-1995	1970-1995	1970-1995	1970-2002	1970-2002	1970-1995	1970-2002	1970-1995	1970-2002
Country sample	Small	Expanded	Expanded	Expanded	Expanded	Small	Small	Expanded	Expanded
Turkey	Aug 70 Jan 80 Mar 94	Aug 70 Jan 80 Mar 94	Aug 70 Jan 80 Mar 91 Mar 94	Aug 70 Jun 79 Jan 80 Mar 94 Feb 01	Aug 70 Mar 78 Jun 79 Jan 80 Apr 94 Feb 01	Jan 80 Dec 81 Mar 94	Jan 80 Dec 81 Jul 83 Mar 94	Jan 80 Dec 81 Mar 94	Jan 80 Mar 94 Feb 01
Uruguay	Dec 71 Oct 82	Mar 72 Nov 82	Mar 72 Nov 82	Mar 72 Nov 82 Jul 02	Mar 72 Nov 82 Jul 02	Nov 82 Nov 84	Nov 82 Nov 84 Jul 02	Nov 82 Nov 84	Nov 82 Nov 84 Jul 02
Venezuela	Feb 84 Dec 86 Mar 89 May 94 Dec 95	Mar 84 Dec 86 Mar 89	Feb 84 Dec 86 Mar 89	Feb 84 Dec 86 Mar 89 May 94 Dec 95 Feb 02	Feb 84 Dec 86 Mar 89 May 94 Dec 95 Apr 96 Feb 02 May 02	Feb 84 Dec 86 Mar 89 May 94	Feb 84 Dec 86 Mar 89 May 94 Apr 96 Feb 02	Feb 84 Dec 86 Mar 89 May 94	Feb 84 Dec 86 Mar 89 May 94 Dec 95 Apr 96 Feb 02
Total number of crisis periods for									
- Small sample:	75	70	79	93	84	55	83	--	--
- Expanded sample:	--	91	104	126	88	--	--	76	101

a Upon the existence of consecutive signals, only the first one is displayed and counted as a crisis. Moreover, according to the proposal of FR (1996, p. 358), there must be at least 2 months in between two signals before being counted as two different crisis periods.

Annex 3.2: Definition, background information, data sources and construction of different indicators

Indicator	Definition	Background information to explanatory power	Threshold percentile	Data sources	Construction particularities[1]
Real exchange rate	Deviation of real exchange rate (RER) from its deterministic trend over the whole sample period: $Dev_{RER_t^i} = \frac{RER_t^i - Trend_t^i}{Trend_t^i} * 100$	An overvalued exchange rate can often be seen as an indication of a possible devaluation of a currency and thus raises the risk of an upcoming currency crisis.	10	IFS line AE IFS line 64	The real exchange rate is the result of multiplying the nominal exchange rate in price quotation, (indicating local currency per USD, line AE) with the consumer price index (CPI, line 64) of the USA divided by the local CPI (line 64). For calculating the trend, we optionally used either a linear, an exponential or a logarithmic function, taking the best fit into consideration.
Exports	Growth rate in reference to the respective month of the preceding year	A weak export sector implies a higher crisis probability as the government might have an incentive to devaluate in order to empower the exports.	10	IFS line 70D	–
Reserves	Growth rate in reference to the respective month of the preceding year	A lost of international reserves stands for central bank market intervention in order to stabilize the exchange rate. Thus a small or even negative growth rate heightens the risk of a crisis.	10	IFS line 1LD	–
M2 / reserves (level)	Level of the ratio of M2 to reserves	This indicator is considered in order to assess the short-term liquidity and convertibility of a country's currency. An increase of the ratio can occur due to a loss of international reserves or to extraordinary monetary expansion. Both can be considered as risk factors.	90	IFS line 34 IFS line 35 IFS line 1LD	The sum of money (line 34) and quasi-money (line 35) divided by international reserves (line 1LD).

Indicator	Definition	Background information to explanatory power	Threshold percentile	Data sources	Construction particularities[1]
M2 / reserves	Growth rate of the ratio of M2 to reserves in reference to the respective month of the preceding year	Similar to M2 / reserves as a level consideration, this indicator also measures whether and to which degree a country is able to convert domestic into foreign currency. An exceptionally high growth rate shows upcoming imbalances and thus heightens the crisis risk for a country.	90	IFS line 34 IFS line 35 IFS line 1LD	The sum of money (line 34) and quasi-money (line 35) is considered to form M2. After dividing M2 by international reserves (line 1LD) the growth rate in reference to the respective month of the preceding year is calculated.
Current account / GDP (level)	Ratio of current account to GDP in reference to the respective month of the preceding year	Emerging Markets often exhibit high current account deficits. In order to finance these deficits they depend on foreign capital inflows. High deficits make the respective country vulnerable to expectation shifts and losses of confidence which might imply a sudden turn in capital inflows and thus sharpens the risk of a crisis.	10	IFS line 78AL IFS line 99B	Both variable series are firstly linearly interpolated from annual and quarterly data, respectively, to monthly data. After dividing current account (line 78AL) by GDP (line 99b), a moving average of the previous for quarters is calculated. The variable is measured in levels only.
Real interest rate[b]	Level of real interest rate	---	---	IFS line 60 IFS line 60B IFS line 60L IFS line 60P IFS line 64	Use of money market rate, discount rate, deposit rate or lending rate according to data availability with prioritization on the money market rate. Real interest rates are calculated with the help of the CPI (line 64).

a All time series were transferred into Millions of USD. Replication efforts imply the reference to details given by Edison (2003, p. 47) and Berg and Pattillo (1999a, p. 567).

b The variable is not used as an indicator but enters the crisis definition of Bussiere and Fratzscher (2002).

Part II:
Financial Markets from a Behavioral Perspective – the Role of Asset Managers' Behavioral Biases, Cultural Background and Gender

Evidence from Country Studies

4 Still Emerging – More Biased? Asset Managers' Behavior in Thailand, Indonesia, and Germany[19]

4.1 Motivation

Around the globe, financial market capitalization keeps steadily beating its own previous years' records. Meanwhile, huge capital inflows to the growing numbers of asset management companies document the boost of entrusted asset volumes worldwide and underline the importance of institutional investors, such as mutual or pension funds, both in mature and emerging markets (cf. Ong and Sy, 2004).

This analysis offers new insights into these important market actors' behavior. To the best of our knowledge, we are the first study to survey professional asset managers in emerging markets, namely Thailand and Indonesia. Being able to compare their answers to mutual fund managers from a more mature market, Germany, and also to control for personal characteristics as well as individual differences in risk propensity and behavior as the basis for every investment decision, we contribute to the literature by analyzing two of the most discussed behavioral puzzles, i.e. herd behavior and home-biased asset allocation, in diverging market environments.

Institutional investors have been equally praised as key contributors to financial markets integration and blamed as culprits in financial crises (cf. Aitken, 1998, Kaminsky et al., 2001). Not surprisingly, research interest in institutional investors' behavior has been vast during the last two decades. The majority of studies focus on findings regarding mutual fund performance, strategies and price impact. Besides, observable anomalies like herd behavior, first modeled by Schafstein and Stein (1990), or the so-called 'home bias puzzle' early documented by French and Poterba (1991), have been widely addressed and point to behavioral biases in mutual fund investments. Nonetheless, studies at the micro-

19 Helpful comments by Lukas Menkhoff and Maik Schmeling are gratefully acknowledged. Furthermore, I would like to thank the surveyed asset managers in Thailand, Indonesia and Germany for valuable ideas contributed in prior interviews as well time offered to respond to the questionnaire. Besides, my thanks goes to the Thai Association of Investment Management Companies "AIMC", the Indonesian Association of Investment Firms "APRDI", and the German Investment Association "BVI" for great recommendation letters and organizational support. Finally, financial support by the VolkswagenStiftung is highly appreciated.

level of the individual asset manager remain comparably scarce – particularly in emerging markets.

Instead, research related to institutional investors often concentrates on aggregated fund flow analyses. While the majority of studies focus on U.S. institutional investors (cf. e.g. Lakonishok et al., 1992, Grinblatt et al., 1995, Carhart, 1997, Wermers, 1999, or Sias, 2004), considerably fewer studies address the Japanese or the European mutual fund industry (cf. e.g. Cai et al. 1997, Otten and Bams, 2002, or Walter and Weber, 2006). Regarding mutual funds in emerging markets, studies concentrate on transactions data explorations of mainly U.S. hosted mutual funds operating in emerging markets: Disyatat and Gelos (2001), Kaminsky et al. (2001) or Ong and Sy (2004) focus on a better understanding of funds' portfolio choice and its impact in a broad set of emerging markets. Borensztein and Gelos (2003) and Kaminsky et al. (2004) concentrate on mutual fund strategies, and find evidence for momentum strategies, i.e. the systematic selling of losers and buying of winners, as well as significant but moderate herd behavior of emerging markets funds. Choe et al. (1999) and Kim and Wei (2002), who focus on the Korean stock market, detect positive feedback trading, i.e. momentum investment, and herd behavior of non-resident institutional investors.

These studies of emerging markets funds have in common that either research motivation or parts of their findings could be attributed to the investment environment. A different market environment might induce a change in market participants' behavior, implying potentially more biased actions in an environment where transparency is scarce and market efficiency is low. Not only from the individual actor's perspective but also from the view of the fund management company, limited information access could lead e.g. to a stronger orientation on other market players. Indeed, the neglect of the own limited information in favor of following better informed market players' actions, could even be rational. In this respect, particularly emerging financial markets can be characterized by scarcity of publicly available information, high asymmetric information distribution and thus often less transparency than more mature financial markets. At the same time, the institutional and regulatory environment is comparably lower (Beim and Calomiris, 2001).

How market transparency affects investor behavior at the fund level has been globally studied by e.g. Gelos and Wei (2005). Measuring government and corporate transparency in several countries for a sample of 300 emerging market funds, they find evidence that international funds invest systematically less in less transparent countries. Herding, however, seems to be more prevalent among them in the latter. In addition, a significant relevance of the quality of accounting standards, shareholder rights, information disclosure and legal frameworks for non-resident emerging market funds' allocation is shown by Aggarwal et al. (2005).

Besides, Ahearne et al. (2004) examine how informational asymmetries affect a home biased asset allocation. By exploiting the cross-sectional variations of U.S. holdings in several countries, they find evidence that information asymmetries, resulting from poor quality and credibility of financial information, are much more important than direct investment barriers like ownership restrictions. Foreign countries whose firms opt into the U.S. regulatory environment by public U.S. listing are significantly less underweighted in U.S. portfolios. Results by Edison and Warnock (2004) regarding security-level holdings of U.S. funds point into the same direction.

Returning to the above mentioned micro-level research, mainly studies of U.S. mutual funds have explored the role of the individual asset manager. Prominent studies are those by e.g. Chevalier and Ellison (1999, 1999a). They do not only relate transactions data to personal characteristics of individual asset managers but also link performance and herding to individual characteristics such as age, experience and education. Their finding that e.g. experience is a significant positive determinant of fund performance is also confirmed by e.g. Ding and Wermers (2004). Niessen and Ruenzi (2006), for example, find evidence of gender-related effects in terms of investment styles and performance distribution of U.S. mutual fund managers. For the European mutual fund industry, knowledge concerning individual asset managers' behavior has been largely complemented by survey studies, such as Menkhoff (1997), Arnswald (2001) or Menkhoff et al. (2006), e.g. for the German market. In contrast to that, however, so far we do not know of any mutual fund study that analyzes data on individual asset managers' characteristics and behavior in emerging markets.

Hence, our contribution to the literature is threefold. Firstly, we enter new data ground that allows us to gain an insight into individual asset managers' behavior in the two emerging markets Thailand and Indonesia. Secondly, by comparing our survey data with similar data generated in the German mutual fund industry, differences in individual characteristics, views, and behavior between asset managers from emerging markets and those acting in a more mature market become evident. Although the industries in all three countries are embedded in rather intermediary-based financial systems (cf. Demirgüc-Kunt and Levine, 2001), differences arising from the industry's history, developmental stage as well as the market environment might also matter. In particular, when taking information availability and market transparency into account, the emerging markets environment can provide a quickly accepted justification while asset managers from emerging markets might behave relatively more cautious and / or more biased. From the perspective of institutional development, aspects like self-perception and self-assessment could be sharpened by offered trainings and career development opportunities. As we expect such mechanisms to be relatively less accessible for the broad majority of asset managers in the two emerging than in the more mature market, asset managers in the former are easily assumed to answer more greenly. Thirdly, as without doubt the individual investor's risk propensity and risk related personal biases are at the center of every investment decision, we contribute to the literature by controlling for self-assessed risk behavioral differences and the role of personal characteristics when analyzing two broadly discussed behavioral biases from the literature: herd behavior and home bias. While we detect a higher risk propensity among asset managers from Thailand and Indonesia, we also confirm risk biases to significantly matter for herding behavior – both in the German market and the two emerging ones. The analysis of home bias confirms the role of professionals' risk biases for asset allocation. Moreover, particularly in the two emerging markets, strong regulatory influence and personal characteristics are found to matter in addition.

The remainder is organized as follows. Chapter 4.2 gives an overview of the industry development in the three surveyed countries. Chapter 4.3 describes our survey methodology and our generated data set. Both, sample representativeness as well as asset managers' personal characteristics are discussed. Chapter 4.4 addresses risk-related behavior, considering it the basis for investor's investment decisions. Chapter 4.5 analyzes herd behavior, and Chapter 4.6 the home bias puzzle, while controlling for several factors in addition. Chapter 4.7 concludes.

4.2 Industry description and development in the three markets

Describing our three selected markets, we find the Thai mutual fund industry to have grown by at least 20 % annually since 2002, summing up to almost 1,122 billion THB (30 billion USD) of net assets in September 2006.[20] In the Indonesian mutual fund industry, the last four years revealed both boom and bust times. By the end of 2004, net asset value managed by Indonesian mutual funds had risen to over 100 trillion IDR (10.8 billion USD), while company and fund numbers peaked. Mainly due to unstable monetary conditions, mutual fund inflows sharply reversed in March 2005 and total net asset value dropped by more than 70% within the next 6 months. Recovering slowly but steadily again, by the end of September 2006 the Indonesian mutual fund industry has reached a net asset value of 39.2 trillion IDR (4.3 billion USD).[21] In contrast to that, the German asset management industry in total keeps track on a steady and comparatively less exceptional growth path: since 2002, assets under management grew

20 Numbers are provided by the "AIMC" – the Association of Investment Management Companies in Thailand. At the time we were conducting our survey, additional private and provident funds taken together added another two third of the mutual funds' volume to the total of net asset value managed by Thai asset management companies.

21 Numbers are given by the Indonesian Capital Market Supervisory Agency "Bapepam".

by at least 4.5 % annually from 862.4 billion EUR (904 billion USD) to lately 1,205 billion EUR (1,545 billion USD).[22]

By the time we collected our survey data as described in Chapter 4.3, mutual fund investment instruments in both considered emerging markets ranged from fixed income funds[23] to money market, equity and balanced or mixed funds, as well as so-called flexible portfolio funds in Thailand. In Germany, mutual fund investment options included real estate and others, e.g. commodities, in addition. As already mentioned above, particularly in Indonesia, fixed income investments clearly dominated the other fund types, while Thailand and especially Germany were much more balanced. Another difference linked to the industry's development becomes evident, when taking a look at institutional and regulatory restrictions: In comparison to German asset management companies that could offer a broad range of globally investing funds to their customers, asset management companies in Thailand and Indonesia faced clearly higher restrictions regarding investment abroad. While in Thailand only five companies were licensed to offer so-called foreign-invested funds, in Indonesia the amount of investment on foreign securities exchanges was not allowed to exceed 15% of the mutual fund investment company's total net asset value.

4.3 Survey data and methodology

Our data comprehends 417 questionnaires, originating from an international written survey project in the Thai, Indonesian and German asset management industry between spring 2003 and spring 2005. In particular, we questioned professional asset managers about their market views and behavior.

Survey studies have the advantage of offering a direct measure of individual attitudes instead of having to rely on assumptions about individual behavior. Nevertheless, they occasionally face criticism in terms of data quality, target group choice and strategic answering. In order to overcome possible skepticism, we did not only prepare our survey by previous oral interviews with asset managers from different investment companies in several German cities, Bangkok, and Jakarta, but also assured in test runs that questions and response categories were well understood and in common wording. Moreover, for planned cross-country comparisons, questions had to be both relevant for the respective market and, if necessary, country-specifically adapted, but still comparable

22 Data is taken from the annual reports of the German Investment Management Association 'BVI'. Numbers comprise round about 50% mutual funds, and 50% restricted/special funds.

23 These include bonds of different maturity (Thailand), and in local currency or USD (Indonesia).

afterwards.[24] Finally, guaranteed anonymity to all participants helped to overcome possible objections, and as in a market sample of over hundred questionnaires the marginal influence of a single person is obviously limited, incentives for strategic answering have been low.

Altogether, we obtained a participation rate of 67.8%[25] of contacted investment companies. In detail, we received responses from 29 of 31 contacted member companies of the "AIMC" – the Thai Association of Investment Management Companies (participation rate of Thai firms: 93.6%, see Table 4.1). Regarding assets under management, this implies Thai market share coverage of our survey of more than 96%. The extraordinary high participation rate is attributable to recommendation and helpful support of the "AIMC". In Indonesia, 19 out of 55 contacted investment management companies contributed to our survey (participation rate of Indonesian firms: 34.6%). Out of these 19, six investment companies belong to the ten biggest market players and already cover a market share of almost 50%. Altogether participating companies comprise 61% share of the market. Again, like in Thailand, a supporting letter by the investment association, here "APRDI" (Asosiasi Pengelola Reksa Dana Indonesia), was key to success. In Germany, 51 of 66 addressed investment companies participated in our survey (participation rate of German firms: 77.3%). As almost

Table 4.1 Comparison of the data sample with the industry structure[a]

	Thailand	Indonesia	Germany
Firm participation rate	93.6%	34.6%	77.3%
Covered market share (by assets under management)	96.5%	60.8%	91.8%
	Correlation[b] with company size (by assets under management)		
Number of answered questionnaires per company	0.534*** (0.000)	0.388*** (0.004)	0.679*** (0.000)

a The market data for Thailand is taken from a market share datasheet provided by selected companies of the Thai asset management industry and private information provided by the AIMC. For Indonesia, we us market data provided by Bapepam, the Indonesian Capital Market Supervisory Agency, as well as APRDI. We refer to June and July 2004 as months of reference. For Germany, market data is taken from the annual report 2003 of the BVI.

b The table gives the coefficient of the Pearson correlation with the p-value in parentheses. Asterisks refer to level of significance: * 10%, ** 5%, *** 1%.

24 An example for country-specific adaptation necessity, e.g. in the sense of regional groups or home country fit in answers, can be found in the annex reflecting an additional question in the Thai questionnaire.

25 Similar surveys by e.g. Shiller and Pound (1989), Oberlechner (2001), Gehrig and Menkhoff (2004), or Menkhoff and Schmidt (2005) report company participation rates of 45%, 54%, 51%, and 59%, respectively.

all big market players took part in our survey, market coverage in terms of assets under management sums up to 92%. All companies are member firms of the German Investment Management Association "BVI", and, once more, the association's letter of recommendation supported high participation rates.

Bigger investment companies with higher asset volumes under management typically employ more asset managers and therefore have a bigger market impact than smaller investment firms. We test whether our sample is representative in this respect as well. Correlation coefficients between number of answered questionnaires and company size are positive, ranging between 0.4 and 0.7 for Indonesia, Thailand and Germany. This confirms that asset managers who work for bigger companies participated significantly more in our survey.

Asset managers' characteristics are shown in Table 4.2. Taken over all three countries, the average asset manager is 36 years old, has seven years of experience, works as senior asset manager, holds a higher educational degree, and is male and most probably married.

Table 4.2 Personal characteristics of surveyed Thai, Indonesian and German asset managers[a]

Age	*< 31*	*31 – 35*	*36 – 40*	*41 – 45*	*> 46*	*Mean*	*N*
(in years)	16.7%	36.5%	33.3%	11.9%	1.6%	~35	126
	10.7%	35.7%	21.4%	28.6%	3.6%	~37	28
	21.0%	35.5%	22.9%	14.9%	5.7%	~36	263
Professional	*< 4*	*4 – 6*	*7 – 9*	*10 – 12*	*> 12*		
experience	24.6%	19.0%	27.8%	20.6%	7.9%	~ 7	
(in years)	28.6%	21.4%	25.0%	17.9%	7.1%	~ 7	
	32.0%	20.7%	19.1%	10.9%	17.2%	~ 7	
Occupational level	*Junior AM*	*Senior AM*	Bonus payments	*Median*		*Std. dev.*	
	38.1%	45.2%		16.0%		47.8	
	7.7%	38.5%		50.0%		152.7	
	32.0%	46.1%		25.0%		24.0	
	Head AM	*CIO / CEO*	Educational level	*Bachelor*		*Master or PhD*	
	11.9%	4.8%		4.0%		96.0%	
	30.8%	23.1%		29.6%		70.4%	
	16.4%	5.5%		13.2%		86.6%	
Gender	*Male*	*Female*	Marital status	*Single*	*Married*	*Other*	
	53.6%	46.4%		55.9%	43.0%	1.1 %	
	85.7%	14.3%		17.6%	82.4%	0.0%	
	90.0%	10.0%		44.1%	53.5%	2.4%	

a Regarding each item, the first row displays responses of Thai asset managers, the second row of Indonesian asset managers and the third one captures our surveyed German asset managers' personal characteristics.

When taking a closer look, however, expected differences from a perspective of developmental progress between the two emerging markets and the more mature one, as well as country-related particularities become evident. First of all, in accordance with market and industry history and development, we find clearly more asset managers with long professional experience, i.e. more than 12 years, in the German than in the emerging markets' sub-samples. The conspicuous high number of Indonesian asset managers older than 40 is linked to an exceptionally high participation of 54% of asset managers in leading positions.[26] Concerning education, the number of asset managers with a master or PhD degree is exceptionally high in Thailand, while Germany and Indonesia meet expectations. Country specific differences are most proponent regarding gender and marital status: while asset managers in Thailand are almost 50% female and, independent from gender in the majority single, Indonesian asset managers are overwhelmingly male and married. Typically (male) German asset managers are almost equally single and married.

4.4 Risk behavior

Undoubtedly, the investor's risk propensity is essential to every investment decision she takes. While standard finance theory assumes the individual investor to be generally risk averse – modeled by concavity of the utility function and expressed by the risk premium as compensation for risk taking –, differences in the individual investor's degree of risk aversion imply different proportionate allocations between investment choices.

Risk aversion is linked to two other risk related behavioral phenomena: Prospect theory, developed by Kahneman and Tversky's (1979), revises assumptions of the traditional expected utility framework and introduces the concept of "loss aversion", expressed as utility functions with concavity in the gain domain and convexity in the loss domain relative to a reference point (cf. Schmidt and Zank, 2005, for an overview and analogies to risk aversion). Indeed, investors seem to be less sensitive to gains than they are to losses: Empirical evidence shows that the latter is weighted twice as strongly (cf. Tversky and Kahnemann, 1992). Besides, there is wide acceptance that investors undergo a so-called "disposition effect" in their investment decision behavior. The tendency to hold losing stocks too long and to sell winning stocks too early was first reported by Shefrin and Statman (1985). Since, it has been largely empirically confirmed for both individual and institutional investors (cf. e.g. Odean, 1998, Grinblatt and Keloharju, 2001, Shapira and Venezia, 2001, Garvey and

26 Mirroring in previous interviews in Indonesia experienced strong hierarchical influence in decision making, the latter is highly appreciated from the perspective of capturing relevant market actors with our data.

Murphy, 2004, Locke and Mann, 2005). Again, prospect theory provides the explanatory description: relying on an S-shaped value function, risk aversion in the gain domain causes the investors to realize profits quickly in order to avoid them turning into losses, while risk seeking behavior in the loss domain lets losses run in hope of asset price recovery and the avoidance of any losses at all.

We therefore start our analysis of asset managers' behavior in the three countries by directly surveying their self-assessment of risk behavior. Table 4.3 reveals the distribution of answers for the three countries:

Table 4.3 Asset managers' risk aversion, loss aversion and disposition affect

Different dimensions of risk behavior [1]-[3]		Very risk averse / complete agreement (in %)					Little risk averse / complete disagreement (in %)	% of risk / loss averse AM[a]	H_0: no specific difference[b]
[1] In respect of professional investment decisions, I mostly act...	Thailand	1.6	25.4	36.5	27.0	8.7	0.8	63.5	-0.513
	Indonesia	0.0	17.9	46.4	25.0	10.7	0.0	64.3	(0.601)
	Germany	1.5	9.2	36.9	42.7	8.5	1.2	47.6	-3.485*** (0.000)
[2] In case of loss positions in my portfolio I generally wait for a price rebound instead of selling those securities	Thailand	0.8	14.4	33.6	24.8	22.4	4.0	48.8	-0.528
	Indonesia	0.0	25.0	14.3	25.0	28.6	7.1	39.3	(0.597)
	Germany	0.0	4.6	19.7	17.8	30.1	27.8	24.3	-6.838*** (0.000)
[3] I prefer to take profits instead of cutting losses, when I am confronted with unexpected liquidity demands.	Thailand	5.6	38.1	23.0	12.7	14.3	6.3	66.7	-1.473
	Indonesia	14.3	39.3	25.0	7.1	14.3	0.0	78.6	(0.141)
	Germany	3.5	12.0	22.4	15.4	21.6	25.1	37.9	-7.277*** (0.000)

a The percentages given are calculated as the sum of the first three answering categories.

b The table gives the z-value of the Mann-Whitney U-test regarding the responses from Thai and Indonesian asset managers and Thai and Indonesian asset managers versus German asset managers, respectively. The p-value is given in parentheses. Asterisks refer to level of significance: * 10%, ** 5%, *** 1%.

Firstly, we are interested in their risk aversion in respect to professional investment decisions. Whereas a clear majority of both Thai and Indonesian asset managers consider themselves to act mostly risk averse, only 48% of the German asset managers do so. Secondly, being asked about the case of loss positions in their portfolio, 49% of the Thai and 39% of the Indonesian asset managers indicate to generally wait for a price rebound instead of selling those securities. In Germany, only 24% of the surveyed asset managers reveal this kind of loss aversion. Thirdly, we survey the existence of investors' disposition between winning and losing assets. In a situation of unexpected liquidity demands, 67% of the Thai asset managers agree about preferring to take profits instead of cutting losses. In Indonesia, agreement among the surveyed asset managers is even up to 79%. German asset managers, in contrast, only agree to 38%. In order to test for significant differences, Mann-Whitney U-tests for each of the three aspects are indicated. Whereas the two emerging markets do not show any significant differences between each other, in all three risk dimensions test results confirm significant differences between Thailand and Indonesia taken together on the one hand, and the more mature market, Germany, on the other. As a consequence, we pool survey data from the two emerging markets and compare it with the more mature market sample.

It has been shown – especially from psychological research on risk – that risk attitude and behavior are influenced by personal characteristics such as gender or experience as well, we control for these characteristics in addition. Thereby we also meet the demand to consider country peculiarities reflected in our samples. As described in Chapter 4.3, sample differences emerge for the highly correlated characteristics experience, age, marital status and position[27], as well as in regards to gender. Besides, as we cannot rely on performance data of the individual manager, the size of bonus payments can be seen as a useful indicator of the asset manager's achievement and success.

Table 4.4 discloses linkages between risk behavior and personal characteristics with the help of Spearman rank correlation coefficients. In the two emerging markets, both higher risk and loss aversion seem to be more pronounced among female asset managers, while a higher disposition effect is significantly related to less experience. In Germany, higher risk and loss aversion are significantly linked to those asset managers who receive lower bonus payments, while the disposition effect is correlated with all three characteristics, i.e. gender, experience and bonus.[28] We concentrate on these three as control variables when addressing further potential biases in investment behavior that are in parts also induced by individual attitudes towards risk and loss themselves.

Firstly, Khorana (1996), Graham (1999) or Hong et al. (2000), for example, interpret a higher degree of herd behavior as lower risk taking induced by reputation and career concerns as well as the fear of worse performance in relation to the peer group. Moreover, empirical work has shown that younger and more inexperienced asset managers tend to herd more often, as they are more at risk to be replaced for a worse performance than their older, more experienced colleagues (Chevalier and Ellison, 1999, Arora and Ou-Yang, 2001).

Secondly, a home-biased asset allocation yet implies the waiving of advantages from international diversification, which from the point of view of ex-

27 Considering experience as the most meaningful variable out of these four, we concentrate on it in the following. For more detailed correlations cf. Table 4.4, footnote b.

28 The three variables also matter when controlled simultaneously in a multivariate framework for Thailand and Indonesia taken together as well as Germany. Results are not explicitly shown here.

pected utility may seem risk seeking. Behavioral explanations, however, such as perceived competence (cf. Kilka and Weber, 2000), shed light on the link between individual risk aversion and a home-biased asset allocation that might at least be perceived less risky by the individual investor (cf. Weber et al., 2005). Hence, we now turn to the two behavioral biases herd behavior and home bias, while searching for influential factors and controlling for risk related behavior as well as personal characteristics.

Table 4.4 Findings on risk behavior and personal characteristics

Correlations with risk behavior	Spearman rank correlation coefficients (p-value)[a]					
	Higher risk aversion		Higher loss aversion		Higher disposition effect	
	TH/IND	GER	TH/IND	GER	TH/IND	GER
Female	0.137* (0.092)		0.201** (0.013)			0.128** (0.041)
Less experienced[b]					0.216*** (0.007)	0.147** (0.020)
Lower bonus[c]		0.172** (0.025)		0.168** (0.028)		0.212** (0.005)

a Asterisks indicate the level of significance: * 10%, ** 5%, *** 1%. Only significant rank correlation coefficients are shown here.

b In all three countries experience is highly correlated with other asset managers' characteristics (Table 4.2). Spearman rank correlation coefficients are as follows on age: TH/IND: 0.596***, GER: 0.744***; position: TH/IND: 0.596***, GER: 0.511***; and marital status: TH/IND: 0.309***, GER: 0.428***.

c Spearman rank correlations among the three control variables reveal experience to be significantly positively linked to bonus payments in Germany (GER: 0.322***); in Thailand and Indonesia, female asset manager are significantly more experienced (TH/IND: 0.179**) but receive on average significantly less bonus payments (TH/IND: -0.264**).

4.5 Herd behavior

Providing comprehensive survey work, Bikhchandani and Sharma (2001) distinguish spurious from intentional herd behavior in the market. As only the obvious intent to copy the behavior of others should be seen critical, we concentrate on the second type of herding. Three explanations of the latter are provided and have received overwhelming research attention: The first is information based herding that can be attributed to the occurrence of informational cascades (cf. Bikhchandani et al., 1992). In a surrounding of imperfect information, investors are only able to observe the behavior of others but not the private information signals the others receive. As soon as the observed behavior seems slightly more informative than their private signals, investors are likely – their own information notwithstanding – to copy the observed investment behavior. The second is the idea of reputation based herding, first modeled by Scharfstein and

Stein (1990). They regard herding and conformity as agency phenomena joined with uncertainty about the asset manager's ability. Investment professionals have an incentive for "sharing-the-blame" and "hiding in the herd" regarding portfolio decision mistakes as those weigh less in case others managers make the same mistakes. Reputation based herding has been confirmed empirically by e.g. Chevalier and Ellison (1999), and Hong et al. (2000). Thirdly, affiliated to the former, compensation based herding can occur if the investor's compensation depends on her performance relative to the performance of other investors, her benchmark – a remuneration scheme that is often applied in asset management. As her compensation decreases in case of underperformance, the investor has a strong incentive to move closest to the benchmark by imitating others (Maug and Naik, 1996). Hence, in all three kinds of herding it can be rational from the individual asset manager's perspective to ignore privately received information signals and to prioritize copying the behavior of other market players (cf. also Devenow and Welch, 1996, for an overview of rational herd behavior in financial markets).

We start our analysis of herd behavior in the two emerging markets and the more mature one by providing evidence of its existence in the three markets (Table 4.5). On the one hand, we ask our surveyed asset managers whether they perceive herding amongst professional asset managers; on the other hand, we request an indication of their own trend following behavior. Agreement on observable herding ranges around 80% among Thai and Indonesian asset managers, and even 91% of the German asset managers perceive herd behavior in the

Table 4.5 Evidence of herd behavior in the market

[1] Perception of herd behavior and [2] own trend following		Complete agreement (in %)					Complete disagreement (in %)	% of agreement[a]	**H₀**: no specific difference[b]
[1] Herding is observable amongst professional asset managers.	Thailand	3.2	35.2	41.6	12.8	4.8	2.4	80.0	-0.196
	Indonesia	7.1	32.1	39.3	17.9	3.6	0.0	78.5	(0.845)
	Germany	20.5	46.4	24.3	2.7	2.3	3.8	91.2	-6.153*** (0.000)
[2] I generally follow the trend.	Thailand	3.2	23.0	32.5	24.6	12.7	4.0	58.7	-1.073
	Indonesia	7.1	25.0	39.3	14.3	10.7	3.6	71.4	(0.283)
	Germany	2.3	13.5	34.4	24.3	17.0	8.5	50.2	-2.999*** (0.003)

a The percentages given are calculated as the sum of the first three answering categories.

b The table gives the z-value of the Mann-Whitney U-test regarding the responses from Thai and Indonesian asset managers, and Thai and Indonesian asset managers versus German asset managers, respectively. The p-value is given in parentheses. Asterisks refer to level of significance: * 10%, ** 5%, *** 1%.

market. In contrast, German asset managers themselves indicate least to follow the trend. Only 50% of them agree on own trend following, and 8.5% of them even complete reject it. Among surveyed Thai asset managers, 59% agree on trend following, whereas agreement amid Indonesian managers sums up to 71%. Again, indicated Mann-Whitney U-tests support similarities between asset managers from the two emerging markets, and discloses convincingly significant differences of the latter in comparison to German asset managers.

This immediately raises the follow-up question of the motives for herd behavior. In order to get a first idea of what might motivate surveyed professionals to herd and whether they differ in diverging market environments, as before, we pool our samples from the two emerging markets and compare it to the German one. Figure 4.1 displays mean answers, categorized by own trend following behavior, to three statements aiming to address compensation, reputation, and information based causes of herd behavior as described in the literature.

Starting with compensation related relevance of relative performance, for Thai and Indonesian managers we find a tendency that the more asset managers agree on following the trend, the higher relevance relative performance has for their remuneration. Seen only from the compensational perspective, a strong benchmark orientation could thus indicate a conservative but rational response to incentives. For German asset managers obvious links between trend following and relative performance importance are missing. At least for those professionals who indicate to herd to some degree, relative performance importance is increasing with own trend following agreement. Findings point towards a question raised by Lütje (2006): do asset managers aim to be only as good as the benchmark which would be in line with "hiding in the herd", or do they aspire to be better by deviating and outperforming others? The latter assumption could explain why some German asset managers who reject trend following judge relative performance to be of high importance for them as well. Furthermore, it depends on how asset managers gain reputation and career benefit in the market – by outperformance or (only) by being as good as the benchmark –, and how much of it they risk in case they underperform their benchmark. Being directly asked whether herding benefits the career, professionals, both from the two emerging markets and the more mature one, show mean values above three, i.e. they disagree on average – independent of their own degree of trend following. Nevertheless, we again find indications of individual rationality in herd behavior: except for those managers that agree the strongest on herding, we reveal that the more professionals indicate to herd, the more they also belief in career benefits of the latter. This applies to German professionals, but surely also to Thai and Indonesian asset managers.

The third explanation of herd behavior is given by information cascades. While we do not know which information signals individual market players receive in the different markets, we are, however, able to directly ask them about the relevant information type used for investment decision making. In particular, we are interested which relevance our surveyed asset managers assign to fundamental information depending on their degree of herd behavior. Fundamental facts about companies cannot only be assumed the least biased information type even in an intransparent market environment but an overall dominant use of fundamental facts by important market players also supports a less psychologically based price formation in the market. This in turn might prevent, or at least mediate, "blind" herd behavior. Asset managers' relevance of fundamentals as information source is also shown in Figure 4.1.

Figure 4.1 Different motives for herd behavior[a]

Herd behavior and its motives

Please assess the following statements / sources of information used in making investment decisions:

"If you receive a performance-based remuneration, which criteria determine the size of that bonus? – Relative Performance?"
"Following the herd benefits the asset manager's career."
"[I use] Fundamental facts about the company / market."

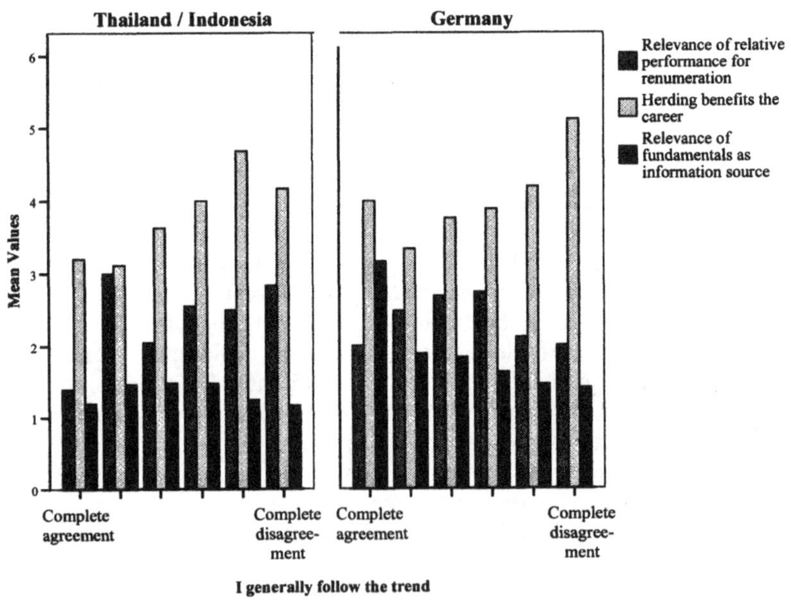

a Mean values for categorical responses ranging from 1=complete agreement / highest relevance to 6=complete disagreement / no relevance.

For German professionals, observations point towards less fundamentally driven behavior of herding asset managers: we find a higher trend following to be accompanied by lower relevance of fundamental information use. For Thailand and Indonesia, however, the pattern is different. In a less transparent environment as assumed in emerging markets, the following observation could be understood as a positive signal towards market efficiency and the role of asset managers in this respect: although fundamentals are of high relevance in all three countries, the level of indicated importance is higher in Thailand and Indonesia than in Germany. Nonetheless, we also find that fundamentals receive the same high level of relevance by those professionals who completely agree on own trend following as by those who completely disagree.

Before jumping to conclusions, we bring herd behavior into a multivariate framework that allows us to control for interdependencies between the different motives of herd behavior as well as for risk behavior and personal characteristics. Table 4.6 shows our findings from pooled ordered probit regressions.

Table 4.6 Herd behavior in a multivariate framework

[1] Common motives for herd behavior and [2] influence of controlled risk-related variables	Ordered PROBIT regressions of herd behavior[a]			
	[1]		[2]	
Career benefit	0.185***	(0.000)	0.137**	(0.015)
Higher relevance of relative performance	0.030	(0.167)	0.093***	(0.004)
Lower relevance of fundamental information	0.286***	(0.000)	0.173*	(0.056)
Higher amount of momentum strategy	0.017***	(0.000)	0.018***	(0.000)
Country dummy TH/IND	0.493***	(0.000)	0.206	(0.238)
Female			0.031	(0.629)
Less experience			0.004	(0.930)
Lower bonus			-0.001	(0.883)
Higher risk aversion			0.236***	(0.001)
Higher loss aversion			0.199***	(0.002)
Higher disposition effect			0.126**	(0.017)
Log likelihood	-577.405		-325.263	
LR statistics	92.50***		81.98***	
(Pseudo)-R^2	0.07		0.11	

a The table gives the coefficients of the respective ordered PROBIT regression with p-values in parentheses. In order to ease understanding, coefficients are adapted to described control variable outcomes in the table. Asterisks refer to level of significance: * 10%, ** 5%, *** 1%.

A higher degree of herding is significantly linked to the belief in a career benefit, and indeed lower relevance of fundamental information. In order to control for possible formal restrictions which individual asset managers might face due to their funds' strategies, we additionally include the amount asset managers attributed to momentum strategy in an extra control question. We reveal a complementary positive and significant impact of the latter on herd behavior.[29] The strong influence of the two emerging markets in our sample is underlined by the significant country variable for Thailand and Indonesia. However, when controlling for risk behavior and personal characteristics in a second regression, the country variable loses significance. Instead, we find higher relevance of relative performance to add up to significant herding motives. Furthermore, and even more important, herd behavior is significantly linked to higher risk aversion, higher loss aversion, and a higher disposition effect.[30]

Taken together, results underline the strong influence of risk propensity for asset managers' herd behavior: confirming compensation related aspects, assumed career benefits and less fundamentally driven information reliance to matter, we particularly find more risk averse and loss sensitive professionals to significantly follow the herd. This finding gives strong support to the above mentioned real "fear" of falling out of the herd (cf. Graham, 1999), and to risk propensity to be more pronounced among professionals from the two surveyed emerging markets and, thus, at least from the individual perspective, rationality in trend following cannot be denied – neither in Germany nor in Thailand and Indonesia.

We now turn to a second behavioral bias that also might be linked to asset managers' risk propensity. Again, we take a closer look at other influencing factors as well.

4.6 Home bias

Although global diversification opportunities have constantly increased over the last decades, it is well documented that investors still neglect capital market theory in this respect and miss chances to increase risk-adjusted returns: they underweight foreign assets in their portfolios and allocate over proportionately high shares to home assets instead. This phenomenon, widely known as 'home

29 As we do not know how causality runs among trend following and momentum strategy, we ran the same regression with and without the momentum variable. In both cases, significant findings for all the other variables as described in the following remain the same.

30 Except for the disposition effect, above findings from the second regression also widely hold when controlling for the set of risk variables in Thailand and Indonesia in particular (results are not explicitly displayed here). Moreover, with coefficients only slightly changing, the significant influence of shown risk variables is also confirmed when regressions are done separately for Thailand and Indonesia on the one hand and Germany on the other. Again, results are not explicitly given here.

bias', has been related to several factors which French and Poterba (1991) divide into two categories: institutional barriers and investor behavior.

While a home biased asset allocation was initially attributed to governmental restrictions and high transactions costs (cf. e.g. Stulz, 1981), strong advances in global financial integration have softened this argument (cf. e.g. Tesar and Werner, 1995, Ahearne et al., 2004). In its place, indirect barriers such as information asymmetries have received both broad research attention and empirical support to fit for the home bias puzzle (cf. e.g. Gehrig, 1993, Coval and Moskowitz, 1999, Edison and Warnock, 2004). Related to the formerly described emerging markets investment environment, the question of whether there is an information advantage either for foreign or domestic investors remains controversial. While Choe et al. (1999) in Korea, and Dvorak (2005) in one of our surveyed countries, Indonesia, find support in favor of domestic investors, Seasholes (2004) finds little evidence of information disadvantages for foreign investors in Taiwan, but indeed discloses outperformance of the latter related to certain stock types.

Among the behavioral explanations for home bias, differences in investor sentiment in support of the domestic market, particularly in forms of differences in return optimism (cf. e.g. French and Poterba, 1991, Strong and Xu, 2003) and felt higher competence (cf. e.g. Kilka and Weber, 2000 as well as Graham et al., 2005, though with contrary findings) are fruitful explanations. Furthermore, analyses of the role of regional proximity (cf. e.g. Coval and Moskowitz, 1999) as well as familiarity (cf. e.g. Huberman, 2001) revealed these two factors to matter as well. Lütje and Menkhoff (2004) who provide survey evidence on German equity managers' home bias bring the different kinds of determinants together and show them holding simultaneously in a multivariate framework.

Similar to our analysis of herd behavior we first test the existence of a home biased asset allocation. We therefore asked our asset managers from the three countries to reveal their preferred international asset allocation despite any fund restrictions. To highlight the latter is important for excluding restrictions which exist in Thailand and Indonesia (see Chapter 4.2).

According to capital market theory, an investor should only hold domestic assets in her portfolio in proportion to her country's share of world market capitalization. Taking the MSCI All Country World Index, Thailand's and Indonesia's current share each amounts to slightly over 0.1%, while Germany represents 3.0% of world market capitalization.[31] Figure 4.2 reveals our findings in regards to the surveyed asset managers' preferred allocation. The histogram in Figure 4.2 [1] shows that 12% of the Thai and Indonesian asset managers and only 8.5% of the German asset managers prefer to allocate less than 5% of their

31 Data referring to October 2006 are given by MSCIBarra. In comparison, the United States' share accounts for 46%, Europe in total represents another 30%, Japan approximately 10 % of world market capitalization.

portfolio to their respective home market. Those managers would thus, if at all, show a very limited home bias.

In contrast, the biggest group (47%) of German asset managers reveals a certain degree of home bias by allocating between 10% and 15% to the home market. Furthermore, in Thailand and Indonesia, the biggest fraction (36%) among Thai and Indonesian asset managers can even be found among those who would still allocate more than 50% to their home market.

Figure 4.2 Evidence of home bias

[1] Histogram of preferred allocation to home market,

[2] preferred allocation to home market relative to other markets.

"Apart from any fund's restriction, please allocate an amount of 500 million Baht / 50 Bio. IDR / 10 million EUR to invest in the following regions (adding up to 100%): _ Home Market: Thailand / Indonesia / Germany; _ United States and Canada; _ Europe; _ China and _ Japan /_ Asia; _ Asian Emerging Markets and _ Other Emerging Markets /_ Emerging Markets."

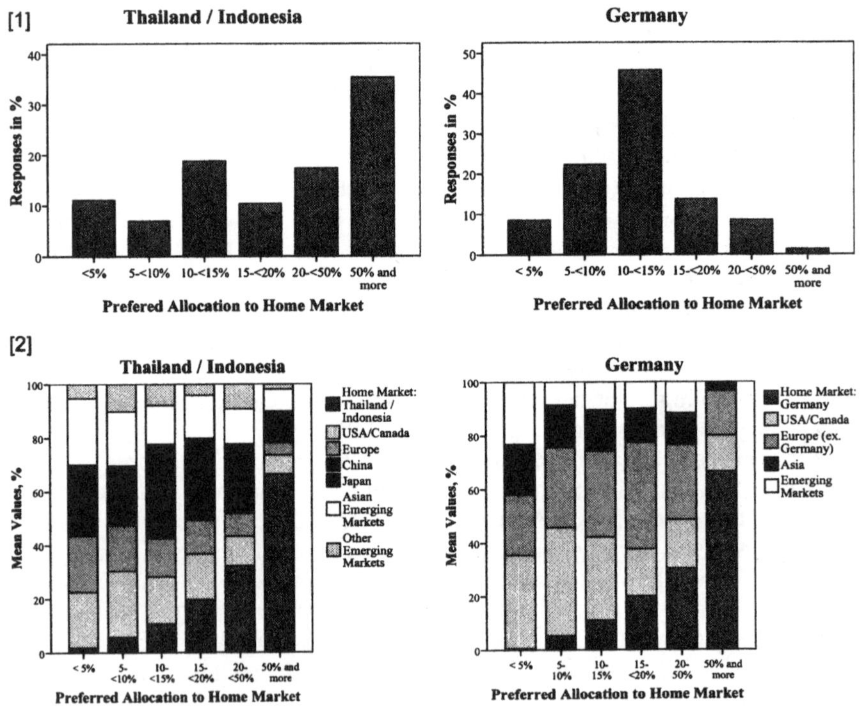

Considering average values of the preferred domestic allocation relative to other markets in Figure 4.2 [2], our findings are threefold. Firstly, in the Thai and Indonesian sample Asia as a whole dominates. Even those asset managers that prefer less than 10% allocation to the domestic market reveal preferred allocation shares of around 50% to Asia in total. Hence, they show at least a strong regional bias, probably driven by geographic and cultural proximity. Among the three big markets, only Japan constantly receives a reasonable allocation share when relying on the MSCI All Country World Index, while North America and Europe are clearly underrepresented.

Secondly, in Germany those asset managers who would allocate less than 10% to the home market are also the least biased in regards to other countries, mirroring the dominance of the USA/Canada and allocating a surprisingly high proportion to Asia and global emerging markets. Then with an increasing preferred allocation share to the home market, particularly North America loses share while, again, regional proximity unfolds its influence: the allocation share to Europe steadily grows and remains relatively high even in the most biased two subgroups. Thirdly, it is interesting to see how attractive emerging markets are perceived. The least home biased asset managers in both samples would allocate the highest proportion to emerging markets (20% in Germany, almost 40% including China in Thailand and Indonesia). Shares of at least 30% in Thailand and Indonesia, and 10% in Germany, remain stable even with increasing home biased allocation, and only German managers with over 50% domestic allocation do not consider emerging markets any more.

In the following, we are interested to know which motives – besides possibly remaining institutional barriers in the two emerging markets – drive the home bias: whether informational advantages and barriers, or behavioral explanations such as return optimism might contribute to its understanding. We thus asked our professionals about their agreement to information advantages as domestic asset managers. In addition, we consider the relevance they attribute to fundamental facts about the company and the market. Moreover, we also requested their long-term expectations for stock and bond market yields for both the home market and the U.S. market as reference. Results are shown in Figure 4.3.

While overall findings for German asset managers do not reveal obvious relations, patterns for Thailand and Indonesia are much more evident. To start with, the agreement to be better informed as a domestic manager is slightly higher in the two emerging markets than in Germany. Nevertheless a clear pattern related to the degree of home biased asset allocation is missing in both samples. However, when taking the relevance of fundamentals into account, we observe the consistently positive coherence between a higher preferred home investment share and higher indicated relevance of fundamental facts in the Thai and Indonesian sample. Return expectations offer more convincing findings. For both, bond and particularly stock yield expectations for the home market, we find a positive trend: the higher the difference in expectations regarding the home versus U.S. markets, the more asset managers prefer to allocate investments to the home market. For German asset managers, yield differences between German and U.S. markets are negative in three subgroups. For a home allocation between 5% and 50%, we do, however, find that an increase in home bias is accompanied by relatively higher stock yield expectations for the domestic market.

Figure 4.3 Different motives for home bias[a]

Home bias and its motives

Please assess the following statements regarding your investment behavior and the sources of information used in making investment decisions:

"As a domestic asset manager I benefit from better information on domes tic securities compared to market players overseas."

"[I use] Fundamental facts about the company / market."

"What are your long-term expectations for the next 10 years? We would like to ask you to estimate the respective development within the next 10 years for the

- Stock market: average stock yield per year (in percent),
- Bond market: average bond yield per year (in percent)."

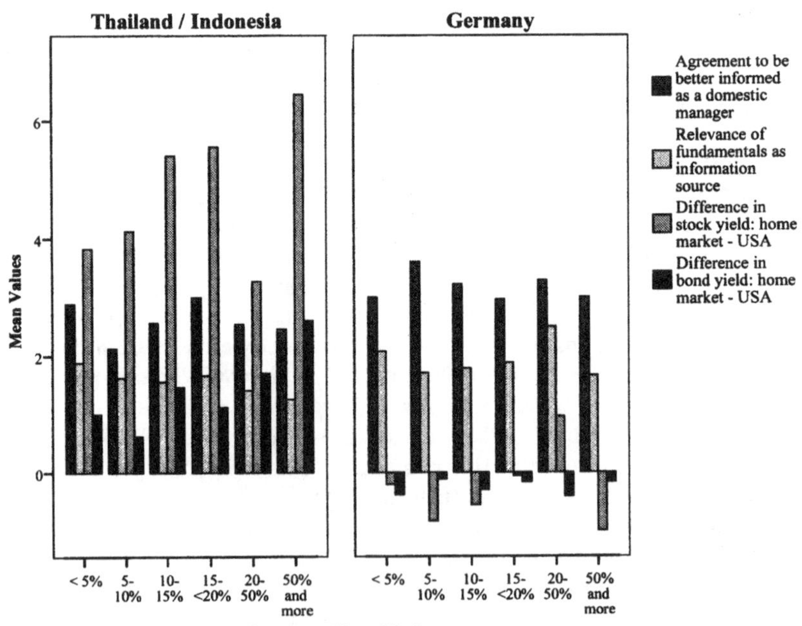

a Mean values for categorical responses range from complete agreement / highest relevance (=1) to complete disagreement / no relevance (=6). Stock and bond yield differences are given on a numerical scale.

Findings from the multivariate framework, i.e. censored tobit regressions, again controlled for personal characteristics and risk variables, are shown in Table 4.7.

Table 4.7 Home bias in a multivariate framework

[1] Common motives for home-biased allocation (whole sample), [2] including emerging market variable, [3]-[4] and the influence of controlled risk-related variables	Censored TOBIT regressions of home investment share[a]			
	[1]	[2]	[3]	[4]
Better informed as domestic manager	0.772	0.174	0.173	0.056
	(0.352)	(0.829)	(0.866)	(0.955)
Higher relevance fundamental information	1.325	0.806	1.234	0.940
	(0.237)	(0.454)	(0.397)	(0.502)
Stock market yield HM-USA	0.730**	0.081	0.301	0.498
	(0.013)	(0.794)	(0.509)	(0.223)
Bond market yield HM-USA	2.327***	1.491**	1.100	1.957**
	(0.001)	(0.034)	(0.205)	(0.021)
Country dummy TH/IND		13.385***	10.016**	
		(0.000)	(0.015)	
Female			2.916***	1.383
			(0.009)	(0.236)
Less experience			-0.873	-0.758
			(0.193)	(0.241)
Lower bonus			-0.010	-0.025
			(0.775)	(0.438)
Higher risk aversion			-0.097	-0.326
			(0.933)	(0.771)
Higher loss aversion			-0.975	-0.967
			(0.331)	(0.319)
Higher disposition effect			2.326***	1.859**
			(0.009)	(0.036)
Female TH/IND				10.187***
				(0.000)
Higher disposition effect TH/IND				3.236**
				(0.021)
Constant	20.434***	14.563***	13.483*	12.333*
	(0.000)	(0.000)	(0.066)	(0.076)
Log likelihood	-1121.66	-1109.89	-724.32	-717.66
R^2	0.16	0.22	0.26	0.31

a The table gives the coefficients of the censored TOBIT regression with p-values in parentheses. In order to ease understanding, coefficients are adapted to described control variable outcomes in the table. Asterisks refer to level of significance: * 10%, ** 5%, *** 1%.

Firstly, a higher preferred home allocation share is significantly linked to higher expected stock and bond yield differences. When secondly controlling for an indeed significant emerging markets effect, only bond yield optimism remains significant.[32] Personal characteristics and risk variables brought into the regression in addition reveal, thirdly, a highly significant gender influence as well as significant positive linkages between home bias and disposition effect. As the emerging markets dummy remains significant, we also test for specific differrences between Thailand and Indonesia on the one hand, and Germany on the other hand in regards to effects from gender and disposition effect. This fourth regression shows two aspects: higher bond yield optimism and a higher disposition effect contribute significantly to a higher home bias. Besides, particularly female asset managers in Thailand and Indonesia as well as those undergoing a higher disposition effect in the two emerging markets show an even higher home investment share than their average sample counterparts.

So far, both linkages between home bias and disposition effect as well as home bias and gender are still scarcely researched. Karlsson and Nordén (2007), for example, analyze the existence of home bias in mutual fund portfolios that are part of the Swedish pension plan. Looking at the individual investor and controlling for age, individual wealth and the amount invested in analyzed pension funds, they do, however, find older male investors slightly more inclined to invest domestically than females. In contrast, Graham et al. (2005) provide evidence that is in line with our findings. Analyzing data from the UBS/Gallup Investor Survey, they link perceived investor competence to trading activity and home bias. Similar to Barber and Odean (2001) who find particular young male investors to trade too much, Graham et al. (2005) detect male investors to be more likely to perceive themselves as competent and thus showing a higher trading activity. Besides, by feeling more competent also about foreign investments, male investors are less likely to exhibit a home biased asset allocation than their female counterparts. Krause et al. (2006) close the circle by their analysis of Chinese stock and fund accounts. Finding active traders to be less prone to display a disposition effect, they do not detect any statistically significant gender difference in their multivariate framework regarding the disposition effect. Further research to reach a more coherent framework linking observed behavioral biases as well as the role of personal characteristics in mutual fund investments, such as gender differences, is clearly needed.

32 At first sight, this finding is somewhat surprising as a home biased allocation is often referred to as equity home bias in particular. Taking into account, however, that the Thai sample is balanced between equity and bond managers and the Indonesian sample mirrors domination of fixed income funds in the industry, we can expect managers to be more familiar with bond yields, i.e. bond yield optimism appears to be dominant.

4.7 Conclusions and outlook

This research offers new insights into asset managers' behavior by presenting comparative survey evidence from two emerging markets, Thailand and Indonesia, and Germany as a more mature market. This implies a comparison of professionals acting in diverging investment environments concerning transparency, institutional development, and regulatory restrictions. After revealing significant differences for risk behavior and biases between Thai and Indonesian asset managers on the one hand and German asset managers on the other, we analyze two widely discussed phenomena, herd behavior and home bias, in more detail.

Starting with herd behavior, we find evidence for two major aspects. Firstly, the imitation of others market players' decisions seems to be both linked to relative performance importance for compensation and reputation concerns. Those managers who herd seem to be afraid of falling out of the herd, and they thus perceive staying within the latter as career protection or even benefit. This finding is robust to controlling for risk and personal variables. We detect a significant influence of higher risk and loss aversion as well as the obvious disposition between winning and loosing stocks at the individual investor's level. From an individual perspective, revealed herding can thus be considered rational at least to some degree – both in the emerging as well the more mature market environment. Secondly, the evidence for information based herding is mixed. We find that herd behavior is significantly linked to lower importance of fundamentals. Though, when controlling for risk variables, we cannot tell, whether herding asset managers really use inferior information and only follow better informed managers. Worrying about the impact of obviously risk driven behavioral biases on market prices and efficiency remains two edged. On the one hand, e.g. short-term price impacts of e.g. loss averse traders have been evidenced by Coval and Shumway (2005). More generally, the danger of uninformed behavior to reinforce market trends and crises has been widely described (cf. e.g. Chari and Kehoe, 2003, Hirshleifer, 2001, or Shiller, 2003). On the other hand, good news comes from surveyed asset managers in emerging markets: Acting risk averse, they consider fundamental information on average more important than their German counterparts do. Besides, we can only speculate how much their risk behavior has been influenced by e.g. experiences from the Asian financial crisis that made both professionals and private investors painfully aware of possible ups and downs of the market.

From our home bias analysis, we want to highlight three findings: Firstly, professionals' risk biases, especially in forms of a disposition effect, are confirmed to also matter for a home biased asset allocation. Secondly, we disclose striking evidence for regional proximity and familiarity preference. Moreover, results confirm significance of return optimism. Thirdly, a surprisingly high influence of institutional barriers could matter as a third factor.

Preferred allocation illustrations have shown that regional relatedness – in line with cultural, language, and geographic proximity – is observable almost independently of the allocation to the domestic market itself, both in the emerging markets and in Germany. We thus confirm findings from the literature. Return expectation differences, a significant determinant of a higher home investment share, can provide a behavioral explanation – either driven by optimism or even by realism. To detect further coherences with risk related biases and to sharpen knowledge about gender influences regarding mutual fund manager's behavior remains open for future research. For policy makers and practitioners, it is helpful to learn about the unmistakable influence of existing foreign investment restrictions in the two emerging markets: Even in a simulated unrestricted framework, more than one third of the surveyed asset managers from Thailand and Indonesia reveal preferred domestic allocation shares of more than 50%. To prepare and promote a reasonable exploitation of the advantages of international diversification in the mid future will be an important task to face for asset management companies and regulators. Finally, considering that asset managers act as agents on behalf of their customers, it will also be interesting to see in which direction customer demand develops. So far, individual investors, similarly to professionals, are still confronted with strong regulatory restrictions regarding investment opportunities. Nevertheless, steady fund inflows to the still limited number of offered foreign-invested funds point towards customer interest not only for domestic investments but also for regional and international allocation opportunities.

5 Evidence for Italian Asset Managers on Overconfidence, Risk Taking and Gender Differences[33]

5.1 Motivation

The Italian mutual fund industry ranges among the global top ten investment businesses. During the last decade, there have been considerable gains in size, and substantial amounts of national households' financial wealth have been entrusted to professional asset managers.[34] However, up to now, this growth market, and in particular attitudes and behavior of its professional market players are comparatively unexplored. This is somewhat surprising compared to depth and conspicuity of findings derived e.g. for important U.S. financial market participants. Indeed, very often market observations contradict the preamble of solely rational behavior in text-book like efficient financial markets and promote research in the mounting field of behavioral finance instead (cf. Shiller, 2003). Especially psychological phenomena like investor overconfidence or risk aversion strongly matter even for professional market players' perception, information processing and investment decisions (cf. Hirshleifer, 2001, Barberis and Thaler, 2003). In addition, individual characteristics such as gender, age or experience have been found to influence behavior (cf. e.g. Chevalier and Ellison, 1999a, Menkhoff et al., 2006). Hence, returning to Italian financial market players, it would be interesting to see, whether behavioral biases also apply to Italian professionals, which role asset managers' personal characteristics play, and if any particularities of the Italian mutual fund industry can be detected to matter.

Surveying Italian professional asset managers, this study concentrates on the three aspects of overconfidence, risk, and gender differences. So far, a wide array of studies addresses gender dissimilarities in risky decision making more generally and, although being less clear cut than often referred to (cf. Schubert

33 I would like to thank my co-authors Torben Luetje and Luca Rebeggiani. Moreover, helpful comments have been provided by Lukas Menkhoff, Marina Nikiforow and Rafael Rebitzky. In addition, financial support by the VolkswagenStiftung is gratefully acknowledged. Besides, we are highly thankful to the Investment Management Associations in Italy and Germany. In particular we are indebted to Fabio Galli, Direttore Generale dell' "Associazione Italiana del Risparmio Gestito" (in short: "Assogestioni"), as well as Stefan Seib and Rudolf Siebel, Managing Directors of the "Bundesverband Investment und Asset Management e.V." (in short: "BVI") for the provision of indispensable recommendation letters. Last but surely not least, we strongly appreciate valuable time and ideas contributed by surveyed professionals.

34 Cf. Khorana et al. (2005) who compare the mutual fund industries around the globe. They relate assets under professional management to the nation's GDP and disclose Italy in this respect to hold the second position in Europe behind Luxemburg as well as the fifth position worldwide.

et al., 1999), derived the stereotype of women to be more risk averse than men.[35] In order to properly frame our study, we briefly review selected studies that link gender to overconfidence, before addressing research on risk related gender differences particularly in the area of professional asset management.

One of the most prominent studies in the field of overconfidence is presented by Barber and Odean (2001). Their paper is motivated by Odean (1998a), who does not only give a broad overview of the literature on overconfidence, but also shows that overconfident investors, i.e. those investors who miscalibrate and overestimate the precision of their own knowledge, trade too much and by doing so forfeit expected utilities.[36] When analyzing common stock investments with the help of a large data set of household accounts, Barber and Odean do not explicitly measure overconfidence, but relying on previous studies (e.g. Lewellen et al., 1977) take gender as a proxy for overconfidence. They find the average portfolio turnover rate for men to be significantly higher than for women. While both male and female investors reduce net returns by trading, performance losses are significantly more pronounced for men. Their findings are contrasted by Deaves et al. (2004) as well as Biais et al. (2005). The former experimentally analyze the relation between overconfidence, trading activity and gender differences with the help of German and Canadian student samples. They provide evidence that greater overconfidence enhances trading activity and thus results in reduced earnings. However, they do not confirm formerly reported gender differences. Biais et al. (2005) find men to trade more than women, but they do not discover any correlation between gender and the overconfidence measure of miscalibration. When splitting their experimentally generated data set by gender, however, they detect miscalibration to significantly worsen male performance, but not the one of their female participants.

Miscalibration, going back to Fischhoff et al. (1977), is not the only form of overconfidence. Overestimation of the own ability going hand in hand with unrealistically positive self-evaluation as well as control illusion in ambiguous situations are further strains of overconfidence that are widely found among individuals (cf. e.g. Deaves et al., 2004, for a survey). Taking the so-called "better than average" effect, e.g. Svenson (1981) revealed that 82% of the surveyed Swedish car drivers believe that their driving skills are among the best 30%.

Returning to gender differences and overconfidence, Lundeberg et al. (1992) provide evidence of dissimilarities for male and female psychology students by requesting confidence judgements on formerly given exam answers. Although they reveal both men and women to be overconfident, in particular young males are found to be especially overconfident when wrong. Similarly, Bengtsson et al. (2005) also reveal significant gender dissimilarities in self-assessments when

35 For an overview cf. the meta analysis by Byrnes et al. (1999) as well as Chapter 7 regarding more recent studies.

36 Similar findings are derived by Odean (1999), as well as Barber and Odean (2000).

studying exam behavior of male and female Swedish economics students. Differences in confidence are most pronounced in younger age groups.

Apart from exam behavior, different kinds of competitive environments could be suitable to analyze the relation between overconfidence and gender. Moreover, assumptions of higher female risk propensity have also been linked to observed competition behavior. Niederle and Vesterlund (2007), for example, present an interesting insight into gender dissimilarities in an experimental tournament frame: women are found to be rather diffident in terms of entering a competitive tournament incentive scheme, whereas men welcome it. The gender gap cannot be explained by performance differences, but male overconfidence is found to be a key factor. Gupta et al. (2005) as well as Dohmen and Falk (2006) confirm findings on gender dissimilarities in competition behavior while attributing them to differences in risk attitudes.

With Bliss and Potter (2002) who link gender differences to both risk aversion and overconfidence, and also consider professional asset managers, we return to the financial market environment. Comparing data from domestic and international U.S. equity funds, the authors expect women to hold less risky portfolios than men. Assuming them to be less overconfident, female asset managers are expected to trade less than their male counterparts, and thus to perform better. However, Bliss and Potter do not find evidence of expected risk taking differences among female and male asset managers. Furthermore, trading activity is not subject to gender differences for domestic but only for international funds. While for the latter male asset managers perform better than their (few) female colleagues, for domestic funds the authors detect female outperformance. When controlling for factors that might influence results like risk or asset managers' tenure, yet lastly performance differences disappear for domestic funds. Remaining with professionally trained investors, Olsen and Cox (2001) provide survey evidence from two groups of U.S. professionals: Chartered Financial Analysts (CFAs) and Certified Financial Planners (CFPs). They reveal that female professionals weight risk attributes, such as possibility of loss and ambiguity, more severely than their male counterparts. Moreover, females put more emphasis on risk reduction in their portfolio construction.

Niessen and Ruenzi (2006), finally, investigate gender differences among U.S. equity mutual fund managers. They disclose only moderately less risky portfolios of female managers but show that women follow more stable investment styles over time. With regards to performance, the authors do not find significant average performance differences. Again, however, male asset managers are rather found in the distributional extremes than women, and more moderate female investment styles lead to a higher performance persistence compared to their male counterparts. In contrast to that, while analysing a sample of U.S. fixed income funds, and controlling for wealth and knowledge differences between female and male asset managers, Atkinson et al. (2003) find no differences in fund performance, risk and other fund characteristics. They do, however, similarly to Niessen and Ruenzi, detect significantly lower customer net inflows to funds that are managed by female professionals.

Our contribution to the literature is twofold: Firstly, we provide a pioneering insight into the Italian mutual fund industry by directly assessing asset managers' views and behavior and comparing their aggregated answers with those given by their German counterparts in a similar survey. Secondly, we shed light on overconfidence, risk taking and typical gender differences – not in an experimental framework with student participants but among professionals in the risky and ambiguous investment environment. While disclosing Italian professionals' overly positive self-assessment in general, we find evidence for male overconfidence in particular – though without being accompanied by control illusion in forms of an excessive overestimation of the own level of information. Asset managers' risk taking reveals further differences: Italian female professionals do not only assess themselves as more risk averse than their male colleagues, they also prefer a more passive portfolio management compared to the level they are allowed to. Moreover, in a competitive tournament scenario near the end of the investment period female asset managers do not try to become the ultimate top performer when they have outperformed their peer group so far. However, in case of underperformance, the risk of deviating from the benchmark makes female professionals more willing than their male colleagues to seize a chance of catching up. Overall, compared to their German counterparts, we find Italian asset managers to be more risk averse. Matching former results on Italian mutual funds, we discuss interdependencies as well as impact of our findings at the individual asset managers' level on trading activity, management style and performance.

The remainder of this chapter is organized as follows: Chapter 5.2 provides an overview of the Italian mutual fund industry's development and related research so far. Chapter 5.3 describes survey methodology and data set. Both, a comparison between the generated sample and the industry structure as well as characteristics of the surveyed asset managers are provided. Chapter 5.4 addresses asset managers' self-assessment regarding their professional success and information level, Chapter 5.5 reveals asset managers' risk propensity. In Chapter 5.6, we disclose Italian professionals' behavior in the tournament they typically face near the end of an investment period. Chapter 5.7 summarizes the main findings and concludes.

5.2 The Italian mutual fund industry

The Italian mutual fund management industry has risen to one of the biggest in the world: since its foundation in 1984, starting with 10 offered funds at the beginning, the industry has experienced meaningful growth rates, particularly by the end of the 1990s. Figure 5.1 sheds a more detailed light on its development. Numbers from the German mutual fund industry are given in comparison as we consider the latter a well suiting reference due to three main factors: Firstly, in both countries, the mutual fund industries are embedded in rather bank-based than market-based financial systems. This implies certain similarities in equity culture, bank presence and pension systems (Cf. Otten and Schweitzer, 2002). Secondly, different from the United States, in both countries a limited number of fund groups have long dominated the domestic market. Combined with considerably higher importance of bank branch distribution channels[37], this reveals a competition environment very different from the one in the U.S. Thirdly, obvious parallels concerning development and fixed income funds dominance in the German and Italian mutual fund industry are shown in the following.

Figure 5.1 Development of the Italian mutual fund industry[a] (assets under management, % of households' wealth entrusted)

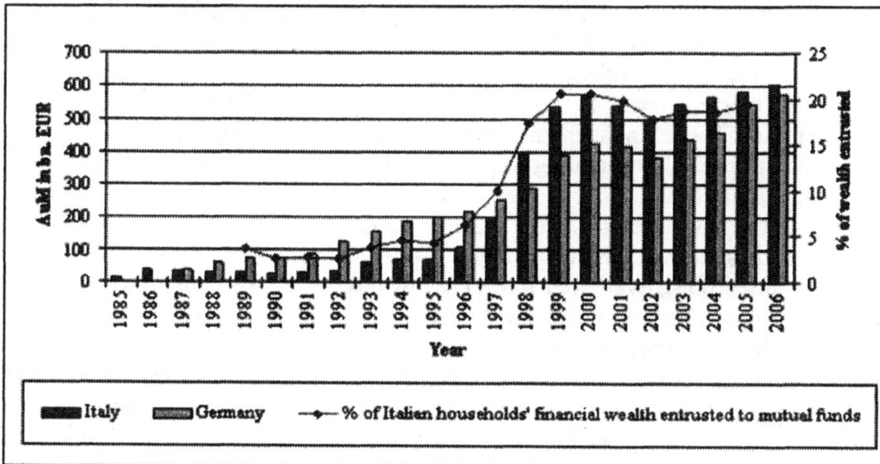

a Numbers on assets under management (AuM) and households' wealth entrusted are provided on the websites of the Italian and the German Investment Management Associations "Assogestioni" and "BVI".

While in the 1980s indirect holdings of financial assets in Italy through mutual fund investments "was virtually absent" (Guiso and Jappelli, 2002) by accounting for less than four percent of household's financial wealth, a shift towards more risky assets as well as mutual fund investments became clearly no-

37 Cf. Walter (1999). Fund distribution in the U.S. has always been strongly dominated by direct sales and full-service brokers, while bank branches have only played a marginal role. In contrast, bank branch distribution has dominated in Germany while in Italy both bank and independent sales force channels have been used.

ticeable in the mid 1990s.[38] By 1995, the number of funds offered by the Italian mutual fund industry has rosen to 459, and in 1996, assets under management by Italian mutual funds passed the EUR 100 billion line. Dramatic growth rates in the following four years positioned Italy among the largest investment businesses in the world. Italian assets under management invested in over one thousand funds peaked in the year 2000, showing 20% of Italian household wealth in the hands of mutual funds. A recovery from the following stock market turbulences appeared in 2003. Since, steady industry growth rates of at least three percent per year led the Italian mutual fund industry to 2,340 offered funds, provided by 63 investment groups and summing up to EUR 604.3 billion of assets under management by September 2006. One fourth of it is invested in equity funds, almost half in fixed income funds, 15% in money market funds, and the rest comprehends balanced, flexible as well as hedge funds.

In comparison, the German mutual fund industry underwent a similar development, though starting to boom a little earlier, in 1992, with slightly more smooth and steady growth rates in the subsequent years and a first peak in 2000. Its quick recovery from the following crisis is best documented by an astonishing industry growth rate of 16% in 2005. By September 2006, the German mutual fund industry accounts for EUR 573.7 billion of assets under management and 3,112 offered funds. 79 member companies of the "BVI" (the German Investment and Asset Management Association) manage equity and bond fund by about one third each, remaining assets comprise money market, real estate, balanced and other funds.[39]

While German asset managers' behavior has been covered by comprehensive survey studies (cf. e.g. Arnswald, 2001, Lütje and Menkhoff, 2005, or Menkhoff and Schmidt, 2005), even after more than twenty years of mutual fund business in Italy, the number of studies explicitly addressing Italian asset managers remains limited. Among previous studies, the majority concentrates on issues of performance, persistence, and market efficiency, some on customer interaction or regulation induced developments, and only very few address – more or less directly – behavioral aspects in the Italian market. Nevertheless, some interesting findings have been derived that can also be linked to our results regarding asset managers' self-assessment and risk behavior in the following and should therefore be reviewed in brief.

38 This move towards higher stock market participation in Italy is part of a general change in portfolio structure observed throughout Europe, confirmed both by aggregate accounts (Guiso et al., 2003) and by household survey data (Sierminska et al., 2006). Among other determinants, like the good performance of stock markets in the 1990s and demographic trends, the growth of the mutual fund industry is regarded as one of its main causes, reducing significantly (real and perceived) participation costs for households.

39 Not considered special funds cover another EUR 650 billion.

Starting with performance findings, Cesari and Panetta (2002) reveal market efficiency in the sense that on the basis of gross returns, risk-adjusted performance[40] is in total positive in the Italian market, thus implying that informed investors are compensated for their information gathering. The authors do, however, not find significant market-timing abilities for analyzed Italian equity funds. Moreover, at the single fund level, they disclose half of funds with negative risk-adjusted performance, but do find the latter to be driven out of the market as a consequence. Casarin et al. (2003) also question whether mutual fund managers are able to generate "extra return" due to market timing and stock-picking ability, and which role performance persistence plays in the Italian market. Different from Grande and Panetta (2002) who provide evidence for weak persistence for their whole sample period from 1987 to 2000, Casarin et al. (2003) do neither find evidence for general outperformance abilities nor return persistence in the long run. They do, however, reveal a short run "hot-hand" effect by showing perseverance in risk-adjusted returns at least for four-month intervals.

Looking from the side of mutual fund investors, Anolli (2005) investigates the costs investors face when holding shares of Italian mutual funds. He discloses the management style and fund portfolio turnover as key determinants of mutual fund costs but shows that a low level of transparency from mutual fund companies meets insufficient awareness of cost importance from fund investors. Both keep competition to a mild degree in this respect.

Savona (2006, 2006a) analyzes the Italian mutual fund industry in terms of competition induced by foreign market players. Comparing return patterns between domestic and foreign mutual funds, his first paper focuses on tax-induced differences while showing that only asymmetric treatment of foreign and domestic funds supports foreign funds' outperformance. In his second paper, Savona finds evidence for different dominant investment styles between home market players and their foreign counterparts. Detected dominance of bond and liquidity investment for Italian funds as well as shifts from bonds to equities especially for foreign funds are attributed to possible changes in clients' risk-return targets.

Caparrelli et al. (2004) finally offer an interesting insight from the behavioral perspective. They test for herd behavior in the Italian stock market and detect the latter to be particularly present in extreme market conditions, i.e. sustained growth rates and high asset price levels. Thus, the role of investors' mentality, rationality and the importance of behavioral psychology are convincingly shown to also matter in Italian financial market decisions.

---

40 While Cesari and Panetta (2002) carefully check different models, Casarin et al. (2005) shed light on the relevance of the chosen performance indicator by e.g. also addressing customized benchmarks that mutual fund companies in Italy, as the first county in Europe, have to disclose by law in their fund's advertisements.

5.3 Survey methodology and data

In financial market analysis, survey studies using data directly derived from professional decision makers have been established as a complementary method to conventional approaches (cf. Shiller and Pound, 1989, or Blinder, 2000, as prominent examples). However, especially in written surveys, quality and explanatory power crucially depend on the reasonable choice of questions as well as correct and unmistakable wording. We therefore discussed preliminary questionnaire versions with asset managers in several cities in advance, and test runs assured comprehensibility. In addition, guaranteed anonymity of participating professionals and limited individual influence on survey results overall are two further factors that strengthen authenticity and explanatory power of the survey.

Between March and July 2004, we collected written questionnaire data of Italian asset managers of all relevant member companies of the "Assogestioni" (Association of Italian Investment Management Companies). A reference letter by the association helped to ensure participation and convinced asset managers in contributing companies to act as multipliers by forwarding blank questionnaires to their colleagues as well. For the German market we received similar support by the "BVI" for an analogous survey conducted in 2003.[41]

Altogether, we base our following analyses on 375 questionnaires, covering both Italian and German asset managers. We are pleased to finally report a participation rate of 58% regarding contacted investment firms in Italy, and even 77% in the German mutual fund industry. Numbers are shown in Table 5.1.[42]

As 29 among the thirty biggest investment firms in Italy participated in our survey, and we mainly missed the smallest companies, participating firms cover almost 97% of the market in terms of assets under management. Regarding the number of funds offered, the covered companies' market share comprehends 90%. For Germany, numbers sum up to 92% and 82%, respectively. Mann-Whitney U tests confirm that the null hypothesis of no difference between the respective industry's structure and our data sample cannot be rejected.

While a clear majority of survey respondents is male, we also received at least 20 percent of the questionnaires from female asset managers. This result might seem somewhat surprising when having stereotypes and cultural descriptions of an alleged male-dominated Italian society in mind. Indeed, in relation to e.g. the U.S. mutual fund industry with constant female shares around 10% (cf. Niessen and Ruenzi, 2006), a share of one fifth appears comparatively high and encourages further analyses. Descriptive sample statistics are therefore given in Table 5.2. They reveal characteristics of the participating Italian asset managers – directly clustered by gender.

---

41 A full description of the German survey can be found in Lütje and Menkhoff (2005).

42 Due to anonymity reasons, we were unable to attribute all questionnaires. Numbers thus refer to those questionnaires without doubt in regards to company assignment.

Table 5.1 Comparison of the data sample with the industry structure[a]

	Italy		Germany	
Investment firm participation rate	58.2%		77.3%	
	Structure of the survey sample in relation to country's asset management industry			
Covered firms' market share		**H₀**: no difference[b]		**H₀**: no difference[b]
- by assets under management	96.6%	-0.403 (0.687)	91.8%	-0.669 (0.503)
- by numbers of funds	89.7%	-0.385 (0.700)	81.8%	-0.821 (0.412)

a The market data for Italy is taken from the Italian Investment Management Association' Website "Assogestioni". We refer to aggregated data by investment firm for January 2004, July 2004 and January 2005. For eleven out of 112 received Italian questionnaires, we are unable to ascribe them to the considered investment firms. Numbers in the following thus refer to 101 out of our total of 112 Italian questionnaires. For Germany, market data is taken from the annual report 2003 of the "BVI". Eight out of 263 questionnaires remain anonymous with respect to the investment company and are thus not attributable.

b The table gives the z-value of the Mann-Whitney U test with the p-value in parentheses.

Table 5.2 Italian asset managers' personal characteristics clustered by gender[a]

Age (in years)	*< 31*	*31 – 35*	*36 – 40*	*41 – 45*	*46 – 50*	*> 50*	*Mean*
	18.8%	32.9%	16.5%	18.8%	7.1%	5.1%	~37
	34.8%	52.2%	13.0%	0.0%	0.0%	0.0%	~32
Prof. experience (in years)	*< 4*	*4 – 6*	*7 – 9*	*10 – 12*	*13 – 15*	*> 15*	
	16.9%	19.3%	24.1%	6.0%	20.5%	13.3%	~9
	21.7%	34.8%	26.1%	13.0%	0.0%	4.3%	~6
Marital status / Educational level	*Single*	*Married*	*Other*		*Non-academic*	*Academic*	
	42.9%	57.1%	0.0%		8.3%	91.7%	
	63.6%	27.3%	9.1%		0.0%	100.0%	
Occupational level / Bonus	*Junior manager*	*Senior manager*	*Head of AM team*	*CIO / CEO*	*Median bonus*	*Std. dev.*	
	13.8%	41.3%	18.8%	31.3%	35.0%	41.5%	
	28.6%	52.4%	9.5%	9.5%	31.0%	26.6%	
Major investment segment / Working hours and info research	*Equities*	*Bonds*	*Money market*		*Mean weekly working hours*	*Mean info research*	
	48.4%	43.0%	8.6%		~49	~21	
	67.5%	32.5%	0.0%		~47	~22	

a Regarding each item, the first row displays response of male asset managers (survey participation rate: 78.9%), whereas the second row displays response of female asset managers (participation rate: 21.1%).

We find a balanced sample regarding age and experience, particularly among the surveyed male asset managers, and also discover immediate gender differences. As we can see, participating female asset managers are significantly[43] younger (none is older than 40), and on average less experienced than their male counterparts (on average six versus nine years). Furthermore, the typical male asset manager is married and in the majority academically educated, while the majority of female asset managers are single, and received by even hundred percent an academic education. The slight female "advantage" in education is not yet reflected in the asset managers' position: training-on-the-job might play a major role as well. So far, the biggest group of asset managers who participated in the survey now holds a position as senior asset manager – this finding is equal among both sexes with even relatively more women in this position than men. Among the surveyed male asset managers, almost one third work as Chief Investment Officers (CIO) or Chief Executive Officers (CEO) in comparison to only ten percent among female respondents. As the bonus payment, which is additionally paid to the fixed basic salary in relation to one's performance, increases with the hierarchical level, it is not surprising that bonus payments are (though not significantly) higher for men than for women, revealing also higher variances among the former. Differences regarding working hours that are assumed to be higher on average for higher positions are minor. We even find women to put more time effort in information research. Finally, regarding the investment segment, significant differences at the 5% level reveal a clear majority of surveyed females to manage equity funds, while male asset managers are more equally distributed among equities and bonds, and to a smaller part also manage money market funds.

5.4 Asset managers' overconfidence

We start the analyses by reviewing how surveyed professional asset managers perceive their own professional success and whether they underlie the "better-than-average" effect of overconfidence identified in former, mainly experimental studies. Both the prevalence of gender dissimilarities in the Italian mutual fund industry as well as differences among Italian and German professionals are addressed. In more detail, on the one hand, we asked surveyed professionals to judge their last year's risk-adjusted investment performance compared to their peer group; on the other hand, we requested them to reveal their perceived overall achievements in relation to colleagues and counterparts. Table 5.3 shows their answers – both split by gender and in aggregated form in comparison to German asset managers.

We find striking evidence for an unrealistically positive self-evaluation – particularly among male asset managers – which are almost comparable to the

43 Also conducted Mann-Whitney U tests are not explicitly shown here.

Table 5.3 Self-assessment of professional success

Performance and achievements		Much better (in %)			Equally good			Much worse (in %)	H_0: no specific difference[a]
[1] Risk-adjusted performance last year compared to your peer group	Italy ♂	9.4	30.6	32.9	22.4	4.7	0.0	0.0	-1.697*
	Italy ♀	5.0	25.0	20.0	35.0	15.0	0.0	0.0	(0.090)
	Italy total	8.5	29.2	31.1	24.6	6.6	0.0	0.0	-2.328**
	Germany total	6.9	17.7	33.1	35.5	4.8	2.0	0.0	(0.020)
[2] Achievement in asset management compared to your peer group	Italy ♂	6.0	29.8	41.7	22.5	0.0	0.0	0.0	-2.000**
	Italy ♀	5.0	25.0	15.0	45.0	10.0	0.0	0.0	(0.046)
	Italy total	5.7	28.6	36.2	27.6	1.9	0.0	0.0	-1.800*
	Germany total	5.2	18.5	41.0	30.9	3.6	0.8	0.0	(0.072)

a The table gives the z-value of the Mann-Whitney U test regarding gender specific differences in Italy as well as between responses from Italian and German asset managers. The p-value is given in parentheses. Asterisks refer to level of significance: * 10%, ** 5%, *** 1%.

findings of Svenson (1981): summing up the first three response categories, 73% of the male asset managers in Italy (but only 50% of their female colleagues) indicate a better risk-adjusted performance relative to their peers. Additional 22% and 35%, respectively, reveal an equally good investment performance and only few asset managers a slightly worse performance than their peer group. As the ultimately achieved fund performance can be seen as the result of a complex, multilevel investment process, it is reasonable not only to ask for the risk-adjusted investment performance but also how asset managers individually evaluate their overall achievement in asset management. Among male managers positive self-perception becomes even more pronounced here: 78% perceive their achievements to be better than their peer group and none of them at all indicates to be worse. Among female asset managers, the percentage of those assessing themselves to be better drops to 45%, while another 45% indicates their achievements to be equally good as other market players in their investment segment. Not surprisingly, indicated Mann-Whitney U tests reveal significant gender differences in both questions.[44]

44 The level of significance is even reinforced when controlling for possible "boldness effects" among professionals arising by the position they hold. As shown in Chapter 3, female professionals are clearly less represented in higher positions. In order to take into account that asset managers in leading positions might indeed show better achievements or at least subjectively assume to be better than their lower positioned counterparts, we repeat Mann-Whitney U tests after excluding the leading position groups of CIO/CEO and head of asset management team. Findings of even pronounced gender differences in the lower position groups do not only reassure male overconfidence in our sample but they are

Taking aggregated data in comparison to German asset managers into account, Italian professionals indeed show an overly positive self-assessment. Although Germans also reveal affirmative self-evaluations, findings seem to be relatively less pronounced. Again, differences are significant in both cases at the 10% and 5% level, respectively.

Although our findings could indeed reflect relatively positive performance developments compared to individually considered benchmarks for (at least some) Italian managers, findings by Cesari and Panetta (2002) of several negatively performing Italian equity funds rather point towards a clearly biased overestimation of own abilities among Italian asset managers in general, and male professionals in particular. The also described absence of expected market mechanisms in response to negative fund performance which would, if existent, mediate completely unjustified self-perceptions, supports our observation in addition.

In order to better assess possible implications, we examine whether detected overly positive self-evaluations are also accompanied by an overestimation of the own level of information, i.e. reflecting a second form of overconfidence: control illusion. Although former research revealed different measures of overconfidence to be not necessarily correlated (cf. e.g. Glaser et al., 2005), in asymmetric information frameworks – as prevailing in international financial markets and hence representing the typical information environment for professional asset manager to make their investment decisions – access to, as well as choice and transparency of relevant information is of key importance. We therefore also surveyed the asset managers' personal information level and tested for control illusion regarding the latter by presenting two statements and evaluating their degree of agreement. The first pronouncement assesses individually perceived novelty of published business news; the second statement questions possible advantages of domestic managers relative to their foreign counterparts. Results are displayed in Table 5.4.

Concerning novelty of news, we again find Italian male asset managers to be slightly more prone to overconfidence than their female colleagues (55% agreement that news do not reveal any surprise at all versus 48%). Differences are, however, not statistically significant. Besides, results turn when assessing the agreement on information advantages as a domestic market player. With 57% versus 42% agreement, females are found to show a considerably higher conviction in this respect. Though, once again, the null hypothesis cannot be rejected, and thus gender dissimilarities among surveyed professionals cannot be confirmed for control illusion. Instead, it is interesting that some professionals (14 percent of both males and females) also completely disagree on informational

---

also in line with reinforced findings in lower age groups by Lundeberg et al. (1992) and Bengtsson et al. (2005) as described in our motivating chapter.

advantages for domestic managers as this conviction can be linked to the belief in efficient markets where home market informational advantages would not exist. Taking into account that Savona (2006) cannot distinguish pre-tax risk-adjusted returns between domestic Italian and foreign funds, surveyed professionals seem to have quite a realistic self-perception in this respect. Accordingly, when comparing Italian professionals to German asset managers at the aggregate level, Italians seem indeed to be much more moderate in their assessment. For both statements, German professionals reveal significantly higher levels of confidence in their own information level.

Table 5.4 Self-assessment of personal informational level

Perception of informational advantages compared to others		Completely agree (in %)					Completely disagree (in %)	**H_0**: no specific difference[a]
[1] Most of the published business news does not surprise me at all	Italy ♂	1.2	20.5	33.7	27.7	14.5	2.4	-1.142
	Italy ♀	0.0	4.8	42.9	33.3	14.3	4.8	(0.253)
	Italy total	0.9	17.0	35.8	29.2	14.2	2.8	-1.848*
	Germany total	1.9	21.0	39.3	28.2	8.0	1.5	(0.065)
[2] As a domestic asset manager I benefit from better information on domestic securities compared to market players overseas	Italy ♂	2.4	18.3	22.0	24.4	19.5	13.4	-0.874
	Italy ♀	4.8	19.0	33.3	19.0	9.5	14.3	(0.382)
	Italy total	2.9	18.1	25.7	22.9	17.1	13.3	-3.172***
	Germany total	5.1	24.9	35.2	15.8	14.2	4.7	(0.002)

a The table gives the z-value of the Mann-Whitney U test regarding gender specific differences in Italy as well as between responses from Italian and German asset managers. The p-value is given in parentheses. Asterisks refer to level of significance: * 10%, ** 5%, *** 1%.

To summarize our findings, we find (unrealistic) overly positive self-assessments of Italian asset managers with regards to professional success and achievements. In particular, male overconfidence is statistically confirmed. Nevertheless, we do neither detect comparably high levels of possessed information overestimation nor gender dissimilarities for control illusion. At least the latter is approvable from the Italian investor's point of view: Bringing to mind the fiduciary character of the asset management industry, it is surely in the investor's interest that asset managers are apparently not too overly convinced about their own performance and their abilities to control uncertain situations. As reviewed, empirical studies have widely shown that overconfidence inclines excessive trading activity, which has turned out to be detrimental to the performance of U.S. funds (cf. i.e. Carhart, 1997, Odean, 1999, Glaser and Weber, 2004). For the Italian market, Anolli (2005) underlines the huge impact of portfolio turnover on mutual fund costs. Besides, overconfidence might drive professionals into overly risky investment decisions. In order to get further insights, we now turn to professionals' risk taking behavior. Again, we analyze possible gender differences as well as divergence to German asset managers' behavior.

5.5 Asset managers' risk taking behavior

Once more, we start the analysis by a self-assessment of the surveyed asset managers. We directly asked them about their risk taking behavior in professional investment decisions. Table 5.5 reveals their responses.

Table 5.5 Self-assessment of risk taking behavior

Risk aversion and compensation for risk taking in simulated bet		Very risk averse (in %)					Little risk averse (in %)	**H_0:** no specific difference[a]
[1] In respect of professional investment decision, I mostly act…	Italy ♂	1.2	15.9	24.4	37.8	18.3	2.4	-1.671*
	Italy ♀	0.0	15.0	55.0	20.0	10.0	0.0	(0.095)
	Italy total	1.0	16.3	29.8	34.6	16.3	1.9	-0.317
	Germany total	1.5	9.2	36.9	42.7	8.5	1.2	(0.751)
[2] Imagine someone offers you a bet and the odds are fifty-fifty. You will have to pay 1,000 € if you lose. What would be the minimum amount you would expect to win to lure you into accepting the bet? At least…		Median answer						
	Italy ♂	2,001 €						-1.392
	Italy ♀	5,000 €						(0.164)
	Italy total	2,750 €						-3.451***
	Germany total	1,750 €						(0.001)

a The table gives the z-value of the Mann-Whitney U test regarding gender specific differences in Italy as well as between responses from Italian and German asset managers. The p-value is given in parentheses. Asterisks refer to level of significance: * 10%, ** 5%, *** 1%.

While the majority of male asset managers, i.e. almost 59%, indicate to rather act little risk averse (indicated by response categories 4 to 6), female professionals seem to behave according to the stereotype. Indeed, females respond slightly less in the extremes than their male colleagues, i.e. indicating neither very high nor very little risk aversion, but nevertheless female agreement on rather risk averse behavior sums up to 70% when taking together the first three response categories. This gender difference is statistically significant.

When looking at the aggregate level, Italian asset managers do not seem to differ from German professionals. In both samples, agreement to risk averse behavior (covered by response categories 1 to 3) adds up to slightly under 50%.

In a second step, we move from the professional investment decision framework to a simulated coin toss bet originated by Tversky and Kahneman (1992). In this abstract gamble, asset managers are asked to indicate the minimum amount to win that would make them accepting a bet where the odds are fifty-fifty to lose EUR 1,000. While we do not test for an explicit (risk-less) certainty equivalent, we nevertheless expect to find that losses loom larger than corresponding gains (cf. Tversky and Kahneman, 1991). Moreover, findings by Schubert et al. (1999), who were the first to disclose mixed evidence regarding gender dissimilarities in financial decisions, confirmed the latter to appear at least in an abstract gambling framework.

Indeed, results for both male and female asset managers point into the expected direction of a pronounced fear of loss – even among professionals. Facing the threat to lose EUR 1,000 Italian male asset mangers demand on average a minimum gain of EUR 2,001 as condition to accept the 50:50 bet. Their female colleagues' required gain equivalent is even five times the loss amount. Although these median numbers point towards greater risk propensity among females again, differences are not confirmed to also be statistically significant.

Turning to aggregate numbers, we find Italian asset managers to show a higher sensitivity to the possible loss of EUR 1,000 than their German colleagues. While Italian professionals demand on average a minimum gain amount of EUR 2,750, Germans reveal a median of EUR 1,750. Here, differences are statistically significant at the 1% level.[45]

So far, gender differences in risk propensity seem to be more pronounced when surveyed asset managers are asked about professional investment decisions. At first sight, this finding deviates from Schubert et al. (1999). However, it might also reflect and imply differences in the risk related management of entrusted assets. Female asset managers might face other institutional restrictions than males in regards to risky behavior by the funds they manage: if female asset managers indeed supervised less risk oriented funds (self-selected or not), this would explain their stronger agreement on risk averse behavior in regards to professional investment decisions. In order to examine the robustness of previous findings, we return to the professional investment decisions framework, and let the surveyed asset managers self-assess their degree of active management. Asking them about their allowed and their actually practiced trading style, we assume that more risk-averse managers would shrink back from exploiting their given leeway, and prefer a more passive management style instead. Figure 5.2 illustrates our comparative results in this respect.

In general, in all four displayed subgroups (Italian males, Italian females, Italian asset managers in total, and their German counterparts) a plurality of asset managers actually uses the tracking error, i.e. the deviation from their benchmark index, as they are allowed to. However, dissimilarities between Italian males and females become, again, clearly evident: While 50% of Italian

45 Given the higher female participation in the Italian sample, we repeat Mann-Whitney U tests for surveyed male professionals only. Differences between German and Italian professionals remain strongly significant.

male asset managers do not show any difference at all, and another 40% reveal to act only slightly more passive in comparison to what they are allowed to, Italian female professionals are obviously more risk averse. While (only) 30% reveal no difference between allowed and actually used tracking error, a clearly right skewed graph demonstrates another 60% of female managers to act either slightly or clearly more passive than allowed. A Mann-Whitney U test reveals significant differences at the 5% level. In contrast, significant differences between German and Italian asset managers overall cannot be detected.

Figure 5.2 Self-assessment of active management style (difference between tracking error allowed and practiced)[a]

Please describe your trading style: I) "What trading style are your allowed?" II) "What trading style do you actually follow?" Six answer categories ranging from 1="high tracking error" to 6="indexing".

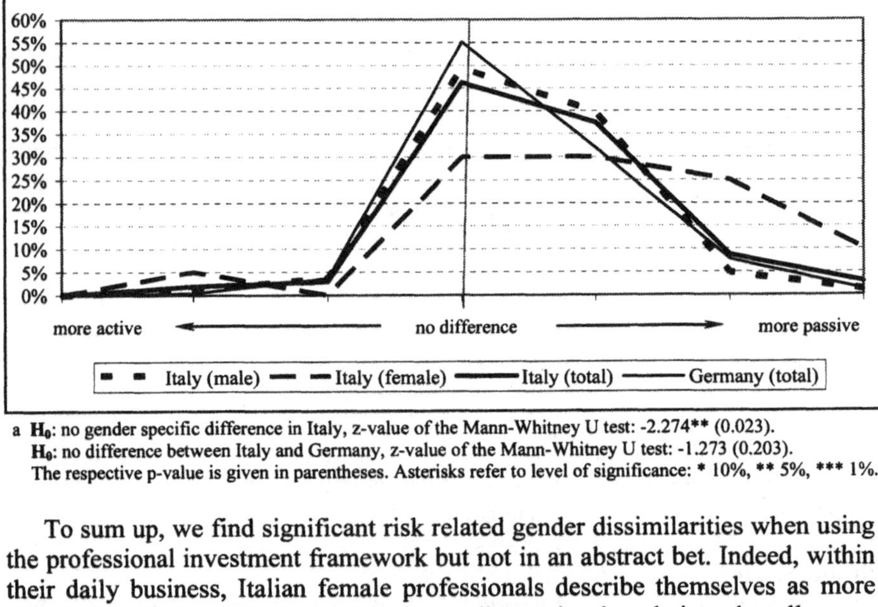

a H_0: no gender specific difference in Italy, z-value of the Mann-Whitney U test: -2.274** (0.023).
H_0: no difference between Italy and Germany, z-value of the Mann-Whitney U test: -1.273 (0.203).
The respective p-value is given in parentheses. Asterisks refer to level of significance: * 10%, ** 5%, *** 1%.

To sum up, we find significant risk related gender dissimilarities when using the professional investment framework but not in an abstract bet. Indeed, within their daily business, Italian female professionals describe themselves as more risk averse and also reveal more passive trading styles than their male colleagues relatively to what they are allowed to. In a strongly competitive environment like the asset management industry where companies and funds compete for client's assets, relative performance is of key importance. So far, we have seen that male asset managers are more confident about their success than women. Does the revealed higher risk propensity also imply female asset managers to shy away from competition as shown by experimental work of Niederle and Vesterlund (2007)? In order to shed light on this question and to detect whether differences among German and Italian professionals in the abstract gamble reveal further implications, we bring our asset managers in a simulated, but typical tournament situation they regularly face in their professional work near the end of the investment period.

5.6 Asset managers in the tournament

Driven by the industry's structure and competitiveness, asset managers could have an incentive to vary the risk level of their managed fund(s) near the end of the valuation period in order to either assure and "lock in" their achieved outperformance, or to guard a chance to "catch up" in case of previous underperformance relative to their benchmark. Indeed, this so-called "tournament behavior", going back to Brown et al. (1996), has been empirically detected, but also controversially discussed by several studies (cf. Lütje, 2006, for an overview of the literature, as well as Li and Tiwari, 2006, for an assessment of possible consequences).

From a gender perspective, findings by Niessen and Ruenzi (2006) underline obvious differences between male and female asset managers in performance distribution and possibly underlying performance ambitions. While female professionals are rather found on medial performance ranks and additionally show higher performance persistence than their male colleagues, male professionals are more often found among the very best, but also among the very worst, with individual manager's performance varying more strongly over time as well. Accordingly, in our survey tournament scenario we would expect female Italian asset managers to act both more risk averse in general, and also to be less inclined than their male counterparts to give all for a star performance rank in case of previous outperformance. This presumption, however, stays in contrast to behavior advised when considering results by Sirri and Turfano (1998). In their study of 20 years of U.S. equity fund data, the authors reveal star performing funds to receive disproportionately high new cash inflows, while bad performance is not similarly punished by outflows. Above described findings by Cesari and Panetta (2002) support similar recommendations to match the Italian market as well.

For a more detailed analysis in the following, we split the tournament situation in two separate scenarios, one reflecting previous outperformance and the other one assuming the case of underperformance so far. Table 5.6 displays the asset managers' response distribution.

In case of outperformance, the majority of both male and female Italian professionals decrease the risk level, i.e. they "lock in". When looking at the response numbers in more detail, however, gender differences as expected are once more uncovered. While among female asset managers, 82% indicate to lock in and another 18% keep their strategy, in comparison only 57% of their male counterparts are willing to decrease risk. Almost 40% keep the previous strategy, and 5% of male asset managers even increase the risk level in order to become top performers.[46] Our gender specific findings from Italian mutual fund managers are not only statistically significant but also completely in line with findings derived for U.S. equity funds by Niessen and Ruenzi (2006) as presented above.

Table 5.6 Tournament behavior

Risk taking behavior in simulated tournament scenarios		Increase risk level	Keep strategy	Decrease risk level	H_0: no specific difference[a]
[1] In case of <u>outperformance</u> near the end of the investment period…	Italy ♂	4.8%	38.6%	56.6%	-2.205**
	Italy ♀	0.0%	18.2%	81.8%	(0.027)
	Italy total	3.8%	34.9%	61.3%	-4.391***
	Germany total	0.8%	65.5%	33.7%	(0.000)
[2] In case of <u>underperformance</u> near the end of the investment period…	Italy ♂	18.1%	59.0%	22.9%	-1.750*
	Italy ♀	36.4%	50.0%	13.6%	(0.080)
	Italy total	21.7%	56.6%	21.7%	-1.765*
	Germany total	9.7%	69.0%	21.8%	(0.078)

a The table gives the z-value of the Mann-Whitney U test regarding gender specific differences in Italy as well as between responses from Italian and German asset managers. The p-value is given in parentheses. Asterisks refer to level of significance: * 10%, ** 5%, *** 1%.

The underperformance scenario discloses further interesting findings. 59% of Italian males and exactly half of the surveyed females keep their strategy in case of negative performance deviation from the benchmark near the end of the period. Being convinced of previous portfolio decisions and thus keeping a chosen strategy notwithstanding hitherto performance developments can quickly be linked to a certain degree of (over)confidence and risk taking. In line with that, at first sight, a slightly higher disclosed percentage among males in this respect matches with male overconfidence and higher female risk propensity. However, when looking as well at those asset managers who change their strategy, we find significantly less females than males to decrease the risk level. Far from it, 36% of the surveyed females (compared to only 18% of the male Italian professionals) even start to gamble by increasing their portfolio risk.

46 Chevalier and Ellison (1997) differentiate between funds that are just slightly ahead of their benchmark and those that are 'well ahead'. While they find the former to decrease risk to assure performance, the latter tend to gamble, attempting to become top performers. We did not distinguish the degree of outperformance any further in our questionnaires, but left the commonly understood term open for individual assessment.

While this finding might seem surprising from the purely stereotyped gender perspective on risk behavior, it could be brought in line with findings from U.S. asset managers by Niessen and Ruenzi (2006) again. By increasing the risk level and using the chance to catch up, females might be successful in saving at least medial performance in the last moment.[47] Besides, Lütje (2006) provides matching evidence with his analysis of German financial market professionals' herd behavior. Although herding asset managers are found to be generally more risk averse, the latter also take more risk near the end of the valuation period after poor previous performance. Their tournament behavior can yet be explained when taking into account the also emphasized stronger orientation on their benchmark and possibly bigger fear of falling out of the herd.

When compared to aggregated data from Germany, Italian asset managers are considerably more cautious in their tournament behavior following previous outperformance on the one hand: significantly more German professionals keep their strategy in first priority instead of locking in as the Italians do in the majority. On the other hand, in case of underperformance, Italian professionals seem more afraid of the risk of deviating from the benchmark than their German counterparts: they are more willing to seize a chance of catching up by increasing the risk level than to keep a formerly chosen strategy. While Anolli (2005) reveals only mild competition from the perspective of Italian mutual fund investors' cost perception and industry transparency, a higher diversification in distribution channels in Italy than in Germany (cf. Walter, 1999) as well as bigger competition induced by foreign competitors[48] might explain detected findings. More detailed research in this respect is clearly needed.

5.7 Conclusions

Based on survey data of Italian asset managers, this study offers new insights into the Italian mutual fund industry. It does not only confirm stereotyped gender differences in terms of overconfidence and risk behavior but also reveals divergence from German counterparts.

---

47 Indeed, Carhart et al. (1999) disclosed a considerable number of analyzed U.S. equity mutual funds to earn large positive returns on the last day of the year; an investment behavior that is supposed to be motivated by both agency issues and the above described flow-performance relation.

48 For Italy, Savona (2006) accounts the foreign firm market share to one third of total assets under management by the end of 2005. In contrast, the German Investment Management Association "BVI" just recently changed their statistics and now also considers funds offered by foreign firms of explicitly non-German provenance. Although considerably growing, by September 2006, in Germany the latter have only reached a market share in terms of assets under management of 6% (cf. www.bvi.de).

While disclosing Italian asset managers' (obviously biased) overly positive self-assessment, evidence for a strong "better-than-average" effect among male professionals is detected in particular. Findings for Italian asset managers' overconfidence are slightly mediated when additionally considering the overconfidence measure of control illusion: Excessive overconfidence and gender differences are not confirmed for the level of information Italian asset managers possess. Their on average somewhat more modest self-assessment in this respect in comparison to their German colleagues is approvable from the Italian investor's perspective when taking into account the fiduciary mandate investment managers accomplish, and former theoretical and empirical studies that relate overestimation of the own information level to excessive trading activity and detrimental performance impact.

When considering asset managers' risk taking behavior, in comparison to their German colleagues, Italian asset managers as a group are found to be more sensitive to risk and losses in both abstract gambles and the simulated tournament scenarios near the end of the investment period. Possible interdependencies of these findings with the industry's transparency, distribution channels and competitive environment are open to future research.

Besides, clear gender differences according to the stereotype of women to be more risk averse than men are revealed in the Italian fund management industry. Despite the somewhat surprising observation that surveyed Italian female professionals manage equity and not bonds or money market funds in the majority, female managers indeed do not only assess themselves as more risk averse than their male colleagues, they also prefer a more passive trading style than their male counterparts, taking into account the level of active portfolio management they are allowed to. Furthermore, in a competitive tournament scenario that asset managers typically face in their business, female Italian asset managers do not try to become the ultimate top performer in case they outperformed their peer group so far. Moreover, in case of underperformance, the risk of deviating from the benchmark makes female professionals more willing than their male counterparts to seize a chance of catching up.

These findings taken together, Italian female professionals seem to be less prone to achieve extreme performances and instead put more emphasis on performance stability. Whether their behavior is driven by the fear of negative career consequences in case of bad performance ranks or rather by missing eagerness to engage in competitive behavior remains an open question. Yet individual investors who entrust parts of their wealth to asset managers' funds might prefer this behavior in comparison to more aggressive and less stable investment styles. On the other hand, by acting not only more risk averse than their male colleagues but also than allowed by the given investment frame of their managed funds, female asset managers might forgo a chance of achieving higher return levels.

When finally looking from the perspective of the individual private investor, as a consequence, although at first sight being often attracted by extreme performance ranks, the former should sharpen her perception of the own financial priorities, of what she expects from her chosen funds and individual fiduciaries in Italy, and how the latter view and accomplish their professional task. This research intends to contribute to a better understanding in this respect.

Cross-Country Evidence

6 Asset Managers' Views and Behavior: Does Culture Matter?[49]

6.1 Motivation

International financial markets have been the outriders of globalization during the last decades. Professional asset managers who manage huge volumes – typically billions of Dollars – for banks, insurance companies or mutual funds invest their entrusted assets globally as a matter of course. Moreover, their decisions are based on theories about capital markets and optimal portfolio allocation which are globally uniform. Thus, we would expect asset managers' behavior to be influenced by incentives resulting from their age, experience and education or from idiosyncratic institutional details, but not really by cultural aspects.

With the help of an international questionnaire survey in the market we analyze asset managers' views and behavior by considering respondents' attributes such as gender, experience, position or their firm's size. At the heart of this research is the question, whether cultural differences matter and thus, as predicted by cultural theory, do have any systematic influence on the professional actors of the international asset management industry.

We do indeed find asset management to be a global business which shows some common global aspects like e.g. strong reliance on fundamental data and related strategies. However, we also find country-specific differences that can hardly be explained by capital market theory but that are consistent with a cultural influence on views and behavior instead.

Defining "culture" has been of scientific interest for centuries (for a critical review, see Kroeber and Kluckhohn, 1952). We rely on the comprehensive, empirically based understanding by Hofstede (1980). He defines culture as collective programming of the mind which is primarily manifested in values and norms, but also more superficially visible in rituals and symbols. This so-called mental programming – also referred to as "software of the mind" – is stable over

---

49 I would like to thank my co-authors Lukas Menhoff and Megumi Suto. We are grateful for enriching comments by Monika Hanswillemenke, Rafael Rebitzky and Maik Schmeling as well as participants at the 2006 Annual Meeting of the European Financial Management Association (EFMA) in Madrid / Spain. In particular Dong Hong offered a very useful discussion of the paper. Furthermore, our thanks go to the VolkswagenStiftung for financial support, to the Investment Associations "BVI" and "AIMC" for referential assistance as well as to Daiwa Research Institute and Michael Melvin for indispensable organizational support.

time and implies the same person showing consistently similar behavior in similar situations. When talking about culture, Hofstede refers to national culture.

There have been several research streams in cultural theory in the past decades and cross-cultural research as a multidisciplinary approach ranges from cognitive and social psychology, sociology, anthropology and history, up to management science and economics. This broad and vivid field of research encompasses a variety of approaches and frameworks for cross-cultural analyses.[50]

In order to examine and compare the viewpoints and behavior of asset managers from four countries, we refer to Hofstede's (1980, 2001) cultural dimension framework and his country scores given as index numbers for each single country.[51] We account for all four of his original dimensions, namely "Individualism" (IDV), "Power Distance" (PDI), "Masculinity" (MAS), and "Uncertainty Avoidance" (UAI). Further explanations of the single dimensions will be given in Chapter 6.4.

Regarding our selection of countries, we consider asset managers from the United States, Germany, Japan, and Thailand. At first glance, one might be tempted to expect a simple eastern-western differentiation. However, when taking a closer look at the exact dimension scores given by Hofstede for the four countries, the differences over all dimensions become clearly evident (see Figure 6.1). According to Hofstede, the United States and Germany are closer to each other than they are to Japan and Thailand. Nevertheless, the latter are far away from being similar. Especially regarding Hofstede's dimension of Masculinity, they deviate significantly. Even without going into detail yet, analyses can be expected to be surely more complex than they might seem at first sight.

This is a major reason why cross-cultural research papers have mostly focused on one cultural dimension only. Especially the Individualism dimension is much researched. It has been (re-)defined, analyzed in detail, and combined with selected topics[52] – both, theoretically and empirically (see Triadis, 1995 or Oy-

50 Approaches to unambiguously distinguish cultural groups from each other could be based on different cultural dimensions as suggested by Hofstede (1980, 2001), Hall (1985), Hall and Hall (1990) or House et al. (2004), on grid/group typologies and cultural prototyping (see e.g. Douglas and Wildavsky, 1982, Rayner and Cantor, 1987, Thompson et al., 1990, or Dake, 1991) or on factors such as professional or ideological affiliations which, as the former, are often used for risk-related cultural research (see e.g. Rohrmann and Renn, 2000, Sjöberg et al., 2000).

51 Hofstede's cultural dimensions are based on a global written survey conducted within the IBM group in the late 1960s and by beginning of the 1970s. Altogether 116,000 questionnaires from more than 70 countries were collected. Though not without pitfalls, this all-time comprehensive data set assures Hofstede's recognition and uniqueness until today (see Kagitcibasi, 1997).

52 Shafiro et al. (2003) or e.g. Nesdale and Naito (2005) combine their analysis of Individualism with gender aspects, Kemmelmeier et al. (2003) take authoritarianism, i.e. the individual degree of compliance with social norms and (political) authority, into additional ac-

sermann et al., 2002, for a broad overview). Among most recent studies Hwang et al. (2003) and Green et al. (2005) provide interesting cross-cultural psychology research input on Individualism. Chui et al. (2005) are the first to apply Hofstede's Individualism index to financial market return patterns.[53]

Figure 6.1 Country scores[a] in cultural dimensions according to Hofstede

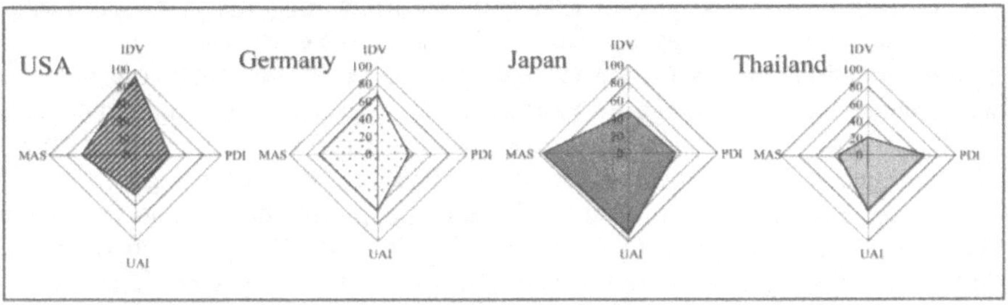

a For the United States, Germany, Japan and Thailand, scores in Hofstede's following four dimensions are shown here: Individualism (IDV), Power Distance (PDI), Masculinity (MAS) and Uncertainty Avoidance (UAI).

Hofstede's study and its dimensions are definitely not without critics (see Berry et al., 2002). Aspects such as the neglected influence of organizational culture keep on setting incentives to test the validity of his dimensions as done by Merritt (2000). Examining the behavior of a broad sample of commercial airline pilots in 19 countries, she was able both to statistically replicate all four dimensions and to find support that culture exerts a non-neglectable influence on professional pilots' behavior.

This encourages relying on Hofstede's dimensions as cultural framework. Analyzing asset manager's viewpoints and behavior with the help of a questionnaire survey designed from an economic point of view, we access Hofstede's work as an analytical grid and aim at deducing structured contributions to the field of cross-cultural research. Indeed, with our analysis we overcome several recent shortcomings in many cross-cultural studies (see e.g. Renn and Rohrmann, 2000, p. 227) and add the following benefits to the existing body of literature: First, we do not analyze another student sample, but we were able to convince asset managers to participate in our survey study.[54] Managing huge

count. Shuper et al. (2004) do not only consider Hofstede's dimension of Individualism but also include Weinstein's (1980) measure of unrealistic optimism as well as Hofstede's dimension of Uncertainty Avoidance.

53 Further recent examples of incorporating culture into economic and financial research are provided by e.g. Grinblatt and Keloharju (2001), Frederking (2002), or Stulz and Williamson (2003).

54 Effects of occupational factors on e.g. subjective risk perception and interpretation have been found by several researchers (see e.g. Rohrmann and Renn, 2000, p. 36).

volumes of assets in international financial markets, these professionals and their ways of perception and behavior exert an influence on prices as well as market developments. Second, we are able to distinguish gender aspects and to consider individual demographic and occupation-related factors like e.g. age, experience, position, working effort, and company size. Third, we highlight that we consider a broad and diverse sample and thus are able to overcome the restrictions implied by the so-called "generation effect" of younger people being on the one hand more prepared to take risks but on the other hand less brave regarding individual behavior due to lacking experience and reputation. Indeed, we consider the whole range of asset managers regarding age, experience and position. Fourth, our sample asset managers are asked about their market perception, their individual behavior and their attitudes, e.g. regarding risk – not from a general perspective related to hazards people might fear and that have been addressed in several studies (see e.g. Slovic et al., 2000, or Sjöberg et al., 2000) but all related to their every day business. Fifth, by considering asset managers from two Asian countries, namely Japan and Thailand, from Germany and the United States, we deviate from an often observable concentration on the United States and are able to critically check an easily done eastern versus western split.

The remainder is structured as follows. Chapter 6.2 describes design and methodology of the survey as well as the generated data set. Chapter 6.3 focuses on common aspects in global asset management. In Chapter 6.4 we analyze differences in asset managers' view points and behavior by relying on Hofstede's dimensions as analytical framework. Chapter 6.5 discusses implications of cultural influences. Chapter 6.6 concludes.

6.2 Survey design and data

Our analyses are based on data from an international written survey conducted with asset managers in four countries in 2003/2004. Altogether, we generated a sample of 1025 questionnaires, comprising 148 questionnaires from the United States, 263 from Germany, 488 from Japan and 126 questionnaires from Thailand.

We prepared our survey by previous oral interviews with asset managers from various investment companies in several cities in the different countries. Especially for an international survey, it is most important to speak in the right language: Both, questions and response categories had to be clearly understandable and in common wording, relevant for the respective market and if necessary country-specifically adapted. A test run of the questionnaire assured its comprehensibility.

As we successfully convinced participating asset managers to act as multipliers within their companies by forwarding blank questionnaires to their colleagues and team members, we do not report a response rate regarding the number of sent out questionnaires. Altogether, however, we obtained a participation rate of 47.5% of investment companies.[55] In detail, we contacted the top 250 US firms ranked by worldwide assets under management and received response from asset managers of 74 different companies (participation rate of US firms: 29.6%). In Germany, we sent questionnaires to 66 member firms of the German Investment Management Association "BVI" with major investment segments in equities and bonds, respectively, and asset managers of 51 different companies participated in the survey (participation rate of German firms: 77.3%). The high participation rate of German companies is also attributable to the letter of recommendation by the "BVI". In Japan, we cooperated with Daiwa Research Institute that provided us access to all major and core asset management companies. Their letter of recommendation encouraged participation and assured aca-

Table 6.1 Comparison of the data sample with the industry's structure[a]

	Structure of the asset management industry in relation to respective country sub sample (by assets under management)			
	USA	GER	JP	TH
H_0: no difference[b]	-1.213 (0.225)	-0.669 (0.503)	-1.183 (0.237)	-0.136 (0.892)
	Correlation[c] with company size (by assets under management)			
Number of answered questionnaires per company	0.256** (0.033)	0.679*** (0.000)	0.545*** (0.000)	0.534*** (0.000)

a The market data for the USA is taken from on the 'Pensions & Investments' money managers directory 2003 (www.pionline.com). For Germany, market data is taken from the annual report 2003 of the BVI. Japanese market data refers to The Trust Companies Association of Japan, Japan Securities Investment Advisors Association, and The Investment Trust Association Japan. Thailand data is taken from a market share datasheet provided by selected companies of the Thai asset management industry and private information provided by the AIMC.

b The table gives the z-value of the Mann-Whitney U-Test with the p-value in parentheses.

c The table gives the coefficient of the Pearson correlation with the p-value in parentheses. Asterisks refer to level of significance: * 10%, ** 5%, *** 1%.

55 Compared to similarly designed surveys as presented by Shiller and Pound (1989) with participation rates of 45% or Menkhoff and Schmidt (2005) with 59% regarding companies, our response rates represent a reasonable result. Moreover, our total number of participants with 1025 altogether is also convincing compared to other cross-cultural survey studies like Shuper et al. (2004) with 535 participants from two countries, Kemmelmeier et al. (2003) with 1018 participants from seven different countries or Kühnen et al. (2001) comprising 422 participants from four countries.

demic purpose only. In the end, 46 of 74 contacted asset management companies took part in our survey (participation rate of Japanese companies: 62.2%). In Thailand, we received responses from 29 of 31 contacted member companies of the "AIMC" – the Thai Association of Investment Management Companies (participation rate of Thai firms: 93.5%). Once again, the extraordinary high participation rate is attributable to recommendation and support of the "AIMC".

Table 6.2 Sample composition and respondents' characteristics[a]

		CEO / CIO	Head of team	Senior asset manager	Junior[b] asset manager	Total / Average
USA	Number of responses	17.9%	20.0%	46.9%	15.2%	N=148
	Age in years	47	42	42	31	42
	Experience in years	15	15	13	4	13
	Weekly working hours	55	53	51	52	52
		Spearman rank correlation[c] of higher position with				
	Higher managed vol.[d]	0.270*** (0.001)				
GER	Number of responses	5.5%	16.4%	46.1%	32.0%	N=263
	Age in years	43	38	37	31	36
	Experience in years	14	8	7	<4	7
	Weekly working hours	54	52	48	49	49
		Spearman rank correlation[c] of higher position with				
	Higher managed vol.[d]	0.469*** (0.000)				
JP	Number of responses	2.3%	17.9%	18.3%	61.5%	N=488
	Age in years	48	41	40	36	38
	Experience in years	15	14	12	9	11
	Weekly working hours	53	55	53	54	54
		Spearman rank correlation[c] of higher position with				
	Higher managed vol.[d]	0.291*** (0.000)				
TH	Number of responses	4.8%	11.9%	45.2%	38.1%	N=126
	Age in years	42	39	37	31	35
	Experience in years	11	10	8	4	7
	Weekly working hours	46	48	45	45	45
		Spearman rank correlation[c] of higher position with				
	Higher managed vol.[d]	0.331*** (0.000)				

a Mean values for age, experience and weekly working hours are given for each position and in each country.

b In Japan the lowest position was entitled more generally as "Asset Manager". This broader classification might imply a bias in favor of a high number of responses in this answering category.

c The table gives the coefficient of the Spearman rank correlation with the p-value in parentheses. Asterisks refer to level of significance: * 10%, ** 5%, *** 1%.

d Higher managed volumes under personal responsibility are also significantly correlated with higher bonus payments and the participation in stock option programs in the United States, Germany and Japan (results are not explicitly shown here). In Thailand, the incentive structure differs from those in the other countries. As especially stock option programs hardly exist in the Thai asset management industry, interviewed Thai asset managers gave the advice to drop the topic for the Thailand survey.

Regarding representativeness of our collected data sample, we compare the structure of the asset management industry in each country with the one of our respective country sample data set. As shown in Table 6.1 the null hypothesis of no difference cannot be rejected in any country's case. Moreover, bigger investment companies typically employ more asset managers and thus have a higher market impact than smaller investment companies. The same can be found in our country sub samples as asset managers working for bigger companies participated significantly more in our survey over all countries. Besides, survey studies may face criticism regarding data quality and target group width and appropriateness. Regarding this study, there are two cogent counterarguments: First, due to guaranteed anonymity of all participants, strategic answering is unlikely. Second, strategic answering would be useless from an individual point of view as the benefit of influencing results is marginal for a single person and as the costs of professionals with limited time are obviously high. As an indication of the usefulness of our data, the current position of respondents within their companies for each country sub sample is shown in Table 6.2.

Obviously, the firms' hierarchy is reflected in the sample. For universality of responses it is of particular significance that answers were not primarily given by less experienced and less influential junior asset managers but by a broad and balanced sample of asset managers. Moreover, additional exemplary data on age, experience and weekly working hours, given in Table 6.2 as well, prove the sample to be consistent in its structure.

6.3 Common aspects in global asset management

In our study we consider asset managers who act as professionals in global financial markets. New approaches from the area of behavioral finance already take behavioral biases of human actors into account and thus contribute to a more complete understanding of financial markets and its participants (Shiller, 2003). Nevertheless, the traditional capital market theory about risk and return of a well diversified financial portfolio – as reflected in the seminal studies by Markowitz (1952), Sharpe (1964) and Fama (1970) – is globally taught and unmistakably understood as the basis of portfolio management. Accordingly, we expect to detect some common worldwide characteristics that are inherent to the asset management industry, its structure, market players' behavior, and strategies.

First of all, as we have seen in Table 6.2, common factors among all four countries apply very generally to the combination of personal characteristics and career development: Overall, holding higher positions in an asset management company seems positively associated with higher age, longer experience, slightly higher working effort and higher managed asset volumes under personal responsibility.

Furthermore, we asked all surveyed asset managers about the relevance of fundamentals and the importance of different investment strategies (see Table 6.3). According to the globally shared theory one would expect large communality in investment approaches, too. Indeed, being questioned about the relevance of fundamentals, an overwhelming majority of asset managers from all four countries agrees on their extremely high relevance. This is substantiated by the fact that fundamental information is also clearly most relevant in comparison to further sources of information used in making investment decisions, such as chart analysis, discussions with colleagues or decisions and opinions of others. Due to this strong orientation towards fundamentals, one may be not surprised that the preferred investment strategy is also derived from theory. In efficient markets it is rational to rely on a long-term orientated buy and hold strategy, especially when facing long-term investment horizons, and thus to refrain from following short-sighted sentiment driven trends and frequent portfolio shifts that might cause high transaction costs.

Table 6.3 Relevance of fundamentals and the importance of different investment strategies

[1] Relevance of fundamental information: "Please assess the following sources of information used in making investment decision." Six response categories, ranging from 1="highest relevance" to 6="no relevance" (coded as 6).

[2] "Which strategies are your investment decision normally based upon? Please assign 100% altogether. If a category does not apply, please assign 0% to it."

		USA	GER	JP	TH
[1]	Share of high relevance[a]	96.0% (-1.074)	95.1% (-0.913)	98.2% (-1.264)	99.2% (-0.945)
[2]	Buy and hold[b]	37.39	26.17	33.17	47.65
	Momentum	17.50	26.61	23.79	21.43
	Contrarian	23.08	15.84	26.02	12.27
	Dividend orientated	6.53	8.61	3.77	16.59
	Other	15.51	22.91	13.60	2.06

a The table shows the share of high relevance of fundamental information, calculated as aggregated distribution to the answer categories 1-3. The mean value difference relative to the second most important information source, namely discussion with colleagues, is given in parentheses, respectively.

b The table shows the mean values for the different strategies, expressed in percentages.

Table 6.3 [2] shows that, indeed, the buy and hold strategy receives highest importance in all four countries (rivaled by the momentum strategy in Germany only). However, it seems interesting to note that despite the strong reliance on fundamental facts and despite the preference for the buy and hold strategy, other strategies receive a surprisingly high amount of attention. Striking is the prominent position of the momentum strategy, i.e. buying past winners and selling past losers, a finding also confirmed by different methods (see Grinblatt et al., 1995) and in different surveys (Menkhoff and Schmidt, 2005). This strategy is definitely not rooted in financial theory and thus provides a clear hint that factors not captured by traditional capital market theory may play a role, too.

In order to take possible cultural factors on asset managers' views, behavior and the industry's structure into account, we introduce a necessary cultural framework below.

6.4 Cross-cultural differences in global asset management

In the following, we rely on Hofstede's (1980) cultural dimensions framework that consists of four dimensions that are explained briefly: The first dimension, "Individualism" (IDV), as opposed to "Collectivism", focuses on the degree of reinforcement of individual or collective achievements and interpersonal relationships. A high Individualism ranking expresses individuality and individual rights being overriding in a society while personal relationships are loose. The second dimension, "Power Distance" (PDI), takes the extent of inequality among members of a country's society into account. A high Power Distance ranking implies that inequalities of power, prestige, and wealth have been allowed to grow within the society and keep being accepted by its members. The third dimension, "Masculinity" (MAS) with its opposite pole of femininity, describes the extent of role division between sexes and its emphasis on the traditional masculine work role model of male achievement, control, and power. A high Masculinity ranking indicates that a country experiences a high degree of gender differentiation. The fourth dimension, "Uncertainty Avoidance" (UAI), finally focuses on the extent to which members of a country's society feel threatened by and thus try to avoid uncertain or ambiguous situations. A high Uncertainty Avoidance ranking implies low tolerance for uncertainty, leading to the creation of a rule-oriented society. Hofstede (2001, p. 29) emphasizes his four dimensions to be statistically independent of each other and to occur in all possible combinations.

6.4.1 Individualism

According to Hofstede, the four considered countries can be clearly ranked regarding their position on a continuum between Individualism and Collectivism. The highest Individualism scoring is given to the United States at 91 as their top dimension, followed by Germany, then Japan and the lowest for Thailand at 20.

We analyze asset managers' behavior in this dimension by taking a closer look at their trend following or so-called "herding" behavior – a phenomenon that remains highly discussed in both academics and practice and yet cannot be totally explained by rational motives (Bikhchandani and Sharma, 2001). Herding behavior in its problematic denotation means that investment decisions are solely based on observed investments of other investors (and not on own fundamental information as assumed by theory). Different types of such behavior can be traced back to informational cascades (Bikhchandani et al., 1998) or reputation based herding (Scharfstein and Stein, 1990). It has been found empirically by Chevalier and Ellison (1999) and Hong et al. (2000) that younger managers who are more likely to be fired due to poor performance than their older colleagues deviate less from the herd than more experienced asset managers.

Figure 6.2 displays the distribution of responses to the statement "I generally follow the trend". Evidently, Japan and Thailand show a much higher approval to collectivistic behavior in forms of trend following than Germany or the United States. While a clear majority of asset managers from Thailand and Ja-

Figure 6.2 Trend following

Country ranking and values according to Hofstede:	Individualism — Collectivism
	USA – Germany – Japan – Thailand
	91 67 46 20

"I generally follow the trend":
Six answering categories from 1="completely agree" to 6="completely disagree".

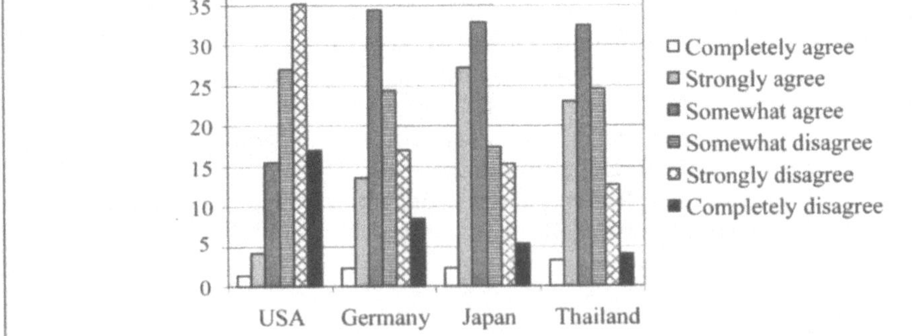

pan and still half of the German asset managers agree on the above mentioned statement, only 20% of the asset managers from the most individualistic country, the United States, affirm it.[56]

56 These differences in behavior over all countries are confirmed to be significant by the Kruskal-Wallis-Test (results are not explicitly shown here).

Following the herd implies the orientation on others. Accordingly, we also ask asset managers about the importance of different information sources for their investment decisions. As we have already seen in Table 6.3, fundamentals have been agreed to be of high relevance by at least 95% of the surveyed asset managers, consistently over all countries. Compared with the results concerning other sources of information shown in Table 6.4, fundamentals are thus judged to be the most important source of information. Furthermore discussions with colleagues take the second position in all countries: An evident majority of the surveyed asset managers judge collegial exchange to be of high importance.

Table 6.4 Importance of different information sources

Country ranking and values according to Hofstede:	Individualism			Collectivism
	USA –	Germany –	Japan –	Thailand
	91	67	46	20
"Please assess the following sources of information used in making investment decision" Six response categories, ranging from 1="highest relevance" to 6="no relevance".				
	USA	GER	JP	TH
Discussion with colleagues[a]	81.8% (2.689)	78.6% (2.701)	80.8% (2.619)	92.1% (2.413)
Other market players	41.2% (3.865)	31.1% (4.171)	60.7% (3.379)	49.6% (3.472)
Opinion leaders (industry)	25.0% (4.514)	19.1% (4.555)	41.2% (3.936)	57.1% (3.357)
Opinion leaders (economy)	33.2% (4.142)	43.3% (3.844)	61.3% (3.289)	89.7% (2.349)

a The table shows the share of high importance calculated as aggregated distribution to the answer categories 1-3. Mean values are given in parentheses. Performed Kruskal-Wallis-Tests show that the Null-hypotheses of no difference between our four considered countries cannot be rejected for discussions with colleagues. However, for the other three infomation sources, significant differences over all countries are confirmed at the 1% level. Test outcomes are not explicitly shown here.

Taking the other three information sources into account, a difference between Germany and the United States on the one hand, and Japan and Thailand on the other hand, becomes obvious. Our results show consistently over all considered information sources where others market players are integrated that asset managers from the more individual western countries seem to orientate themselves less on others than the more collectivistic eastern countries do.[57]

57 A comprehensive theoretical discussion of the influence of social and cultural norms on individual's decision making processes as well as the individual orientation on reference groups can be found in Hayakawa (2000). Returning to our findings, we also controlled our sample for possible biases e.g. due to an extraordinary high participation among higher positions as it can be found in the United States sample (see Table 6.2). CEOs and

Before jumping to conclusions, however, we want to look at possible causes of herd behavior. Might it be beneficial for an asset manager's career and thus be rational for the individual asset manager to "hide in the herd"? What role do personal characteristics as age or experience play? Does the industry incentive structure matter? In the following, we therefore apply a multivariate ordered probit approach in order to detect possible reasons behind asset managers' herding behavior. Results are shown in Table 6.5. The first regression [1] contains single country dummies and several variables, including those related to the herding literature as addressed above as well as a set of control variables. We will refer to the latter whenever we return to multivariate considerations. All factors included for control purpose are specific to the individual asset manager and, in parts, have also been treated in the herding literature before. In detail, these factors are the asset manager's experience, age, and position, all implying her degree of establishment and self assessment (see e.g. Avery and Chevalier, 1999, and Lamont, 2002), her educational background, the size of company the asset manager is working for (expressed in worldwide assets under management) as a proxy of her individual information and research facilities access, and finally the asset manager's working effort.

The second regression [2] of Table 6.5 is restricted to those variables that are at least significant at the 10% level, including a summarized Individualism indicator.

So what do we learn about the determinants of herding behavior? First of all, the fact that herding is regarded as beneficial for the asset manager's career proves to be an important and highly significant determinant of herding behavior. Second, the above mentioned orientation on other market players as well as on opinion leaders from both, the economy and the asset management industry itself, all show the expected positive coefficients, though partly lack significance. Third, the formerly addressed coherence of herding behavior with a significant lower reliance on fundamentals is also confirmed by our multivariate regression results. All these outcomes are in line with theory and expectation. However, what appears most interesting for us is the question whether culture inform of an individualism factor also matters. As described above, we firstly include country dummies to capture country specific factors [1], before secondly taking a pooled Individualism factor into account [2]. In accordance with cultural theory and the Hofstede framework, we find culture to matter significantly: The United States dummy, standing for the most individualistic country, shows a significant negative coefficient while the country dummies of the more collec-

CIOs would be expected to orientate less on others than their younger counterparts. However, except for a weak correlation among position and orientation on opinion leaders of the industry, correlations are not at all significant. This indicates that cultural differences might indeed play an important role here.

tivistic countries Thailand and Japan have positive coefficients. Moreover, we detect the same correlation when summarizing Individualism in one variable: The more individualistic the home country of the surveyed asset manager is, the less likely she is to show herding behavior. We find this cohesion to be significant at the 1% level.

Table 6.5 Herding in a multivariate framework

Ordered PROBIT regressions of herding behavior[a]

[1] including different country dummies and diverse variables

[2] with a summarized Individualism variable and reduced number of variables (restricted to the 10% level of significance)

	[1]		[2]	
Career benefit	0.222	(0.030)***	0.212	(0.029)***
Orientation on other market players	0.072	(0.034)**	0.091	(0.030)***
Orientation on opinion leaders (industry)	0.022	(0.034)		
Orientation on opinion leaders (economy)	0.048	(0.030)		
Relevance of fundamental information	-0.168	(0.049)***	-0.191	(0.045)***
Dummy USA	-0.601	(0.128)***		
Dummy TH	0.041	(0.133)		
Dummy JP	0.458	(0.132)***		
Higher Individualism			-0.292	(0.043)***
Longer experience	-0.090	(0.034)**	-0.077	(0.032)**
Higher age	0.118	(0.046)**	0.104	(0.045)**
Higher position	-0.070	(0.053)	-0.106	(0.050)*
Higher educational degree	-0.036	(0.052)***	-0.158	(0.022)***
Bigger company	-0.064	(0.024)***	-0.042	(0.022)*
Longer weekly working hours	-0.045	(0.034)		
Log likelihood	-1266.45		-1309.396	
LR statistics	222.341***		195.098***	
(Pseudo)-R^2	0.081		0.069	

a The table gives the coefficients of the ordered PROBIT regression with standard errors in parentheses. In order to enhance comprehensibility, coefficients are adapted to described control variable outcomes in the table. Asterisks refer to level of significance: * 10%, ** 5%, *** 1%.

Regarding our set of control variables, we find the asset manager's experience – consistently with expectation and theory – to matter significantly in both regressions. More experienced asset managers feel more skillful and surely less threatened by the industry's "hire and fire" career menace than their inexperienced colleagues. As a logical consequence the negative coefficient implies that experienced asset managers are less keen on hiding in the herd than their less experienced and – as we have seen in Table 6.2 – on average younger and lower positioned counterparts. This is in line with a negative coefficient for position. Interestingly, we find higher age to positively influence herding behavior. At first glance, this finding seems contradictive. However, if the degree of herding behavior could also be understood as a proxy for risk taking (see e.g. Graham, 1999, Hong et al., 2000), our finding might be explained by a negative correlation of risk taking with age as found in several studies (see e.g. Andersen, 2001 or Dohmen et al., 2005). Regarding education, we find those asset managers with a lower educational degree to be more prone to herding behavior. Moreover, asset managers who work for bigger companies are expected to be or at least to feel better informed than their colleagues working for smaller firms and they thus tend to herd less than their counterparts. The same can be found for weekly working hours. The negative, though not significant coefficient implies those asset managers who show more effort also to herd less.

Summarizing our results so far, we find several factors – as predicted by earlier work – to determine the observed herding phenomenon. Additionally, as proposed by our applied cultural framework, our results also show that the cultural dimension of Individualism exerts an independent, stable and significant influence on asset managers' (herding) behavior.

6.4.2 Power Distance

In the following we take a closer look at Hofstede's dimension of Power Distance, generally speaking the degree of inequalities of power, wealth, and prestige, and its tolerance within a country's society. According to Hofstede, Thailand shows the highest scoring at 64, followed by Japan, with some distance the United States, and finally Germany with a scoring of 35 in this dimension. Different from the dimension of Individualism, however, where the United States hold the global leading position, the top scorers of Power Distance in Hofstede's original results (2001, p. 127) can be found among other countries like Malaysia in the global lead (PDI score of 104), followed by the Philippines (94), Mexico (81) and Indonesia (78). Compared to these scores, our four considered countries are relatively close to each other around the global mean in this dimension. Accordingly, Power Distance is harder to capture than the Individualism dimension. Nevertheless, we find three hints for cultural differences among our four countries that we summarize in the following.

First of all, we use the illustrational example of the hierarchical distribution of occupied positions by our surveyed asset managers. Although hierarchy and unequal distributions of power among members of an organization are the essence of the latter (Hofstede, 2001, p. 82), cross-country comparisons of the observed hierarchical structure reveal some striking differences. Holding a higher position implies higher influence within the asset management company, higher decision power and – as higher positions are also related to higher bonus payments – higher income and wealth. Accordingly, in countries that score higher in Power Distance, we would expect to find power more unequally distributed, implying comparably fewer asset managers in top positions who face a wider basis of asset managers in non leading positions. Splitting the sample therefore into asset managers (junior and senior) and leading positions (head of asset management team or CIO/CEO), Thailand shows the lowest share of leading positions with 16.7%, followed by Japan, then Germany, and the United States with the highest share of leading positions at 37.9% (see Figure 6.3). Only the latter disrupt Hofstede's country classification in this dimension. The results in the United States are mainly based on the exceptionally high share of responses by CEOs/CIOs in the country's subsample. In parts, its longer asset management history, especially in comparison to Germany or Thailand, might also have helped the industry to mature in its structure and contributed to a more balanced distribution among all four positions.

Figure 6.3 Hierarchy structure, age and Power Distance

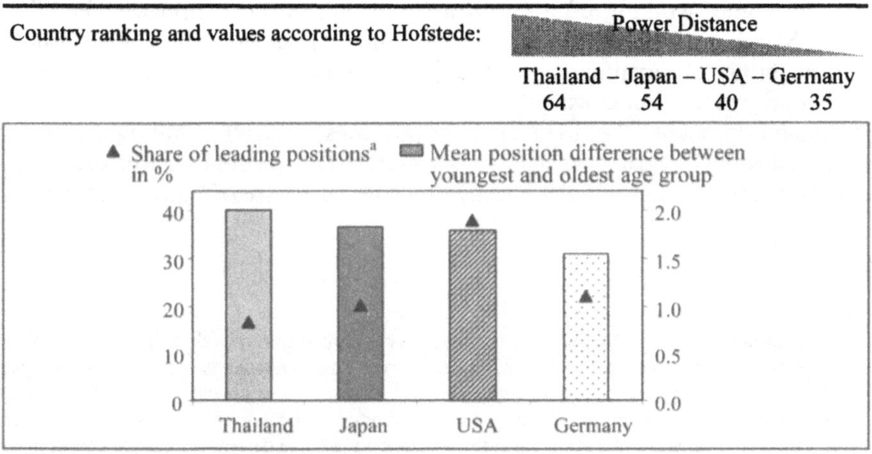

a The share of leading positions is calculated as aggregated distribution to the answer categories 3 (= "Head of Asset Management Team") and 4 (= "CEO/CIO").

Second, we are able to observe a complete fit to Hofstede's dimension scoring when taking the asset managers' age additionally into account (see also Figure 6.3). Considering the mean position difference between the youngest and the oldest age group in all countries separately, Thailand shows the highest position mean difference regarding age groups, Germany the lowest. This could indicate a less rigid and less age dependent hierarchy in the latter country and thus quicker career advancement opportunities for younger asset managers due to lower Power Distance occurrence and preservation.[58]

Third, we test our hypothesis by analyzing position and its determinants in a multivariate framework. Possible influencing factors to be tested for holding a higher position refer to our standard set of control variables and are intuitive, including longer experience, higher age, higher education or higher working effort.[59] We first estimate the model for the whole sample [1] before allowing for country specific variable considerations [2]. Estimation output is shown in Table 6.6.

As expected and in line with Table 6.2, our estimation reveals highly significant positive coefficients for experience, age and educational degree while working effort is positively related to position, but significance is missing over all countries. Going more into detail in Table 6.6 [2], however, we can detect striking differences among the four countries, particularly regarding the relative importance of age versus experience: While for Thailand and Japan age is found to be the single most important determinant for reaching a higher position, in the United States and Germany a higher position is predominantly depending on the asset manager's experience. Additionally, in Germany a higher educational degree and higher working effort exert a significant positive influence. For the United States, working effort is almost as important as age. Therewith, results confirm former observations and underline an apparently different role of age and seniority in the four considered countries.

To sum up, taking the distribution of positions, controlling for age, experience, educational degree and weekly working hours, we find significant differences that seem to confirm a culturally predicted influence of Power Distance.

---

58 A comparison of maximum and minimum age for each position reveals further results that are briefly summarized here: In the US sample, no junior manager is older than 40 years, indicating that either an asset manager works her way up by the end of her 30s or she leaves the business. Holding a junior position is limited to the age of 45 in the German and the Thai sample, while in Japan, asset managers from all age categories can be found in a junior position. In senior positions of the two countries that score higher in power distance, namely Thailand and Japan, sample asset managers are at least 31. For Germany and the United States no age restrictions are found. As to the head of asset management team position, Germany is also an exception with a minimum age below 31. This is interesting when taking into account that Germany still has the longest education times among OECD countries, implying relatively later career entries (see NCES, 2005; OECD, 2005). Finally for the CIO/CEO position, the minimum age found is 36 in Thailand, Japan and Germany, and only 31 in the United States. Altogether, this also points to a more age dependent hierarchy for the Thailand and Japan than for the United States and Germany.

59 Due to questionable explanation power, we exclude company size from our set of control variables here.

Table 6.6 Position in a multivariate framework

Ordered PROBIT regressions[a] of position

[1] over the whole sample

[2] with country specific consideration included for age and experience

	[1]		[2]	
Longer experience	0.183	(0.034)***		
Longer experience TH			0.380	(0.107)***
Longer experience JP			0.188	(0.053)***
Longer experience USA			0.324	(0.086)***
Longer experience GER			0.308	(0.070)***
Higher age	0.413	(0.046)***		
Higher age TH			0.765	(0.138)***
Higher age JP			0.546	(0.073)***
Higher age USA			0.246	(0.095)***
Higher age GER			0.262	(0.094)***
Higher educational degree	0.321	(0.041)***		
Higher educational degree TH			-0.161	(0.145)
Higher educational degree JP			0.012	(0.073)
Higher educational degree USA			0.053	(0.106)
Higher educational degree GER			0.229	(0.087)***
Longer weekly working hours	0.018	(0.032)		
Longer weekly working hours TH			0.054	(0.118)
Longer weekly working hours JP			-0.024	(0.043)
Longer weekly working hours USA			0.233	(0.065)***
Longer weekly working hours GER			0.223	(0.066)***
Log likelihood	-926.944		-871.542	
LR statistics	393.643***		504.447***	
(Pseudo)-R^2	0.175		0.224	

a The table gives the coefficients of the ordered PROBIT regression with standard errors in parentheses. In order to enhance comprehensibility, coefficients are adapted to described control variable outcomes in the table. Asterisks refer to level of significance: * 10%, ** 5%, *** 1%.

6.4.3 Masculinity – Femininity

We now turn to the third of Hofstede's cultural dimensions, namely Masculinity, i.e. the degree of gender differentiation and traditional role models. While Masculinity is Japan's top dimension with a scoring of 95 and Japan is according to Hofstede among the global top scorers, respectively, Germany and the United States are found in between, and Thailand's score in this dimension is considerably low at 34.

We find evidence in favor of cultural influences on the asset management industry and its participants also in this dimension. To start the analysis, we refer to the gender distribution related to the asset manager's position in the four surveyed countries. Figure 6.4 shows essential differences between the considered countries that can be simply summarized as follows: The more masculine a country is, the less women can be found in highly-paid asset management positions. While Japan has only a minority (around 3%) of female junior or senior asset managers, Germany, also lacks women in the leading positions, but we find at least around 18% of female junior asset managers. In the United States sample we find women in all four positions (up to 18% female heads of an asset management team) but the sample is still far away from being equally distributed. This can only be said about Thailand, the clearly most feminine country

Figure 6.4 Gender distribution

Country ranking and values according to Hofstede: Masculinity — Femininity

Japan – Germany – USA – Thailand
95 66 62 34

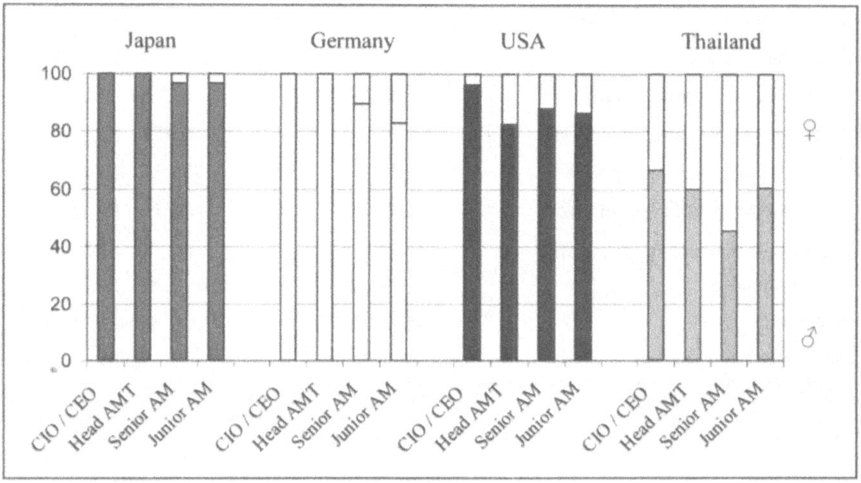

among the four, where women hold about 40% of all asset management positions, almost independent of the hierarchical level.[60]

Besides position, managed asset volumes and responsibilities are a second aspect where gender differentiation might be observable. With the help of an ordered probit model, we therefore examine whether gender matters in this respect and include a gender variable besides our familiar set of control variables (namely experience, age, position, educational degree, company size and working effort). Gender differentiation thus brought into a multivariate framework is shown in Table 6.7.

The first regression [1] is estimated over all countries, the second estimation [2] allows for country specific gender considerations. While a longer experience shows a positive and highly significant coefficient, implying more experienced asset managers to be more likely to be responsible for higher asset volumes, the age coefficient shows a negative sign but lacks significance in both regressions. As expected and in line with Table 6.2, a higher position also leads to significantly higher asset volumes under personal responsibility. Regarding a higher educational degree and longer weekly working hours, we find negative and partly highly significant coefficients: While the first aspect points towards a "learning on the job" practice, higher working efforts obviously do not automatically imply higher responsibilities. However, working for a bigger company is, as expected, linked to significantly higher asset volumes under personal responsibility. Coming to the most interesting point: Being male can be considered as a systematic career advantage. A positive and highly significant coefficient over all countries is also confirmed when allowing for country specific gender considerations. For all countries, we find male asset managers to manage significantly higher volumes than their female counterparts. Moreover, in line with cultural predictions, we reveal that the more masculine a country is, the higher is the coefficient of the gender variable.

To summarize, both, descriptive distributional comparisons of position and multivariate regressions, show that gender differences are more important career determinants for societies like Japan and Germany that also score high in

60 Mann-Whitney-test results (not explicitly shown here) for gender differences regarding position reveal significant differences at the 1% level for Germany. For Japan, weak significance only may be due to the very small number of females in the Japanese sample. Among the relatively more female cultures, neither the United States nor Thailand show significant gender differences. Though these results suit well to cross-cultural predictions, we also consider additional aspects as education or experience. No significant gender differences can be found for education. In terms of experience, we only find significant differences for the two poles, Japan and Thailand. In detail, we find junior positions to be the driving force in Japan, observing male junior asset manager to be significantly more experienced then their female counterparts. For Thailand, female asset managers are slightly more experienced over all positions but differences are never significant.

Hofstede's dimension of Masculinity than for those that are judged to be relatively more feminine societies like the United States or Thailand.

Table 6.7 Gender differences in a multivariate framework

Ordered PROBIT regressions[a] of asset volume under personal responsibility
[1] over the whole sample
[2] with country specific gender consideration

	[1]		[2][b]	
Longer experience	0.157	(0.034)***	0.128	(0.035)***
Higher age	-0.052	(0.046)	-0.055	(0.047)
Higher position	0.228	(0.052)***	0.291	(0.053)***
Higher educational degree	-0.201	(0.043)***	-0.090	(0.048)*
Longer weekly working hours	-0.067	(0.032)**	0.041	(0.033)
Bigger company	0.213	(0.029)***	0.230	(0.025)***
Male asset manager	0.116	(0.059)**		
Male asset manager GER			0.495	(0.079)***
Male asset manager USA			0.323	(0.082)***
Male asset manager TH			0.177	(0.058)***
Log likelihood	-1314.345		-1294.405	
LR statistics	239.562***		279.442***	
(Pseudo)-R^2	0.084		0.097	

a The table gives the coefficients of the ordered PROBIT regression with standard errors in parentheses. In order to enhance comprehensibility, coefficients are adapted to described control variable outcomes in the table. Asterisks refer to level of significance: * 10%, ** 5%, *** 1%.

b We refrained from including a gender specific consideration for Japan due to the very limited number of female respondents.

6.4.4 Uncertainty Avoidance

The last considered dimension, Uncertainty Avoidance, deals with the way of societal coping with uncertainty. Depending on the respective tolerance level, societies have brought up different coping measures of e.g. technology, institutional structure, law and (decision) rules to overcome uncertainty. Hofstede explicitly refrains from equating Uncertainty Avoidance with risk avoidance. For him, risk is focused on a specific event, its probability and its outcome, whereas uncertainty is a more diffuse sentiment. According to Hofstede, Japan shows by far the highest Uncertainty Avoidance scoring results at 92, being followed by Germany and Thailand and finally the United States with the relatively lowest scoring of 46.

Before analyzing the degree of uncertainty avoidance, a brief background information on asset managers' environment appears necessary. In general, asset managers do not invest on their own accounts but manage entrusted assets on behalf of their customers. Depending on the company's risk-return policies, individual performance as well as factors as experience or position, asset managers might be more or less allowed to freely compose their portfolios. To put it in the extremes: They might either be forced to stick to the benchmark, i.e. a market index, or be allowed to clearly deviate from it, showing a so-called high tracking error, i.e. accepting higher risks and higher outcome uncertainty by deviating from the benchmark. However, given a wide leeway does not necessarily imply to play on it. Especially a more uncertainty avoidant asset manager might wish to refrain from deviating too much from the market index even if she would be allowed to do so in order to be on the safer side. Accordingly, we consider the mean difference between the tracking error that asset managers would be allowed to and the one they actually take a chance on. As we can see from Figure 6.5, the difference between the allowed level and the actual tracking error is maximal for Japan, indicating that Japanese asset managers stick relatively

Figure 6.5 Tracking Error difference and research hours as proxies for Uncertainty Avoidance[a]

Country ranking and values according to Hofstede: Uncertainty Avoidance

Japan – Germany – Thailand – USA

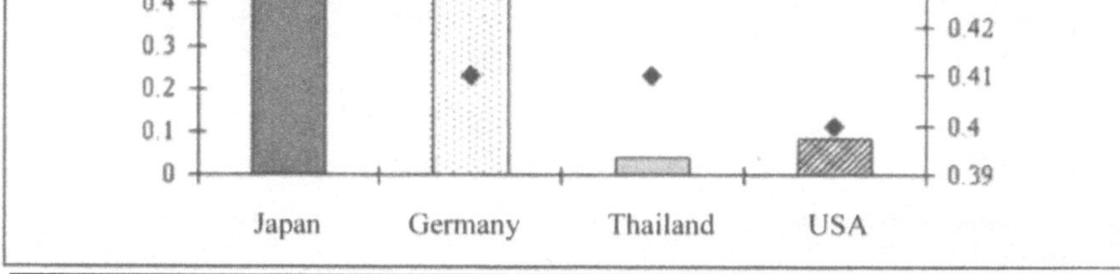

a Mean values are given for each country. The tracking error scale in the questionnaire ranges from "1" (high tracking error) to "5" (low tracking error = indexing). Thus, the lower the value the more the asset managers tend to accept outcome uncertainty by deviating from the benchmark in forms of a market index. Here, only the difference between the actual and the possible tracking error is shown. Weekly research time comprises time for "data procurement and information research". It is shown here in relation to weekly working hours.

closest to their benchmarks. Germany shows the second biggest difference, followed by the USA, and Thailand. Except for the last two, this matches the order of Hofstede regarding the avoidance of uncertainty and ambiguity.

In the asset management industry where decisions are made under uncertainty and risk, comprehensive information research is essential. Nevertheless, different degrees of Uncertainty Avoidance might imply different effort intensities to solve uncertainty in order to fulfill the individual desire to maintain clarity. While information quality itself is unobservable, the survey allows us to compare asset managers' efforts by the time they spend on information research relative to their overall working hours. Results are also shown in Figure 6.5. Asset managers from Japan, the most uncertainty avoidant country, spend with 45% the most time of their already in absolute numbers higher weekly working hours (see Table 6.2) on explicit information research. They are followed by Germany and Thailand, whereas asset managers from the relatively least uncertainty avoidant country, the United States, spend the smallest portion on average of their working hours on information research.

Table 6.8 Tracking error difference in a multivariate framework

Ordered PROBIT regressions[a] of tracking error difference

[1] including different country dummies and diverse variables

[2] with a summarized Uncertainty Avoidance variable included

	[1]		[2]	
Longer experience	0.022	(0.036)	0.020	(0.035)
Higher age	-0.026	(0.049)	-0.018	(0.048)
Higher position	0.007	(0.056)	0.009	(0.054)
Higher educational degree	-0.023	(0.060)	-0.027	(0.050)
Longer weekly working hours	0.066	(0.035)*	0.077	(0.033)**
Bigger company	0.044	(0.025)*	0.054	(0.025)**
Dummy JP	0.247	(0.134)*		
Dummy TH	-0.541	(0.136)***		
Dummy USA	-0.598	(0.138)***		
Higher Uncertainty Avoidance			0.303	(0.046)***
Log likelihood	-937.196		-938.986	
LR statistics	107.496***		103.915***	
(Pseudo)-R^2	0.054		0.052	

a The table gives the coefficients of the ordered PROBIT regression with standard errors in parentheses. In order to enhance comprehensibility, coefficients are adapted to described control variable outcomes in the table. Asterisks refer to level of significance: * 10%, ** 5%, *** 1%.

These results fit well into the culture framework. Nevertheless, univariate considerations always lack control for interferences as e.g. the considered tracking error difference might be influenced by a variety of factors. Especially shifts over the asset managers' career advancement and age should be accounted for. We therefore, once again, apply our set of control variables. Additionally, we also test the single countries' impact [1] as well as the cultural factor's impact [2]. As Table 6.8 shows, only longer weekly working hours and working for a bigger company exert a significant positive influence on the asset manager's tracking error difference. Besides, we find all three considered country dummies to matter significantly (see Table 6.8 [1]). While Japan, the most uncertainty avoidant country, shows a significantly higher tracking error difference, the relatively to Germany less uncertainty avoidant countries, namely Thailand and the United States, reveal negative coefficients at the 1% level of significance. Captured in one variable [2], high significance remains, implying Uncertainty Avoidance to positively influence the tracking error difference.

To sum up, we find evidence that also the last of Hofstede's dimensions, Uncertainty Avoidance, matters. Asset managers from more uncertainty avoidant countries refrain from composing their portfolios as freely as they might be allowed to and try to countervail missing certainty by higher information research effort.

6.5 Discussion of cultural influences' possible implications

The preceding Chapter 6.4 has shown that asset managers' views and behavior as well as the industry's structure differ between countries in a way that is clearly related to expectations derived from Hofstede's cultural dimensions. In this chapter we discuss to which extent these cultural differences may be important for financial markets: Not only herding behavior, influenced by the degree of Individualism, could have a direct impact on market prices and efficiency, but also Power Distance, Masculinity, and Uncertainty Avoidance affect strategic investment decisions and behavior.

Starting with the Individualism dimension, there emerges the clear relation that more individualistic countries have asset managers who follow less the trend in the market, i.e. they show less herding. Analyzing different aspects of herding behavior reveals, first, some relation to rational opportunistic behavior, i.e. following the trend because this may support one's career. Second, herding is seen as an instrument to learn from others (importance of other market players etc.). Third, herding seems to be performed because asset managers do believe in psychological forces in the market (less importance of fundamentals). Fourth, another strong relation exists between herding and having an information disadvantage (less education or working for a smaller company) and fifth, personal experience and career steps matter significantly. In addition to these many influences Individualism provides a sixth statistically significant determinant in understanding herding. There is thus useful evidence that cultural differences cause different behavior. Yet the way how behavior is changed may be complex due to further factors like e.g. the type of financial system and its degree of development, the information surrounding or the regulatory framework.

One may speculate that herding in Germany is more opportunistically career driven and possibly in Thailand comparatively more caused by the motivation to learn from opinion leaders. As these motivations are weaker in Japan, it may be that the cultural norm is strongest there (for theoretical considerations see Hayakawa, 2000). Additionally, in their empirical work Kim and Nofsinger (2005) assume Japanese institutional investors, due to the regulative and relational setting, to suffer less from the asymmetric information framework than asset managers in the United States. Kim and Nofsinger thus attribute herding in the Japanese market to superior information, so-called investigative herding (see also Froot et al., 1992, Hirshleifer et al., 1994). Accordingly, judging the impact of herding critically depends on the kind of herding that is supported by the cultural dimension. Herding being rooted in opportunistic and uninformed behavior will reduce price efficiency, it will induce the danger of contagion and thus the spread out of financial crises (see e.g. Calvo and Mendoza, 2000, Borensztein and Gelos, 2003, Shiller, 2003 or Chari and Kehoe, 2003). However, herding that is based on fundamental information gathering, can speed up the process in which information is reflected in prices.

The second cultural dimension, Power Distance, was identified in asset management mainly in the role that age plays in getting into the upper hierarchy. Countries with more Power Distance put more emphasis on seniority so that the bosses who decide about strategic investment directions are comparatively older. This may be important as we know that age influences investment behavior, especially risk taking, and might thus lead to a more conservative portfolio allocation. Moreover, there are systematic differences regarding the relative importance of age and experience in receiving leading positions: Societies scoring higher in Power Distance do not only prefer older managers for promotion, they also consider experience less. Experience is known to have some favorable impact on investment behavior in a way that it reduces herding (see Chevalier and Ellison, 1999), enhances learning about one's own competences (see Prendergast and Stole, 1996), and dilutes overconfidence to some degree (see e.g. Gervais and Odean, 2001, Locke and Mann, 2003, Menkhoff et al., 2006).

Masculinity, the third cultural dimension, is also clearly important for investment decisions. There is some research demonstrating that men invest differently from women, basically by a more aggressive stance which is identified by generating higher amounts of turnover. Male overconfidence is assumed to be the driving force there (see Barber and Odean, 2001).[61] Higher male presences in leading positions as well as comparably higher asset volumes under personal responsibility substantiate the influence of Masculinity.

Finally, also the fourth cultural dimension of Uncertainty Avoidance impacts investment behavior. The above analysis has shown that Uncertainty Avoidance is related to the degree of an underutilized tracking error, i.e. a safety margin. This leads to the problem that asset managers will not invest as actively as allowed. According to theory, a higher tracking error will lead – on average and in the longer run – to higher returns compared to the benchmark. Thus, Uncertainty Avoidance may be a reason for lower returns generated by affected asset managers. There is, however, also a positive side to this cultural dimension: In order to reduce uncertainty, it seems plausible that asset managers in these societies put more effort into information research. Whether this is always efficient may be another question but at least it can help to gain more information and thus to invest more successfully.

Again, we see – like for other dimensions – that cultural differences translate into different behavior and that these differences are relevant for investment behavior. Unfortunately, the relations are complex, first because countries have different orderings in the four cultural dimensions, and second because cultural influences do not always impact behavior to the same extent and in the same direction. Thus, one cannot draw the conclusion that asset managements' behavior will in a simple way differ between two culturally different countries but influences will be diverse. Nevertheless, they seem to be important enough to be considered.

6.6 Concluding remarks and future prospects

This research enters new ground by presenting comparative survey evidence on asset managers' views and behavior in four countries, i.e. the United States, Germany, Japan and Thailand. According to the globalization of financial markets, evident for example by the same theories used to support portfolio allocation and by the international operation of asset management firms, the question emerges whether cultural differences between countries would play any role in this worldwide business.

---

61 Further empirical research is provided by Bengtsson et al. (2005) or Schubert et al. (1999). While the former confirm male overconfidence, the latter underline that gender differences found in financial decision making experiments might strongly depend on the decision frame: For abstract gambles they reveal gender differences indeed, for contextual and covenant investment and insurance decisions, however, they do not. In contrast, Eckel and Grossman (2005) find women to be significantly more risk averse than man in both, gambles as well as investment treatments. Further research in this respect is needed.

Relying on Hofstede's four cultural dimensions, we find cultural differences to be most helpful in understanding country differences which cannot be explained by pure economic reasoning alone. In short, even when controlled for various determinants, more Individualism explains less herding behavior, more Power Distance leads to relatively older managers in the upper hierarchy, Masculinity generates men in top positions and implies a strong gender influence on managed asset volumes under personal responsibility, and higher Uncertainty Avoidance is related to higher safety margins against the tracking error allowed and more research effort. These consequences, i.e. the culturally different importance of herding, age, experience, gender, active asset management style and information research effort, clearly impact investment behavior. Unfortunately, the impact is complex. Thus, it may be interesting not only to test robustness of our findings but also to further examine consequences for each country.

7 Will Women Be Women? Asset Managers' Struggle between Nature and Incentives[62]

7.1 Motivation

We tend to have established stereotypes in mind when thinking about the behavior of women and men. A prominent case is behavior towards risk in which women are often seen to be more risk averse than their male counterparts. Indeed, there are reams of carefully designed experiments which exactly detect risk-related gender dissimilarities and thus approve it being fair to say that women are different by nature in this respect (cf. Byrnes et al., 1999, Eckel and Grossman, 2007). While virtually all of these studies reflect students' behavior, it is reassuring that survey evidence from households confirms experimental findings (cf. e.g. Barsky et al., 1997, Donkers et al., 2001). However, groups of students and households may be representative for certain parts of the population but not necessarily for those professionals who are experts in managing risks. As we know that familiarity with risk changes behavior towards the latter (cf. e.g. Slovic et al., 2000a, Dwyer et al., 2002), the question emerges whether the change of focus from laymen to experts also impacts the gender difference. We therefore conduct a survey among professional fund managers, which is possibly the first among financial experts to analyze differences between women and men in their behavior towards risk.

Fund managers are not only worth a detailed analysis because they are experts in managing risks but also because they work in an environment with high financial incentives. There is some evidence that decisions in financial affairs may differ from decisions in abstract gambles, possibly because financial decisions involve clear incentives. This framing effect has been found in experiments and reduces the gender difference in risk aversion (cf. Schubert et al., 1999). Clearly, fund managers are familiar with risk and subject to potentially high financial rewards. It is thus difficult to imagine that a more risk averse behavior of women compared to men will survive in professional fund management. Instead, we rather expect the gender-specific nature regarding risk behavior to lose the struggle against uniform incentives for both sexes. In a sense, we

62 I would like to thank my co-author Lukas Menkhoff. We very much appreciate the contributions made by the fund managers who were available for interviews and took time to respond to the survey. We thank the Investment Management Associations in Germany, Italy, and Thailand for the provision of indispensable recommendation letters. Furthermore, we are grateful to Michael Melvin, Luca Rebeggiani and in particular Torben Lütje in helping us to conduct the survey. Last, but not least, financial support by the VolkswagenStiftung is gratefully acknowledged.

thus test the hypothesis that strong financial incentives overcome natural differences in behavior.

The hypothesis on "incentive dominance" is not restricted to risk behavior alone but we also test it with respect to two further phenomena: (over)confidence and tournament behavior. Both are important for financial decision making and women have been found to differ from men here as well: People are tentatively overconfident but women less than men (cf. e.g. Lenney, 1977, Lundeberg et al., 1992). Barber and Odean (2001) regard stronger overconfidence of men as absolutely undisputed while using gender as a proxy for overconfidence in order to explain excessive, detrimental trading behavior. Successive studies have questioned, however, whether it is really male overconfidence that drives the outcome. Deaves et al. (2004) and Biais et al. (2005) confirm that overconfidence drives trading (and men trade relatively more) but do not find male students to be more overconfident in their miscalibration measures. There is thus some doubt whether male overconfidence is robust in financial affairs; indeed, it motivates to extend evidence to professionals – here fund managers – whose performance would be affected by excessive trading. Finally, there is emerging evidence that women "shy away from competition" to quote Niederle and Vesterlund (2007). This pattern has been also found e.g. by Gneezy et al. (2003) or Dohmen and Falk (2006). As it seems to be typical for young children already (cf. Gneezy and Rustichini, 2004), less competitive behavior of women may be seen as part of their nature. This stands in contrast to tournaments in the fund management industry (cf. Brown et al., 1996) and thus raises the question whether female nature holds in an environment of tough incentives. Again, we are not aware of any evidence yet on gender-related differences in fund management tournaments.

There are, however, a few studies analyzing gender-related performance among U.S. fund managers. Their finding that women achieve about the same performance as their male colleagues is consistent with the hypothesized dominance of incentives over nature (cf. Atkinson et al., 2003, Niessen and Ruenzi, 2006).[63]

We design our research on gender differences in order to extend (most) former studies towards the realm of professional fund managers. Aiming to extract information undistorted by (unobservable) legal, customer or company restrictions, we directly ask fund managers via a questionnaire survey. Obviously, this kind of information is not superior to revealed preferences via transaction data

---

63 Unfortunately, Chevalier and Ellison (1999a) who carefully analyze a large sample of fund managers do not include a gender variable because they regard their seven percent share of females being too small. Atkinson et al. (2003) rely on a sample of 70 women managing bonds which is compared to a matching sample of men. Niessen and Ruenzi (2006) rely on a share of female professionals in their sample of around 10%, which equals approximately between 130 and 170 over the whole sample period.

but we regard it as useful complementary evidence. The survey approach has a further advantage by compiling a wide range of data, covering the above mentioned three areas of gender differences – each by several proxies – as well as a full set of relevant control variables. Finally, as we are interested in generally valid gender differences, we provide information on fund managers in four countries, i.e. the United States, Germany, Italy and Thailand. The resulting response from 649 fund managers, among them 125 women, yields three main findings.

First, testing the "incentive dominance hypothesis" surprisingly ends with a victory for nature. Taking the full sample, women will indeed be women even under the demanding incentives of fund management as they keep a more risk averse behavior and somewhat shy away from competition. Second, we reject the view that men are more overconfident than women for the case of fund managers. This finding is robust to an extension of three different measures of overconfidence, i.e. overoptimistic self-assessment, illusion of control and miscalibration. Third, gender-related differences seem to vary systematically with overall economic and financial market development of a country. So, the difference does not systematically exist for the U.S., increases somewhat for Germany, even more for Italy and is relatively the largest for Thailand. This is consistent with an impact of incentives from a cross-country perspective in the sense that incentives gain power with market development.[64] This allows some speculation whether the "natural" gender-related behavior will possibly disappear in the future.

The remainder of this study is organized as follows: Chapter 7.2 describes the data set. Chapter 7.3 addresses risk behavior, while Chapter 7.4 focuses on overconfidence and Chapter 7.5 on tournament behavior. Chapter 7.6 concludes.

7.2 Data

Utilized data consist of a unique set of responses from 649 fund managers in four countries particularly compiled for our research.

We conducted the written survey with professional fund managers in the United States, Germany, Italy, and Thailand between spring 2003 and winter 2004. With the help of the respective investment association[65] in three out of the

64 It is not important here in this respect whether female fund managers adapt their behaviour to the market standard or whether there is a self-selection of those becoming fund managers. Incentives dominate in both alternatives.

65 We received helpful support by the "Bundesverband Investment und Asset Management e.V.", in short: "BVI" for Germany, the "Associazione Italiana del Risparmio Gestito", in short: "Assogestioni" for Italy and the "Association of Investment Management Compa-

four countries, we generate 649 valid questionnaires, where gender splits into 125 women and 524 men. Prior oral interviews in all four countries with fund managers of different hierarchies and of both sexes, previous test runs for clarity, and guaranteed anonymity were factors to ensure useful responses.

In order to control for representativeness of the generated country data sets, we compare assets under management covered by the surveyed firms with the market structure in total. Test results are shown in Table 7.1. In all four countries, we find that responses by and large reflect the market with respect to the representation of firm size.

Table 7.1 Comparison of the data sample with the industry's structure[a]

	Structure of the asset management industry in relation to respective country sub sample (assets under management)			
	USA	GER	ITA	THA
H_0: no difference[b]	-1.213 (0.225)	-0.669 (0.503)	-0.403 (0.687)	-0.136 (0.892)
Firm participation rate	29.6%	77.3%	58.2%	93.5%
Number of questionnaires	148	263	112	126
Share of female participants	11.4%	10.0%	21.1%	46.4%

a The U.S. market data is taken from the 'Pensions & Investments' money managers directory 2003 (www.pionline.com). For Germany, we use market data from the annual report 2003 of the BVI. The Italian market data for 2004/2005 is taken from the Italian Investment Management Association's Website "Assogestioni". Thailand data for 2004 emanates from a market share datasheet provided by the Thai Association of Investment Management Companies "AIMC" as well as selected companies' information.

b The table gives the z-value of the respective Mann-Whitney U test with the p-value in parentheses.

Furthermore, Table 7.1 reveals firm participation rate, number of questionnaires and share of female participation for each country. Indeed, as fund managers sometimes passed questionnaires to colleagues, we cannot report response rates in terms of sent out questionnaires. We know, however, that we generated a participation rate of 64.7% altogether at the company level.[66] While participation among contacted firms is highest in Thailand with 93.5% (29 of 31 contacted companies participated), it is relatively lowest in the United States where at least 74 out of 250 contacted companies responded (29.6%). In absolute numbers, generated country samples cover between 112 questionnaires in Italy and 263 in Germany.

---

nies", in short "AIMC" for the Thai market. In the USA, Professor Michael Melvin, at that time at Arizona State University, supported this research.

66 Survey studies have been established as a complementary approach in financial market analysis. Comparable studies like e.g. Shiller and Pound (1989), Blinder (2000) or Menkhoff et al. (2006) report participation rates between 45% and 59%.

Regarding representation of gender, the global mutual fund industry can undoubtedly be seen as a male-dominated field. Nevertheless, the share of female respondents varies considerably among the surveyed four countries. While the U.S. and German samples comprise slightly over ten percent of female participants, in Italy one fifth of the surveyed managers are women, and in Thailand the sample is almost equally balanced. Indeed, taking the U.S. mutual fund industry on the one hand, female shares have constantly been around 10% within the last twelve years (cf. Chevalier and Ellison, 1999a, Niessen and Ruenzi, 2006). In Thailand on the other hand, interviewed fund managers highlighted that female work force, different from some other East Asian countries, has been comparably strong in banking and financial service sectors during decades and that several women have reached considerable influence in the financial industry. This is in line with the substantial female share in our sample.

In order to learn more about surveyed asset managers' characteristics, Table 7.2 provides descriptive statistics concerning age, experience, marital status, education, position, managed assets and working hours, split by gender and explicitly testing for significant differences.

We do not only uncover differences in mean asset managers' age and experience that match the country's industry development in a cross-country comparison, but also consistently find women to be younger and less experienced than their male counterparts in the U.S., Germany and Italy. Mann-Whitney U tests confirm statistically significant differences in the latter two countries. In Thailand, however, we find our data to match with what fund managers told us during previous interviews: women are on average as old as their male colleagues and even significantly more experienced. While the majority of female fund managers is single, differing significantly from their male counterparts in Germany and Italy, only in the U.S. (the comparatively older) fund managers of both sexes are by majority married. In terms of education, our sample discloses female professionals to be better educated than their male colleagues in all four countries. Their on average higher educational degree is not yet reflected in a higher position. While women hold significantly lower positions than men in Germany and Italy, going hand in hand as well with significantly lower personal assets under management, only in Thailand, experience seems to have paid off for women so far: female professionals hold both slightly higher positions and more assets under personal responsibility. Finally, in all four countries, women work on average less than their male colleagues, the difference being significant in Germany and Italy at the 10% and 5% level, respectively. Taken together, for the U.S. and for Thailand, we reveal trends, but hardly significant gender differences, while for the two other markets, female and male fund managers significantly differ in their personal characteristics. Whether this implies women to be women in terms of risk taking, overconfidence and tournament behavior will be analyzed in the following when we use relevant variables from this section as controls.

Table 7.2 Descriptive statistics of asset managers' characteristics

Characteristics split by country and gender	H₀: no gender difference[a]			
	USA ♂ ♀	GER ♂ ♀	ITA ♂ ♀	THA ♂ ♀
Age[b] in years	~42 ~40 -1.263 (0.206)	~36 ~34 **-2.002*** (0.045)**	~37 ~32 **-3.115*** (0.002)**	~35 ~35 -0.527 (0.598)
Experience[b] in years	~13 ~12 -1.008 (0.313)	~7 ~6 -1.386 (0.166)	~9 ~6 **-2.098** (0.036)**	~6 ~8 **-2.110**(0.035)**
Single[c] in %	17.5 17.6 -0.039 (0.969)	42.1 62.5 **-1.816* (0.069)**	42.9 63.6 **-2.173** (0.030)**	52.1 61.4 -0.783 (0.434)
Academic Education[c] in %	80.3 93.8 -1.308 (0.191)	86.5 88.0 -0.206 (0.837)	91.7 100.0 -1.394 (0.163)	95.5 96.6 -0.292 (0.771)
Position[d]	2.43 2.24 -0.636 (0.525)	2.01 1.46 **-3.172***(0.002)**	2.63 2.00 **-2.398** (0.017)**	1.82 1.84 -0.536 (0.592)
Personal AuM[e]	4.00 3.60 -0.843 (0.399)	3.52 2.45 **-3.332***(0.001)**	3.56 2.15 **-4.170*** (0.000)**	3.16 3.18 -0.070 (0.944)
Working hours[f]	~52 ~51 -1.097 (0.273)	~50 ~47 **-1.811* (0.070)**	~49 ~47 **-2.035** (0.042)**	~46 ~45 0.928 (0.354)

a The table gives the mean value for male and female asset managers in comparison as well as the z-value of the respective Mann-Whitney U test regarding gender specific differences in the four displayed countries. The p-value is given in parentheses. Asterisks refer to level of significance: * 10%, ** 5%, *** 1%.

b Mean age and experience are derived from six response categories that range from 1=<31 years old, and 1=<4 years of experience, respectively, to 6=>older than 50 years, and 6=more than 15 years of experience.

c Marital status and education are binary variables. While marital status is classified by 1=single and 3=married, education is divided into 1=non-academic and 3=academic.

d Position ranges from 1=junior asset manager, over 2=senior, 3=head of team to 4=CIO/CEO.

e Assets under personal responsibility / management (AuM) are classified into six response categories from 1 (lowest) to 6 (highest) with amounts that are country specifically adapted.

f Working hours are assessed by six response categories ranging from 1=<41 hours to 6=>60 hours.

7.3 Risk behavior

Analyzing fund managers' behavior towards risk by five measures, we reveal women to behave more risk averse than men. This finding holds for comparisons between sexes for the single measures in each country as well as for multivariate regression evidence where countries are pooled and the gender variable is controlled by a set of determinants.

We start the analysis of gender differences among professional financial market players with a first most direct measure of risk behavior, i.e. self-stated risk aversion (cf. Kapteyn and Teppa, 2002, in support of ad hoc questions and intuitive measures). As a second measure, we assess the degree of loss aversion as in particular modeled by Kahneman and Tversky's (1979) prospect theory; experimental work by Schmidt and Traub (2002) shows women to be more loss averse. Next, the empirically detected tendency of investors to hold losing stocks too long and sell winning stocks too early, the so-called disposition effect (cf. Shefrin and Statman, 1985) is considered by a questionnaire item. Fourth, we question both female and male fund managers about their average investment horizon, anticipating more risk averse asset managers to be less inclined to commit for long-term financial decisions. Finally, the degree of active management is assessed by comparing effective activism in relation to allowed activism. The degree of activism is understood as deviation of the portfolio from its benchmark, i.e. the so-called tracking error. We expect more risk averse managers to be more chary about completely exploiting their given leeway. Table 7.3 shows our results.

Directly asked about risk taking in professional investment decisions, females in Italy reveal to act more risk averse to a statistically significant degree than their male colleagues while female Thai fund managers tend into the same direction. Turning to loss aversion women show a significantly higher loss aversion in Thailand and tend into the same direction in Germany and Italy, although not in the U.S. Furthermore, women agree significantly more in three out of four countries on their behavior being consistent with the disposition effect than their male colleagues. Moreover, throughout all surveyed countries and statistically significant at the 5% level for Thailand, female professionals indicate a shorter investment horizon than male professionals. For the degree of active management, finally, results are mixed and only in the case of Italy statistically significant while pointing towards a higher female risk aversion in forms of more passive management than actually allowed. As an intermediate summary, there is an obvious tendency by female fund managers to behave more risk averse as all significant results support this tendency (7 out of 20 cases). Interestingly, in terms of cross-country considerations, we reveal significant differences for the Italian and Thai market, only one for the German but none for the U.S. market.

So far, we have not controlled for fund manager's characteristics. The latter, however, do not only mediate gender differences as previously described for studies like e.g. Atkinson et al. (2003) for wealth and investment knowledge, or Sunden and Surrette (1998) in case of marital status, but they have also been shown to exert significant influence on individual's risk behavior by itself (cf. e.g. Jianakoplos and Bernasek, 1998). In order to be on the safe when analyzing gender impact, we use – in addition to *marital status* – the following variables as controls: Dohmen et al. (2005) detect willingness to take risk to decrease with higher *age* (although Dwyer et al., 2002, do not find this effect). Graham (1999) finds that risk aversion decreases with *experience* of analysts, which is tentatively confirmed by Menkhoff et al. (2006) for fund managers. Moreover, e.g. Dwyer et al. (2002) find that more *educated* investors tend to take more risk than their less educated. Finally, we use some proxies to capture the effect from wealth and knowledge on risk taking which has been identified for individual investors. In our analysis we thus control for a higher *position*, for more *personal assets under management* and for more *working hours*. Finally, as we pool the total sample of 649 cases, we have to include dummy variables to control for country-specific effects.

Table 7.3 Risk behavior and gender

Asset managers' risk behavior	H_0: no gender difference[a]							
	USA		GER		ITA		THA	
	♂	♀	♂	♀	♂	♀	♂	♀
Risk taking[b]	3.55	3.59	3.50	3.50	3.63	3.25	3.30	3.05
	-0.139	(0.890)	-0.070	(0.944)	**-1.671***	**(0.095)**	-1.451	(0.147)
Loss aversion[c]	4.18	4.47	4.58	4.39	4.29	4.05	3.83	3.45
	-0.925	(0.355)	-0.790	(0.430)	-0.640	(0.522)	**-1.953***	**(0.051)**
Disposition effect[c]	3.82	3.53	4.22	3.54	3.96	3.35	3.31	2.90
	-0.856	(0.392)	**-2.043****	**(0.041)**	**-1.667***	**(0.095)**	**-1.716***	**(0.086)**
Investment horizon[d]	4.14	3.77	3.19	3.15	3.41	3.33	2.52	2.19
	-1.500	(0.134)	-0.387	(0.699)	-0.549	(0.583)	**-2.351****	**(0.019)**
Active management[e]	3.91	4.00	3.53	3.55	3.53	3.00	4.03	3.86
	-0.801	(0.423)	-0.023	(0.982)	**-2.274****	**(0.023)**	-1.158	(0.247)

a The table gives the mean value for male and female asset managers in comparison as well as the z-value of the respective Mann-Whitney U test regarding gender specific differences in the four displayed countries. The p-value is given in parentheses. Asterisks refer to level of significance: * 10%, ** 5%, *** 1%.

b Risk taking is addressed by the following question: "In respect of professional investment decisions, I mostly act..."; response categories range from 1=very risk averse to 6=little risk averse.

c Response categories range from 1=complete approval to 6=complete contradiction. Statements cover loss aversion: "In case of loss positions in my portfolio I generally wait for a price rebound instead of selling those securities." and the disposition effect: "I prefer to take profits instead of cutting losses, when I am confronted with unexpected liquidity demands."

d The length of investment horizon is addressed as follows: "What is your personal forecasting horizon when making investment decisions?". Five response categories cover 1=days, 2=weeks, 3=2-6 months, 4=6-12 months, and 5=years.

e Active management displays the difference of: "How actively (i.e. high tracking error) do you manage your portfolio in fact?", and "How actively can you manage your portfolio at most?", with response categories for both questions ranging from 1=high tracking error to 6=indexing. To make categories comparable to the other questions and avoid negative numbers, we constructed the active management variable to range between 1 and 6 with smaller numbers thus indicating a less active, i.e. more risk averse, management style.

Results of the multivariate ordered probit regressions are given in Table 7.4. Overall, we find the gender variable to reveal significant explanatory power on four out of five risk behavior variables.[67] Although controlling for the seven variables just discussed above, female professionals behave consistently more risk averse than their male colleagues.

Although controlling for the seven variables just discussed above, female professionals behave consistently more risk averse than their male colleagues. In detail, directly questioned higher risk averse behavior is significantly and positively influenced by being female and being older. The disposition effect is significantly higher for female asset managers as well as those with relatively inferior characteristics of being less educated, in a lower position, with lower volumes of assets under personal responsibility, and showing less working effort. For the investment horizon, the explanatory contribution by chosen variables is highest: shorter investment horizons are significantly confirmed for female professionals as well as for fund managers with less experience, shorter working hours and holding a higher position. For the degree of active management, it is only the gender variable that matters aside from country dummies.

It seems noteworthy, that many of the coefficients have the expected sign: older fund managers tend to be rather more risk averse, experienced fund managers less. Regarding the variables proxying qualification – i.e. education, position, assets – we would like to mention that some of our risk behavior measures do not only indicate risk aversion but also distorted decision making, such as the disposition effect. From this perspective it makes sense that the coefficients tend to show negative signs because more qualified fund managers are expected to decide better.

Discussing country dummies, the multivariate approach closely mirrors the simple comparison presented in Table 7.3 above: Thai fund managers show an almost consistently higher risk aversion, Italians do this to some degree and Germans show mixed results when comparing them to their U.S. colleagues.

Overall, our primary attention is on the gender variable and this gives a clear result: female fund managers tend to show consistently more risk averse behavior. However, when we consider the size of this effect, the difference between women and men is smaller than between countries. We now turn to the relation between overconfidence and gender.

67 The non-significance of the gender variable in the loss aversion-regression is driven by the U.S. sample. When checking the chosen framework of control variables and dummies for robustness by exchanging the three country dummies for Germany, Italy and Thailand with only one for the U.S., the variables for gender, volume of assets under management, and the latter dummy become significant additionally, revealing female professionals to be indeed more loss averse with significance at the 1% level.

Table 7.4 Risk behavior in a multivariate framework

Risk behavior controlled for personal characteristics	Ordered PROBIT regressions[a]				
	Higher risk aversion	Higher loss aversion	Higher dispos. Effect	Shorter investment horizon	Less active management
Female	**0.113*** **(0.097)**	0.092 (0.171)	**0.165**** **(0.014)**	**0.145**** **(0.040)**	**0.137*** **(0.061)**
Older	**0.157**** **(0.011)**	0.015 (0.807)	0.026 (0.667)	0.104 (0.104)	-0.047 (0.474)
More experienced	-0.064 (0.209)	-0.012 (0.814)	-0.011 (0.832)	**-0.142***** **(0.008)**	-0.014 (0.795)
Single	0.034 (0.547)	**0.160***** **(0.004)**	0.069 (0.211)	-0.041 (0.472)	-0.022 (0.714)
Better educated	0.009 (0.910)	-0.076 (0.311)	**-0.172**** **(0.021)**	**-0.205***** **(0.009)**	0.040 (0.629)
Higher position	-0.075 (0.325)	-0.048 (0.531)	**-0.207***** **(0.006)**	**0.172**** **(0.027)**	0.032 (0.702)
More personal AuM	0.029 (0.458)	**-0.111***** **(0.005)**	**-0.068*** **(0.078)**	-0.023 (0.598)	0.059 (0.170)
More working Hours	-0.040 (0.394)	-0.051 (0.280)	**-0.090*** **(0.057)**	**-0.110**** **(0.024)**	0.065 (0.201)
Dummy GER	0.163 (0.239)	**-0.410***** **(0.003)**	**-0.281**** **(0.040)**	**1.274***** **(0.000)**	**0.652***** **(0.000)**
Dummy ITA	0.194 (0.273)	-0.136 (0.436)	-0.081 (0.642)	**0.878***** **(0.000)**	**0.756***** **(0.000)**
Dummy THA	**0.356**** **(0.040)**	**0.324*** **(0.061)**	**0.299** **(0.082)**	**2.306***** **(0.000)**	-0.006 (0.973)
LR statistic	19.29*	77.66***	83.46***	237.85***	47.30***
(Pseudo-)R^2	0.01	0.05	0.05	0.18	0.05

a The table gives the coefficients of the ordered PROBIT regressions with p-values in parentheses. In order to ease reading and comprehensibility at first sight, coefficients are adapted according to described control variable outcomes in the table. Asterisks refer to level of significance: * 10%, ** 5%, *** 1%. Explanations of the five dependent variables can be found in Table 3, information about the control variables is given in Table 2. Country dummies for Germany, Italy and Thailand are binary coded.

7.4 Overconfidence

Addressing overconfidence, we use three measures and find that female fund managers do not differ significantly from their male colleagues.

Previous studies have shown that different measures of overconfidence are not necessarily correlated.[68] Therefore, we choose to independently address all three forms of overconfidence, covering a measure of the better-than-average effect, illusion of control, and miscalibration, respectively. In detail, we ask the surveyed professionals to self-assess their achievements in fund management compared to their peer group; we question them about their approval or contradiction of surprise on business news; and finally, taking into account that overconfident individuals have been found to miscalibrate by giving too narrow confidence intervals, we confront them with the task of 90% probability forecasts of their respective home market equity index for the following month.[69] Again, as performed in Chapter 7.3 on risk behavior, we first show comparisons between sexes for three measures in all four countries surveyed and then give regression results on the pooled sample. Table 7.5 shows our findings, split by gender and with indications of statistical significance.

Table 7.5 Overconfidence and gender

Evidence for male overconfidence?	H_0: no gender difference[a]							
	USA		GER		ITA		THA	
	♂	♀	♂	♀	♂	♀	♂	♀
Management Performance[b]	2.67	2.75	3.13	3.00	2.81	3.30	3.09	3.22
	-0.046 (0.964)		-0.587 (0.557)		**-2.000** (0.046)**		-0.879 (0.380)	
News novelty[c]	3.08	3.53	3.23	3.42	3.41	3.71	3.06	3.19
	-1.418 (0.156)		-1.338 (0.181)		-1.142 (0.253)		-0.855 (0.392)	
Home index range[d]	17.63	21.52	22.16	37.37	11.79	8.39	15.59	16.25
	-1.331 (0.183)		**-1.934* (0.053)**		-0.894 (0.371)		-0.251 (0.802)	

a The table gives the mean value for male and female asset managers in comparison as well as the z-value of the respective Mann-Whitney U test regarding gender specific differences in the four displayed countries. The p-value is given in parentheses. Asterisks refer to level of significance: * 10%, ** 5%, *** 1%.

b Surveyed asset managers are asked to assess their management performance in order to test for unrealistically positive self-evaluation as follows: "How do you assess your achievement in asset management – compared to other asset managers' achievement in the same investment segment?" Response categories range from 1=much better to 7=much worse.

c Control illusion is assessed by: "Most of the published business news does not surprise me at all." Response categories cover 1=complete approval to 6=complete contradiction.

d Miscalibration is tested by 90% probability performance forecasts of home indices: "Please estimate the development of the S&P 500 (EuroSTOXX 50 / SET, respectively) within the next month." Index ranges are calculated by relating the difference of maximum and minimum level estimations to the actual level.

---

68 A thorough experimental assessment of different measures is given by Glaser et al. (2005). Neither them nor e.g. Deaves et al. (2004) and Oberlechner and Osler (2004) find positive correlations between e.g. miscalibraton and an overly positive self-assessment.

69 Cf. e.g. Biais et al. (2005), Glaser et al. (2005) or Menkhoff et al. (2006) for using similar measures.

Asked about their achievements relative to their peers, surveyed asset managers across all four countries and both genders reveal on average overly positive self-assessments: while a value of four would indicate asset managers to be equally good as their benchmark, surveyed professional groups show means between 2.7 and 3.3 and thus describe themselves on average to be better than their benchmark. For the United States, Italy and Thailand, we find a tendency of slightly worse female self-assessments relative to their male colleagues while for Germany, females are even more confident about themselves. Only in the case of Italy, the gender difference is significant. Addressing control illusion among professionals, we assume more confident managers to experience lower surprise about upcoming news in financial markets. We find, first, both women and men on average to agree to the statement that "Most of the published business news does not surprise me at all", thus indicating a form of overconfidence. Second, albeit a tendency towards lower agreement of women relative to their male counterparts, we do not detect any significant gender difference. For the third type of overconfidence, miscalibration, a comparison between female and male professionals concerning estimated broadness of equity index ranges, calculated from maximum and minimum level estimations in relation to the actual index level, reveals further insights: expecting more confident professionals to indicate a more narrow equity index range, in the U.S., German and Thai sample, we find women to give broader ranges than men. Yet, only in the German case gender differences are significant at least at the 10% level, whereas in Italy the sign is even opposite. To summarize, there is only a slight tendency across the three measures that women are less overconfident than men and the gender difference is, indeed, hardly significant.

In order control for the possible influence of personal characteristics, we choose the same set of control variables as before when moving towards the multivariate approach. Again, controlling for several factors is well justified by previous research and derived controversies: Bengtsson et al. (2005) or Deaves et al. (2004) confirm e.g. *age* to be a relevant factor in observed gender differences in their experimental work. While e.g. Gervais and Odean (2001) theoretically and Locke and Mann (2001) empirically argue that overconfidence is highest for *inexperienced* traders, experts have been found to be more likely than inexperienced subjects to show overconfident behavior (cf. e.g. Heath and Tversky, 1991 or Glaser et al., 2005). Moreover, Barber and Odean (2001) have highlighted the influence of *marital status* on their results, revealing differences to be greatest between single women and men. Finally, Estes and Hosseini (1988) reveal the significant role of *education* and familiarity – proxied by our *qualification* variables – for confidence in investment decisions.

The multivariate estimation results are shown in Table 7.6 and confirm our previous finding from Table 7.5. To cut a long story short: we do not find the gender variable to significantly matter for any of the three overconfidence measures.[70] Our findings are thus in line with the student experiments by Deaves et al. (2004) and Biais et al. (2005), rejecting the assumption used by Barber and Odean (2001) to take gender as a generally good proxy for overconfidence. Further significant variables indicate that the self-assessment measure of overconfidence may also capture justified confidence as more experienced and harder working fund managers feel more successful. Moreover, the plausibility of our survey as well as the importance of control variables appears to be underlined by the last regression in Table 7.6: more qualified fund managers give indeed broader – i.e. here better – equity index estimates.

Table 7.6 Overconfidence in a multivariate framework

Overconfidence controlled for personal characteristics	Ordered PROBIT / TOBIT regressions[a]					
	Better assessment of management performance		Lower surprise about business news		Broader home index estimation	
Female	-0.060	(0.381)	-0.043	(0.518)	-0.512	(0.615)
Older	**-0.146****	**(0.018)**	0.059	(0.327)	0.460	(0.618)
More experienced	**0.135*****	**(0.009)**	-0.027	(0.592)	-0.343	(0.646)
Single	-0.013	(0.820)	-0.038	(0.490)	-1.061	(0.187)
Better educated	0.041	(0.594)	-0.031	(0.681)	1.694	(0.144)
Higher position	0.090	(0.234)	0.007	(0.928)	-1.127	(0.326)
More personal AuM	-0.032	(0.415)	0.037	(0.338)	**1.003***	**(0.089)**
More working hours	**0.135*****	**(0.005)**	0.029	(0.533)	**1.231***	**(0.090)**
Dummy GER	**-0.362*****	**(0.009)**	0.154	(0.261)	3.600	(0.101)
Dummy ITA	-0.145	(0.410)	-0.138	(0.422)	**-5.725****	**(0.041)**
Dummy THA	-0.281	(0.108)	**0.386****	**(0.025)**	-0.277	(0.916)
Constant	-		-		5.497	(0.294)
LR statistic	42.18***		14.86		-	
(Pseudo-)R^2	0.03		0.01		0.09	

a The table shows the coefficients of the ordered PROBIT regressions for the first two dependant variables, testing for unrealistically positive self-evaluation and control illusion, and a TOBIT regression for the home index estimation range that addresses miscalibration, respectively. P-values are given in parentheses. Asterisks refer to level of significance: * 10%, ** 5%, *** 1%. Coefficients are again adapted according to described control variable outcomes in the table to ease understanding at first sight. Further explanations of the three dependent variables can be found in Table 7.5, information about the control variables is given in Table 7.2. Country dummies for Germany, Italy and Thailand are binary coded.

The third part of our analysis sheds light on possible gender difference in fund managers' competition behavior in a tournament situation.

70 Besides, country specific dummies reveal a mixed picture across the three overconfidence measures as only for the unrealistically positive self-evaluation, in all three countries covered by dummies, the level of overconfidence is consistently lower than in the U.S.

7.5 Tournament

Regarding tournament behavior we confront fund managers with two realistic scenarios and find that women behave differently from men as they change their strategy more often when they are above or behind the market.

We translate the literature's finding that women shy away from competition more than men into tournament situations which often happen near the end of the investment period (cf. Brown et al., 1996). In these situations, fund managers are aware of the opportunity, on the one hand, to receive disproportionately high new cash flows into "their" fund for extraordinary performance (cf. Sirri and Tufano, 1998). Seeking such performance requires to deviate from the market benchmark. On the other, bad investments decisions – i.e. performance below the market – are punished with negative career consequences (cf. Chevalier and Elisson, 1999). In the survey we give two scenarios: achieved benchmark outperformance or underperformance near the end of the valuation period.

In both scenarios – over- or underperformance – fund managers face a two-stage decision. First, they could stick to their earlier investment strategy which should actually be the one derived from their (private) information. The only piece of new information to be considered here is their fund's position relative to the benchmark. This information might motivate them to change their strategy. Then, there is a second decision to be made: in the case of outperformance, professionals could either intend to "lock in" their achieved outperformance or even aggressively welcome competition by increasing the risk level in order to become top performer. In the second case, underperforming their benchmark might lead them to guard a chance at "catching up" relative to their benchmark or decrease the risk level to save them from further (hurtful) performance losses.

Former mutual fund studies do not provide undisputed expectations on fund managers' behavior in such tournaments (e.g. Busse, 2001, Goriaev et al., 2005). From a gender perspective, however, less competitive behavior of women (Gupta et al., 2005, Dohmen and Falk, 2006) may lead them to orientate themselves stronger towards the benchmark and less seek competition by sticking to their preferred strategy (which deviates from the benchmark). This is consistent with the finding that U.S. female fund managers show less often very good or bad performance ranks (Niessen and Ruenzi, 2006).

Starting with the scenario of outperformance, Table 7.7 shows female professionals in Italy and Thailand to be significantly more likely than their male colleagues to change instead of keeping their previous strategy. Indeed, they "lock in" achieved outperformance. Looking at the "second" decision – that is the direction of riskiness conditional on change –, only a very limited number[71] of

71 We refrain from integrating this specific scenario in following multivariate regressions as the number of observations is too small for meaningful estimations.

professionals choose an increase of the risk level. Turning to the second scenario – previous underperformance – we disclose women again to be more likely to vary the risk level than men. This time, findings are consistent across all four countries, being most pronounced and highly significant at the 1% percent level for Thailand. Concerning the second decision, whether to increase or decrease riskiness in the future, we reveal interesting findings: females are more prone than men to increase the relative risk level, with statistical significance for Germany and Thailand. This seems somewhat surprising at first sight, but is consistent with a strong ambition to stick close to the benchmark's performance. Concerning a decrease in risk level, gender evidence is mixed, with a few U.S. female professionals significantly preferring this behavior.

Table 7.7 Tournament behavior and gender

Gender differences in tournament behavior[b]	H_0: no gender difference[a]			
	USA	GER	ITA	THA
	♂ ♀	♂ ♀	♂ ♀	♂ ♀
Scenario 1: If the portfolio has *outperformed* its benchmark so far…				
Change instead of keeping strategy[c]	0.20 0.06 -1.409 (0.159)	0.34 0.46 -1.191 (0.234)	0.61 0.82 **-1.781* (0.075)**	0.39 0.60 **-2.393** (0.017)**
- Increase risk	0.01 0.00 -0.390 (0.696)	0.01 0.00 -0.415 (0.678)	0.11 0.00 -0.694 (0.488)	0.11 0.12 0.09 (0.93)
- Decrease risk	0.19 0.06 1.363 (0.173)	0.33 0.46 -1.253 (0.210)	0.59 0.82 **-1.924* (0.054)**	0.34 0.58 **-2.625*** (0.009)**
Scenario 2: If the portfolio has *underperformed* its benchmark so far …				
Change instead of keeping strategy[c]	0.15 0.24 -0.852 (0.394)	0.30 0.38 0.714 (0.475)	0.41 0.50 -0.758 (0.449)	0.47 0.74 **-3.065*** (0.002)**
- Increase risk	0.13 0.13 -0.069 (0.945)	0.10 0.25 **-1.940* (0.052)**	0.23 0.42 -1.587 (0.113)	0.33 0.69 **-3.668*** (0.000)**
- Decrease risk	0.04 0.13 **-1.692* (0.091)**	0.24 0.21 -0.326 (0.744)	0.28 0.21 -0.498 (0.619)	0.29 0.38 -0.766 (0.444)

a The table gives mean percentages for male and female asset managers in comparison as well as the z-value of the respective Mann-Whitney U test regarding gender specific differences in the four displayed countries. The p-value is given in parentheses. Asterisks refer to level of significance: * 10%, ** 5%, *** 1%.

b Tournament behavior is assessed by requesting the surveyed asset managers to imagine that – apart from any fund's restriction – their portfolio's performance differs from its benchmark near the end of the period. We then address two scenarios as follows: "If my portfolio has *outperformed* (*underperformed*, respectively in the second scenario) its benchmark so far, I would... a) increase the relative risk level to become a top performer, b) decrease the relative risk level to lock in the performance, c) not change my strategy."

c Variables are binary coded with 1=change (overall, increase or decrease, respectively) and 0=keep strategy.

Table 7.8 Tournament behavior in a multivariate framework

Tournament behavior controlled for personal characteristics	Binary PROBIT regressions[a]				
	Scenario 1: Outperformance		*Scenario 2: Unperformance*		
	Change strategy	Decrease risk	Change strategy	Increase risk	Decrease risk
Female	**0.178** **(0.035)**	**0.204** **(0.018)**	**0.212** **(0.012)**	**0.325***** **(0.001)**	0.042 (0.719)
Older	-0.064 (0.427)	-0.057 (0.479)	-0.077 (0.348)	-0.099 (0.348)	-0.015 (0.877)
More experienced	0.031 (0.632)	0.035 (0.601)	0.003 (0.962)	0.019 (0.830)	0.020 (0.797)
Single	0.065 (0.349)	0.080 (0.251)	0.046 (0.513)	0.076 (0.392)	0.038 (0.659)
Better educated	-0.080 (0.404)	-0.082 (0.399)	-0.151 (0.120)	**-0.281**** **(0.015)**	0.047 (0.720)
Higher position	-0.054 (0.580)	-0.066 (0.508)	0.044 (0.656)	-0.024 (0.844)	0.092 (0.448)
More personal AuM	-0.052 (0.325)	-0.046 (0.371)	**-0.108**** **(0.036)**	**-0.124*** **(0.054)**	-0.100 (0.124)
More working hours	-0.001 (0.997)	-0.017 (0.779)	0.052 (0.402)	0.118 (0.129)	-0.034 (0.661)
Dummy GER	**0.519***** **(0.005)**	**0.515***** **(0.005)**	**0.340*** **(0.070)**	-0.198 (0.379)	**1.001***** **(0.001)**
Dummy ITA	**1.262***** **(0.000)**	**1.218***** **(0.000)**	**0.588**** **(0.010)**	0.406 (0.126)	**0.925***** **(0.005)**
Dummy THA	**0.750***** **(0.001)**	**0.584**** **(0.011)**	**1.098***** **(0.000)**	**1.016***** **(0.000)**	**1.304***** **(0.000)**
Constant	-0.418 (0.347)	-0.369 (0.413)	-0.339 (0.449)	-0.267 (0.620)	**-1.605**** **(0.011)**
LR statistic	67.12***	62.54***	71.14***	85.21***	32.65***
(McFadden) R^2	0.10	0.10	0.11	0.20	0.08

a The table gives the coefficients of the binary PROBIT regressions with p-values in parentheses. Again, coefficients are adapted according to described control variable outcomes in the table. Asterisks refer to level of significance: * 10%, ** 5%, *** 1%. Further explanations of the five binary dependent variables can be found in Table 7.7, information about the control variables is given in Table 7.2. Country dummies for Germany, Italy and Thailand are binary coded.

As we did in the sections before, we test these results in multivariate binary probit models while controlling for the usual set of variables. Table 7.8 shows that our findings on gender differences also hold in a multivariate framework. Gender is the only variable consistently explaining the first decision to be made as women more often change their strategy in both scenarios. Looking at the second decision, i.e. the sign of change, women consistently decrease the risk level in the outperformance scenario. When confronted with underperformance near the end of the valuation period, women are significantly more likely to increase the risk level. Only in terms of a risk level decrease, the gender variable is not significant. Besides, significant country variables reinforce effects in Germany, Thailand and Italy in comparison to the United States.

Overall, female fund managers seem to confirm competitive behavior which is found for women in general, i.e. that they shy away from competition more often then men.

7.6 Conclusions

The question whether women behave differently from men has been extensively researched and reveals some robust gender differences. Women are significantly more risk averse and behave less competitively oriented in tournaments – i.e., women behave different in these respects which seem to affect their behavior as fund managers. This raises the question whether the extremely strong incentives in the fund management industry overcome the nature of female fund managers?

We provide evidence on this important question that is different from earlier approaches. Most interesting, our survey covers fund managers and reaches thus beyond mainly addressed students or individual investors. This feature of our research is key because incentives must be strong in their struggle with nature to succeed.

We find that fund managing women will be women in their profession as expected from general gender studies: they are more risk averse and shy away from competition. However, the mostly found lesser overconfidence of women is not confirmed in fund management where a gender difference is insignificant. Finally, the international study reveals a clear country pattern in the sense that the U.S. market does not really show any gender difference whereas differences increase in the following order: from Germany over Italy to Thailand. It seems plausible to relate this pattern to the degree of market development, so that the possibly highest degree of incentives – in the U.S. – is strong enough to completely erase the natural gender difference.

Obviously, this interpretation of the country pattern rivals with a cultural view in that U.S. women may behave different from women in other countries because cultures are different. Cultural patterns, however, are not one-dimensional whereas we tend to find for all three phenomena – risk behavior, overconfidence and competitive behavior – always the same country pattern. Another concern may refer to the studies finding the same investment performance for both sexes, whereas lower risk aversion and less competitive behavior might translate into lower performance. We argue, however, that gender-differentiated performance studies rely on U.S. data, which is exactly that market where we find no gender difference in fund managers' behavior. Moreover, due to tentatively higher overconfidence of men it does not seem clear ex ante whether either women or men will perform better.

Our research thus suggests a kind of temporary result: the natural gender difference is strong enough to partially persist even in fund management but market development may bring about forceful incentives that finally overcome the gender difference. No question, it would be most interesting to contrast this finding with further evidence.

Annex

International Survey in Professional Asset Management

By answering this questionnaire you are supporting an academic research project, which focuses on the personal viewpoints, perceptions and investment behavior of professional asset managers. Please fill in this questionnaire and send it to: Prof. Dr. Lukas Menkhoff, University of Hanover, Department of Economics: Money and International Finance, D – 30167 Hannover, Germany (or by email to: beckmann@gif.uni-hannover.de).
We would kindly ask you to answer the following questions completely and truthfully. This data will be kept in strictest confidence and anonymity. Besides, we will provide the results of our analysis to you on request.

Personal Data

Gender: ☐ Male ☐ Female

Marital status: ☐ Single ☐ Married ☐ Other

How old are you?
☐ < 31 ☐ 31 - 35 ☐ 36 – 40 ☐ 41 - 45 ☐ 46 - 50 ☐ > 50

Professional experience in asset management (in years):
☐ < 4 ☐ 4 - 6 ☐ 7 – 9 ☐ 10 - 12 ☐ 13 - 15 ☐ > 15

Average working hours per week:
☐ < 41 ☐ 41 - 45 ☐ 46 – 50 ☐ 51 - 55 ☐ 56 - 60 ☐ > 60

Average period of data procurement and research: __ Hours per week

Educational level: ☐ Non-academic education ☐ Academic education

Current position within your company: ☐ Junior Asset Manager ☐ Senior Asset Manager ☐ Head of AM team ☐ CIO / CEO

Average bonus you receive in addition to your fixed salary: ___ %

Type of managed fund: ☐ Mutual fund ☐ Restricted / special / pension fund

Major investment segment: ☐ Equities ☐ Bonds ☐ Money market

Your company's total volume of assets under management (in billion of $):
☐ < 5 ☐ 5 - 10 ☐ 10- 20 ☐ 20 - 50 ☐ 50 - 100 ☐ > 100

Your personal responsibility for assets under management (in million of $):
☐ < 50 ☐ 50 - 250 ☐ 250- 1,000 ☐ 1,000 – 2,500 ☐ 2,500 - 10,000 ☐ > 10,000

Performance Incentives

Do you get a share participation option plan / stock option programme? ☐ Yes ☐ No

If you receive a performance-based remuneration, which criteria determine the size of that bonus?	highest relevance					no relevance
Absolute fund performance	☐	☐	☐	☐	☐	☐
Relative fund performance	☐	☐	☐	☐	☐	☐
Business development of the investment company	☐	☐	☐	☐	☐	☐
Subjective assessment by superiors and colleagues	☐	☐	☐	☐	☐	☐

Please describe your investment performance and assess your achievement in asset management:	much better						much worse
How was your risk-adjusted performance last year – compared to other asset managers' performance in the same investment segment?	☐	☐	☐	☐	☐	☐	☐
How do you assess your achievement in asset management – compared to other asset managers' achievement in the same investment segment?	☐	☐	☐	☐	☐	☐	☐

Your opinion on the general behavior of asset managers

Please assess the investment behavior of professional asset managers:	complete approval					complete contradiction
People are not machines; thus security prices are clearly more determined by psychological influences than by fundamentals.	☐	☐	☐	☐	☐	☐
Herding is observable amongst professional asset managers.	☐	☐	☐	☐	☐	☐
Asset Managers often disregard some information, if it does not complement their opinion.	☐	☐	☐	☐	☐	☐
Following the herd benefits the asset manager's career.	☐	☐	☐	☐	☐	☐

Your personal investment behavior and information processing

Please describe your investment behavior by responding to the following statements:	complete approval					complete contradiction
I prefer to take profits instead of cutting losses, when I am confronted with unexpected liquidity demands.	☐	☐	☐	☐	☐	☐
As a domestic asset manager I benefit from better information on domestic securities compared to market players overseas.	☐	☐	☐	☐	☐	☐
I often trade too much, as my clients demand short-term performance.	☐	☐	☐	☐	☐	☐
Most of the published business news does not surprise me at all.	☐	☐	☐	☐	☐	☐
In case of loss positions in my portfolio I generally wait for a price rebound instead of selling those securities.	☐	☐	☐	☐	☐	☐
I generally follow the trend.	☐	☐	☐	☐	☐	☐

What is your personal forecasting horizon when making investment decisions?

☐ Days ☐ Weeks ☐ 2-6 Months ☐ 6-12 Months ☐ Years

Please assess the following sources of information used in making investment decision:	highest relevance					no relevance
Fundamental facts about the company / market	☐	☐	☐	☐	☐	☐
Chart analysis / technical indicators	☐	☐	☐	☐	☐	☐
Discussions / exchange of views with colleagues	☐	☐	☐	☐	☐	☐
Investments decisions of other market players	☐	☐	☐	☐	☐	☐
Statements of opinion leaders within the industry (e.g. Warren Buffett)	☐	☐	☐	☐	☐	☐
Statements of economic opinion leaders (e.g. Alan Greenspan, Wim Duisenberg)	☐	☐	☐	☐	☐	☐

Please describe your management style:

	high tracking error					Indexing
How actively (i.e. high tracking error) can you manage your portfolio at most?	☐	☐	☐	☐	☐	☐
How actively (i.e. high tracking error) do you manage your portfolio in fact?	☐	☐	☐	☐	☐	☐

Please classify your personal risk-taking:

	very risk averse					little risk averse
In respect of professional investment decisions, I mostly act…	☐	☐	☐	☐	☐	☐

Which strategies are your investment decisions normally based upon?

Please assign **100 % altogether**. If a category does not apply at all, please assign 0 % to it.

___ % Momentum Strategy ___ % Buy-and-Hold Strategy ___ % Others

___ % Contrarian Strategy ___ % Dividend-oriented Strategy

How much importance do you attach to the following categories of information?

Please assign **100 % altogether**. If a category does not apply at all, please assign 0 % to it.

___ % **Fundamentals** (economic and political hard facts)

___ % **Technical analysis** (charts and quantitative indicators)

___ % **(Order) Flows** (observed transactions)

What is your personal forecasting horizon when using this information?

Fundamentals:	☐ Intraday	☐ Days	☐ Weeks	☐ 2-6 Months	☐ 6-12 Months	☐ Years
Technical Analysis:	☐ Intraday	☐ Days	☐ Weeks	☐ 2-6 Months	☐ 6-12 Months	☐ Years
(Order) Flows:	☐ Intraday	☐ Days	☐ Weeks	☐ 2-6 Months	☐ 6-12 Months	☐ Years

Apart from any fund's restriction – Imagine your portfolio's performance differs from its benchmark near the end of the period.

If my portfolio has outperformed its benchmark so far, I would...

☐ increase the relative risk level to become a top performer ☐ decrease the relative risk level to lock in the performance ☐ not change my strategy

If my portfolio has underperformed its benchmark so far, I would...

☐ increase the relative risk level to reach the benchmark ☐ decrease the relative risk level to avoid further deficits ☐ not change my strategy

Imagine someone offers you a bet and the odds are fifty-fifty. You will have to pay 1000 $ from your personal account, if you lose. What would be the minimum amount you would expect to win to lure you into accepting the bet?

At least _____ $.

Please estimate the development of the *S&P 500*, the *Dow Jones* and the *EuroSTOXX 50* within the next month. Please forecast the performance of the respective index with a probability of 90 %:

Date: __.__.2003 (mm/dd)	S&P 500	Dow Jones	EuroSTOXX 50
Today's level:			
Expected minimum level:			
Expected maximum level:			

Thank you very much for your support!

Country-specific adaptations:

The question on performance incentives "Do you get a share participation option plan / stock option programme?" was excluded from the Thai questionnaire after previous oral interviews with Thai asset managers due to missing evidence in the Thai market.

Besides, the following question was included for the survey in Thailand, Indonesia and Germany. The Thai questionnaire is presented here; home countries and regional groups were country specifically adapted:

What are your long-term expectations for the next 10 years?

Even if it is difficult to forecast long-term developments, we would like to ask you to estimate the respective development within the next 10 years.

		Thailand	China	Japan	USA / Canada	Europe	Other Emerging Markets
Stock market	average stock yield per year (in percent):						
Bond market	average government bond yield per year (in percent):						

The following question was next to Thailand, Indonesia and Gemany also posed in the Italian questionnaire. Again, the Thai questionnaire is shown here; home countries and regional groups were country specifically adapted:

Apart from any fund's restriction – Please allocate an amount of 500 million Baht to invest in the following regions: (adding up to 100%):

___ Thailand ___ China ___ Japan ___ Asian Emerging Markets

___ United States and Canada ___ Europe ___ Other Emerging Markets

References

Abiad, Abdul (2003), Early Warning Systems: A Survey and a Regime-Switching Approach, *IMF Working Paper* No. 03/32, Washington D.C.

Aggarwal, Reena, Leora Klapper and Peter D. Wysocki (2005), Portfolio Preferences of Foreign Institutional Investors, *Journal of Banking and Finance*, 29:12, 2919-2946.

Ahearne, Alan G., William L. Griever and Francis E. Warnock (2004), Information Costs and Home Bias: An Analysis of U.S. Holdings of Foreign Equities, *Journal of International Economics*, 62:2, 313–336.

Aitken, Brian (1998), Have Institutional Investors Destabilized Emerging Markets?, *Contemporary Economic Policy*, 16:2, 173-184.

Alvarez Plata, Patricia and Mechthild Schrooten (2003), The Argentine Currency Crisis: A Markov Switching Model Estimation, *DIW Discussion Paper* 348.

Alvarez Plata, Patricia and Mechthild Schrooten (2004), Misleading Indicators? The Argentinean Currency Crisis, *Journal of Policy Modeling*, 26:5, 587-603.

Andersson, Björn (2001), Portfolio Allocation over the Life Cycle: Evidence from Swedish Household Data, Working Paper, 2001:4, Uppsala University, Department of Economics.

Anolli, Mario (2005), Italian Open End Mutual Fund Costs, *Working Paper*, Università Cattolica, Milan.

Arnswald, Torsten (2001), Investment Behaviour of German Equity Fund Managers, An Exploratory Analysis of Survey Data, *Deutsche Bundesbank Discussion Paper*, No. 08/01, Frankfurt.

Arora, Navneet and Hui Ou-Yang (2001), Explicit and Implicit Incentives in a Delegated Portfolio Management Problem: Theory and Evidence, *Working Paper*, University of North Carolina.

Atkinson, Stanley M., Samantha Boyce Baird and Melissa B. Frye (2003), Do Female Mutual Fund Managers Manage Differently, *The Journal of Financial Research*, 26:1, 1-18.

Avery, Christopher N. and Judith A. Chevalier (1999), Herding over the Career, *Economics Letters*, 63:3, 327-333.

Barber, Brad M. and Terrance Odean (2000), Trading is Hazardous to Your Wealth: The Common Stock Investment Performance of Individual Investors, *The Journal of Finance*, 55:2, 773-806.

Barber, Brad M. and Terrance Odean (2001), Boys will be boys: gender, overconfidence, and common stock investment, *The Quarterly Journal of Economics*, 116:1, 261-292.

Barberis, Nicholas and Richard Thaler (2003), A Survey of Behavioral Finance, *Handbook of the Economics of Finance*, Vol. 1B, edited by George M. Constantinides, Milton Harris and Rene M. Stulz, Amsterdam et al., 1051-1121.

Barro, Robert J. (2001), Economic Growth in East Asia Before and After the Financial Crisis, *NBER Working Paper* No. 8330, Cambridge, MA.

Barsky, Robert B., Thomas F. Juster, Miles S. Kimball and Matthew D. Shapiro (1997), Preference Parameters and Behavioral Heterogeneity: An Experimental Approach in the Health and Retirement Study, *The Quarterly Journal of Economics*, 112:2, 537-579.

Bauer, Christian, Bernhard Herz and Volker Karb (2003), The Other Twins: Currency and Debt Crises, *Review of Economics*, 54:3, 248-267.

Beim, David O. and Charles W. Calomiris (2001), Emerging Financial Markets, New York, NY.

Bengtsson, Claes, Mats Persson and Peter Willenhag (2005), Gender and Overconfidence, *Economics Letters*, 86:2, 199-203.

Berg, Andrew, Eduardo Borensztein, Gian M. Milesi-Ferreti and Catherine Pattillo (2000), Anticipating Balance of Payments Crises: The Role of Early Warning Systems, *IMF Occasional Paper* 186.

Berg, Andrew, Eduardo Borensztein and Catherine Pattillo (2005), Assessing Early Warning Systems: How Have They Worked in Practice?, *IMF Staff Papers*, 52:3, 462-502.

Berg, Andrew and Catherine Pattillo (1999), Predicting Currency Crises: The Indicators Approach and an Alternative, *Journal of International Money and Finance*, 18:4, 561–586.

Berg, Andrew and Catherine Pattillo (1999a), Are Currency Crises Predictable? A Test, *IMF Staff Papers*, 46:2, 107–138.

Berry, John W., Ype H. Poortinga, Marshall H. Segall and Pierre R. Dasen (2002), *Cross-Cultural Psychology*, 2nd Edition, Cambridge.

Bias, Bruno, Denis Hilton and Karine Mazurier (2005), Judgemental Overconfidence, Self-Monitoring, and Trading Performance in an Experimental Financial Market, *Review of Economic Studies*, 72:2, 287-312.

Bikhchandani, Sushil and Sunil Sharma (2001), Herd Behavior in Financial Markets: A Review, *IMF Staff Papers*, 47:3, 279-310.

Bikhchandani, Sushil, David Hirshleifer and Ivo Welch (1992), A Theory of Fads, Fashion, Custom and Cultural Change as Informational Cascades, *Journal of Political Economy*, 100:5, 992-1026.

Bikhchandani, Sushil, David Hirshleifer and Ivo Welch (1998), Learning from the Behavior of Others: Conformity, Fads, and Informational Cascades, *Journal of Economic Perspectives*, 12:3, 151-170.

Blinder, Alan S. (2000), Central-Bank Credibility: Why Do We Care? How Do We Build It?, *The American Economic Review*, 90:5, 1421-1431.

Bliss, Richard T. and Mark E. Potter (2002), Mutual Fund Managers: Does Gender Matter?, *Journal of Business and Economic Studies*, 8:1, 1-15.

Bordo, Michael, Barry Eichengreen, Daniela Klingebiel and Maria Soledad Martinez-Peria (2001), Is the Crisis Problem Growing More Severe?, *Economic Policy*, 16:32, 52-82.

Borensztein, Eduardo and Gaston Gelos (2003), A Panic-Prone Pack? The Behavior of Emerging Market Mutual Funds, *IMF Staff Papers*, 50:1, 43-63.

Broner, Fernando A., R. Gaston Gelos and Carmen M. Reinhart (2006), *When in Peril, Retrench: Testing the Portfolio Channel of Contagion*, Journal of International Economics, 69:1, 203-230.

Brown, Keith C., W. Van Harlow and Laura T. Starks (1996), Of Tournaments and Temptations: An Analysis of Managerial Incentives in the Mutual Fund Industry, *The Journal* of Finance, 51:1, 85-110.

Brueggemann, Axel and Thomas Linne (2002), Are the Central and Eastern European transition countries still vulnerable to a financial crisis? Results from the signals approach, *BOFIT Discussion Papers* 5/2002, Bank of Finland.

Busse, Jeffrey A. (2001), Another Look at Mutual Fund Tournaments, *Journal of Financial and Quantitative Analysis*, 36:1, 53-73.

Bussiere, Matthieu and Marcel Fratzscher (2006), Towards a New Early Warning System of Financial Crises, *Journal of International Money and Finance*, 25:6, 953-973.

Byrnes, James P., David C. Miller and William D. Schafer (1999), Gender Differences in Risk-Taking: A Meta-Analysis, *Psychological Bulletin*, 125:3, 367-383.

Cai, Jun, K. C. Chan and Takeshi Yamada (1997), The Performance of Japanese Mutual Funds, *Review of Financial Studies*, 10:2, 237-273.

Calvo, Guillermo A. and Enrique G. Mendoza (2000), Rational Herd Behavior and the Globalization of Securities Markets, *Journal of International Economics*, 51:1, 79-113.

Caparrelli, Franco, Anna M. D' Arcangelis and Alexander Cassuto (2004), Herding in the Italian Stock Market: A Case of Behavioral Finance, *Journal of Behavioral Finance*, 5:4, 222-230.

Carhart, Mark M. (1997), On Persistence in Mutual Fund Performance, *The Journal of Finance*, 52:1, 57-82.

Carhart, Mark M., Ron Kaniel, David Musto and Adam Reed (1999), Mutual Fund Returns and Market Microstructure, *Wharton Working Paper* No. 11.

Caramazza, Francesco, Luca A. Ricci and Ranil Salgado (2000), Trade and Financial Contagion in Currency Crisis, *IMF Working Paper* No. 00/55, Washington D.C.

Caramazza, Francesco, Luca Ricci and Ranil Salgado (2004), International Financial Contagion in Currency Crises, *Journal of International Money and Finance*, 23:1, 51-70.

Casarin, Roberto, Lorianna Pelizzon and Andrea Piva (2003), Italian Equity Funds: Efficiency and Performance Persistence, *Atti della giornata di studio Metodi Numerici per la Finanza*, 30 May 2003, Applied Mathematics Department, University of Venice.

Casarin, Roberto, Marco Lazzarin, Lorianna Pelizzon and Domenico Sartore (2005), Relative Benchmark Rating and Persistence Analysis: Evidence from Italian Equity Funds, *The European Journal of Finance*, 11:4, 297-308.

Cerra, Valerie and Sweta C. Saxena (2002), Contagion, Monsoons, and Domestic Turmoil in Indonesia's Currency Crisis, *Review of International Economics*, 10:1, 36–44.

Cesari, Riccardo and Fabio Panetta (2002), The Performance of Italian Equity Funds, *Journal of Banking and Finance*, 26:1, 99-126.

Chari, Varadarajan and Patrick J. Kehoe (2003), Hot Money, *Journal of Political Economy*, 111:6, 1262-1292.

Chevalier, Judith and Glenn Ellison (1997), Risk Taking by Mutual Funds as a Response to Incentives, *Journal of Political Economy*,105:6, 1167-1200.

Chevalier, Judith and Glenn Ellison (1999), Career Concerns of Mutual Fund Managers, *The Quarterly Journal of Economics*, 114:2, 389-432.

Chevalier, Judith and Glenn Ellison (1999a), Are some Mutual Fund Managers Better than Others? Cross-Sectional Patterns in Behavior and Performance, *The Journal of Finance*, 54:3, 875-899.

Choe, Hyuk, Bong-Chan Kho and Rene M. Stulz (1999), Do Foreign Investors Destabilize Stock Markets? The Korean Experience in 1997, *Journal of Financial Economics*, 54:2, 227–64.

Chui, Andy C.W., Sheridan Titman and K.C. John Wei (2005), Individualism and Momentum around the World, *AFA 2006 Boston Meetings Paper*.

Choueiri, Nada and Graciela L. Kaminsky (1999), Has the Nature of Crises Changed? A Quarter Century of Currency Crises in Argentina, *IMF Working Paper* 99/152.

Ciarlone, Alessio and Giorgio Trebeschi (2005), Designing an Early Warning System for Debt Crises, *Emerging Markets Review*, 6:4, 376-395.

Clarida, Richard H., Lucio Sarno, Mark P. Taylor and Giorgio Valente (2003), The Out-of-Sample Success of Term Structure Models as Exchange Rate Predictors: A Step Beyond. *Journal of International Economics*, 60:1, 61–83.

Coval, Joshua D. and Tobias J. Moskowitz (1999), Home Bias at Home: Local Equity Preference in Domestic Portfolios, *The Journal of Finance*, 54:6, 2045-2073.

Coval, Joshua D. and Tyler Shumway (2005), Do Behavioral Biases Affect Prices?, *The Journal of Finance*, 60:1, 1-34.

Dake, Karl (1991), Orienting Dispositions in the Perception of Risk: An Analysis of Contemporary Worldviews and Cultural Biases, *Journal of Cross-Cultural Psychology*, 22:1, 61-82.

Deaves, Richard, Erik Lüders and Guo Ying Luo (2004), An Experimental Test of the Impact of Overconfidence and Gender on Trading Activity, *Working Paper*, Center for European Economic Research (ZEW) and Rutgers University.

Demirgüc-Kunt, Asli and Ross Levine (2001), Bank-Based or Market Based Financial Systems: Cross-Country Comparisons, in: Demirgüc-Kunt, Asli and Ross Levine (Eds.), *Financial Structure and Economic Growth: A Cross-Country Comparison of Banks*, Markets, and Developments, Cambrigde, MA, 81-140.

Devenow, Andrea and Ivo Welch (1996), Rational Herding in Financial Economics, European Economic Review, 40:3-5, 603-615.

Ding, Bill and Russel Wermers (2004), The Performance and Risk-Taking Behavior of Mutual Fund Managers and the Role of Fund Directors, *Working Paper.*

Disyatat, Piti and Geston Gelos (2001), The Asset Allocation of Emerging Markets Mutual Funds, *IMF Working Paper* No. 01/111, Washington D.C.

Dohmen, Thomas and Armin Falk (2006), Performance, Pay and Multi-Dimensional Sorting: Productivity, Preferences and Gender, *IZA Discussion Paper* No. 2001, Bonn.

Dohmen, Thomas, Armin Falk, David Huffmann, Uwe Sunde, Jürgen Schrupp and Gert G. Wagner (2005), Individual Risk Attitudes: New Evidence from a Large, Representative, Experimentally-Validated Survey, *IZA Discussion Paper* 1730, Bonn.

Donkers, Bas, Bertrand Melenberg and Arthur van Soest (2001), Estimating Risk Attitudes Using Lotteries: A Large Sample Approach, *Journal of Risk and Uncertainty*, 22:2, 165-195.

Douglas, Mary and Aaron Wildavsky (1982), *Risk and Culture: An Essay on the Selection of Technological and Environmental Dangers*, Berkeley et al.

Dreher, Axel, Bernhard Herz and Volker Karb (2006), Is There a Causal Link Between Currency and Debt Crises?, *International Journal of Finance and Economics*, 11:4, 305-325.

Dvorák, Tomás (2005), Do Domestic Investors Have Information Advantage? Evidence from Indonesia, *The Journal of Finance*, 55:2, 817-839.

Dwyer, Peggy D., James H. Gilkeson and John A. List (2002), Gender Differences in Revealed Risk Taking: Evidence from Mutual Fund Investors, *Economics Letters*, 76:2, 151-158.

Eckel, Catherine C. and Philip J. Grossman (2005), Forecasting Risk Attitudes: An Experimental Study of Actual and Forecast Risk Attitudes of Women and Men, *Working Paper*, Presented at Europäisches Forum Alpbach.

Eckel, Catherine C. and Philip J. Grossman (2007), Men, Women and Risk Aversion: Experimental Evidence, in: Plott, Charles R., and Vernon L. Smith (Eds.), *Handbook of Experimental Economics Results*, New York, forthcoming.

Edison, Hali J. (2003), Do Indicators of Financial Crises Work? An Evaluation of an Early Warning System, *International Journal of Finance and Economics*, 8:1, 11–53.

Edison, Hali J. and Francis E. Warnock (2004), U.S. Investors' Emerging Market Equity Portfolios: A Security-Level Analysis, *The Review of Economics and Statistics*, 86:3, 691-704.

Eichengreen, Barry J. (1999), *Toward a New International Financial Architecture*, A Practical Post-Asia-Agenda, Institute for International Economics, Washington, D.C.

Eichengreen, Barry J., Andrew K. Rose and Charles Wyplosz (1995), Exchange Market Mayhem: The Antecedents and Aftermath of Speculative Attacks, *Economic Policy*, 21:10, 249–312.

Eichengreen, Barry J., Andrew K. Rose and Charles Wyplosz (1996), Contagious Currency Crises: First Tests, *Scandinavian Journal of Economics*, 98:4, 463–484.

Estes, R. and J. Hosseini (1988), The Gender Gap on Wall Street: An Empirical Analysis of Confidence in Investment Decision Making, *Journal of Psychology*, 122:6, 577-590.

Esquivel, Gerardo and Felipe Larrain (1999), Currency Crises: Is Central America Different?, *CID Working Paper* 26, Center for International Development at Harvard University.

Fama, Eugene F. (1970), Efficient Capital Markets: A Review of Theory and Empirical Work, *The Journal of Finance*, 25:2, 383-417.

Faust, Jon, John H. Rogers and Jonathan H. Wright (2003), Exchange Rate Forecasting: the Errors We've Really Made, *Journal of International Economics*, 60:1, 35–59.

Fischhoff, Baruch, Paul Slovic and Sarah Lichtenstein (1977), Knowing with Certainty; The Appropriateness of Extreme Confidence, *Journal of Experimental Psychology*, 3:4, 552-564.

Frankel, Jeffrey A. and Andrew K. Rose (1995), Empirical Research on Nominal Exchange Rates, *Handbook of International Economics*, Vol. 3, 1689-1729.

Frankel, Jeffrey A. and Andrew K. Rose (1996), Currency Crashes in Emerging Markets: An Empirical Treatment, *Journal of International Economics*, 41:4, 351–366.

Frankel, Jeffrey A. and Andrew K. Rose (1996a), A Panel Project on Purchasing Power Parity: Mean Reversion Within and Between Countries, *Journal of International Economics*, 40:1-2, 209-224.

Fratzscher, Marcel (2003), On Currency Crises and Contagion, *International Journal of Finance and Economics*, 8:2, 109–129.

Frederking, Lauretta C. (2002), Is there an Endogenous Relationship between Culture and Economic Development?, *Journal of Economic Behavior and Organization*, 48:2, 105-126.

French, Kenneth R. and James M. Poterba (1991), Investor Diversification and International Equity Markets, *American Economic Review*, 81:2, 222-226.

Frenkel, Michael and Lukas Menkhoff (2000), *Stable World Finances? The Debate for a New International Financial Architecture* [Monography in German], Springer, Berlin et al.

Frenkel, Michael, Alexander Karmann, Bert Scholtens (Eds.) (2004), *Sovereign Risk and Financial Crises*, Berlin et al.

Froot, Kenneth A., David S. Scharfstein and Jeremy C. Stein (1992), Herd on the Street: Informational Inefficiencies in a Market with Short-term Speculation, *The Journal of Finance*, 47:4, 1461-1484.

Garvey, Ryan and Anthony Murphy (2004), Are Professional Traders Too Slow to Realize Their Losses?, *Financial Analysts Journal*, 60:4, 35–43.

Gehrig, Thomas (1993), An Information Based Explanation of the Domestic Bias in International Equity Investment, *Scandinavian Journal of Economics*, 95:1, 97-109.

Gehrig, Thomas and Lukas Menkhoff (2004), The Use of Flow Analysis in Foreign Exchange: Explanatory Evidence, *Journal of International Money and Finance*, 23:4, 573-594.

Gehrig, Thomas and Lukas Menkhoff (2005), The Rise of Fund Managers in Foreign Exchange: Will Fundamentals Ultimately Dominate? *The World Economy*, 28:4, 519-540.

Gelos, R. Gaston, and Shang-Jin Wei (2005), Transparency and International Portfolio Holdings, *The Journal of Finance*, 60:6, 2987-3020.

Gervais, Simon and Terrance Odean (2001), Learning to be Overconfident, *Review of Financial Studies*, 14:1, 1-27.

Glaser, Markus and Martin Weber (2004), Overconfidence and Trading Volume, *Working Paper,* University of Mannheim.

Glaser, Markus, Thomas Langer and Martin Weber (2005), Overconfidence of Professionals and Lay Men: Individual Differences Within and Between

Tasks, *Sonderforschungs-bereich 504 Publications* No. 05-25, University of Mannheim.

Glick, Reuben and Andrew K. Rose (1999), Contagion and Trade: Why Are Currency Crises Regional?, *Journal of International Money and Finance*, 18:4, 603-617.

Gneezy, Uri, Muriel Niederle and Aldo Rustichini (2003), Performance in Competitive Environments: Gender Differences, *The Quarterly Journal of Economics*, 118:3,1049-1074.

Gneezy, Uri and Aldo Rustichini (2004), Gender and Competition at a Young Age, *American Economic Review*, 89:2, 386-391.

Goldfajn, Ilan and Rodriguez O. Valdés (1998), Are Currency Crises Predictable? *European Economic Review*, 42:3-5, 873–885.

Goldstein, Morris, Graciela L. Kaminsky and Carmen M. Reinhart (2000), *Assessing Financial Vulnerability – An Early Warning System for Emerging Markets*, Institute for International Economics, Washington, D.C.

Goriaev, Alexei P., Theo E. Nijman and Bas J. M. Werker (2005), Yet Another Look at Mutual Fund Tournaments, *Journal of Empirical Finance*, 12:1, 127-137.

Graham, John R. (1999), Herding among Investment Newsletters: Theory and Evidence, *The Journal of Finance*, 54:1, 237-268.

Graham, John R., Campbell R. Harvey and Hai Huang (2005), Investor Competence, Trading Frequency, and Home Bias, *NBER Working Paper* No. 11426, Cambridge, MA.

Grande, Guiseppe and Fabio Panetta (2002), The Performance of Italian Equity Funds, *Journal of Banking and Finance*, 26:1, 99-126.

Green, Eva G. T., Jean-Claude Deschamps and Dario Páez (2005), Variation of Individualism and Collectivism within and between 20 Countries – A Typological Analysis, *Journal of Cross-Cultural Psychology*, 36:3, 321-339.

Grinblatt, Mark and Matti Keloharju (2001), What Makes Investors Trade?, *The Journal of Finance*, 56:2, 589–616.

Grinblatt, Mark, Sheridan Titman und Russ Wermers (1995), Momentum Investment Strategies, Portfolio Performance, and Herding: A Study of Mutual Fund Behavior, *American Economic Review*, 85:5, 1088-1105.

Guiso, Luigi and Tullio Jappelli (2002), Stockholdings in Italy, *Working Paper* No. 82, Centre for Studies in Economics and Finance, University of Salerno.

Guiso, Luigi, Michael Haliassos and Tullio Jappelli (2003), Household Stockholding in Europe: Where Do We Stand and Where Do We Go?, *Economic Policy*, 18:36, 123–170.

Gupta, Nabanita D., Anders Poulsen and Marie-Claire Villeval (2005), Male and Female Competitive Behavior – Experimental Evidence, *CNRS Working Paper* No. 05-12, Ecully.

Hall, Edward T. (1985), *Hidden Differences: Studies in International Communication*, Hamburg.

Hall, Edward T. and Mildred R. Hall(1990), *Understanding Cultural Differences: Germans, French and Americans*, Yarmouth, ME.

Hartmann, Philipp, Stefan Straetmans and Caspar G. de Vries (2004), Fundamentals and Joint Currency Crises, *ECB Working Paper Series* 324, March.

Hayakawa, Hiroaki (2000), Bounded Rationality, Social and Cultural Norms, and Interdependence via Reference Groups, *Journal of Economic Behavior and Organization*, 43:1, 1-34.

Heath, Chip and Amos Tversky (1991), Preferences and Belief: Ambiguity and Competence in Choice under Uncertainty, *Journal of Risk and Uncertainty*, 4:1, 5-28.

Hey, John D. and Andrea Morone (2004), Do Markets Drive out Lemmings – or Vice Versa? *Economica*, 71, 637-659.

Hirshleifer, David (2001), Investor Psychology and Asset Pricing, *The Journal of Finance*, 56:4, 1533-1597.

Hirshleifer, David, Avanidhar Subrahmanyam and Sheridan Titman (1994), Security Analysis and Trading Patterns when some investors receive information before others, *The Journal of Finance*, 49:5, 1665-1698.

Hofstede, Geert H. (1980), *Culture's Consequences: International Differences in Work-Related Values*, Beverly Hills, CA.

Hofstede, Geert H. (2001), *Culture's Consequences: Comparing Values, Behaviors, Institutions, and Organizations across Nations*, Thousand Oaks, CA.

Hong, Harrison, Jeffrey D. Kubrik, and Amit Solomon (2000), Security analysts' career concerns and herding of earnings forecasts, *RAND Journal of Economics*, 31:1, 121-144.

Hong, Kiseok and Aaron Tornell (2005), Recovery from a Currency Crisis, *Journal of Development Economics*, 76:1, 71-96.

House, Robert J., Paul J. Hanges, Mansour Javidan, Peter W. Dorfman and Vipin Gupta (Eds.) (2004), *Culture, Leadership, and Organizations, The GLOBE Study of 62 Societies*, Thousand Oaks, CA.

Huberman, Gur (2001), Familiarity Breeds Investment, *The Review of Financial Studies*, 14:3, 659-680.

Hwang, Alvin, Anne Marie Francesco and Eric Kessler (2003), The Relationship between Individualism-Collectivism, Face, and Feedback and Learning Processes in Hong Kong, Singapore, and the United States, *Journal of Cross-Cultural Psychology*, 34:1, 72-91.

Jianakoplos, Nancy A. and Alexandra Bernasek (1998), Are Women More Risk Averse?, *Economic Inquiry*, 36:4, 620-630.

Kagitcibasi, Cigdem (1997), Individualism and Collectivism, John W. Berry, Marshall H. Segall, Cigdem Kagitcibasi (Eds.) *Handbook of Cross-Cultural Psychology Vol. 3* , Boston et al., 1-49.

Kahnemann, Daniel and Amos Tversky (1979), Prospect Theory: An Analysis of Decision under Risk, *Econometrica*, 47:2, 263–291.

Kamin, Steven B., John W. Schindler and Shawna L. Samuel (2001), The Contribution of Domestic and External Factors to Emerging Market Devaluation Crises: An Early Warning Systems Approach. Board of Governors of the Federal Reserve System (U.S.), *International Finance Discussion Paper* No. 711, Washington D.C.

Kaminsky, Graciela L. (1998), Currency and Banking Crises: The Early Warnings of Distress, Board of Governors of the Federal Reserve System (U.S.), *International Finance Discussion Paper* No. 629, Washington D.C.

Kaminsky, Graciela L. (2006), Currency Crises: Are They All the Same?, *Journal of International Money and Finance*, 25:3, 503-527.

Kaminsky, Graciela L., Saul Lizondo and Carmen M. Reinhart (1998), Leading Indicators of Currency Crises, *IMF Staff Papers* 45:1, 1–48.

Kaminsky, Graciela, Richard K. Lyons and Sergio L. Schmukler (2001), Mutual Fund Investments in Emerging Markets: An Overview, *World Bank Economic Review*, 15:2, 315-340.

Kaminsky, Graciela, Richard K. Lyons and Sergio L. Schmukler (2004), Managers, Investors, and Crises: Mutual Fund Strategies in Emerging Markets, *Journal of International Economics*, 64:1, 113-134.

Kaminsky, Graciela L. and Carmen M. Reinhart (1999), The Twin Crises: The Causes of Banking and Balance of Payments Problems, *American Economic Review*, 89:3, 473–500.

Kaminsky, Graciela L. and Carmen M. Reinhart (2000), On Crises, Contagion, and Confusion, *Journal of International Economics*, 51:1, 145–168.

Kaminsky, Graciela L., Camen M. Reinhart and Carlos A. Végh (2003). The Unholy Trinity of Financial Contagion, *Journal of Economic Perspectives*, 17:4, 51-74.

Kapteyn, Arie and Federica Teppa (2002), Subjective Measures of Risk Aversion and Portfolio Choice, *Center for Economic Research Discussion Paper* No. 11, Tilburg University.

Karlsson, Anders and Lars Nordén (2007), Home Sweet Home: Home Bias and International Diversification among Individual Investors, *Journal of Banking and Finance*, forthcoming.

Karolyi, Andrew G. (2003), Does International Financial Contagion Really Exist? *International Finance*, 6:2, 178-199.

Kemmelmeier, Markus, Eugene Burnstein, Krum Krumov, Petia Genkova, Chie Kanagawa, Matthew S. Hirshberg, Hans-Peter Erb, Grazyna Wieczorkowska and Kimberly A. Noels (2003), Individualism, Collectivism, and Authoritarianism in Seven Societies, *Journal of Cross-Cultural Psychology*, 34:3, 304-322.

Kilka, Michael and Martin Weber (2000), Home-Bias in International Stock Return Expectations, *Journal of Psychology and Financial Markets,* 1:3/4, 176-193.

Kim, Kenneth A. and John R. Nofsinger (2005), Institutional Herding, Business Groups, and Economic Regimes: Evidence from Japan, *Journal of Business*, 78:1, 213-242.

Kim, Woochan and Shang-Jin Wei (2002), Foreign Portfolio Investors before and during a Crisis, *Journal of International Economics*, 56:1, 77-96.

Khorana, Ajay (1996), Top Management Turnover: An Empirical Investigation of Mutual Fund Managers, *Journal of Financial Economics*, 40:3, 403-427.

Khorana, Ajay, Henri Servaes and Peter Turfano (2005), Explaining the Size of the Mutual Fund Industry Around the World, *The Journal of Financial Economics*, 78:1, 145-185.

Komulainen, Tuomas and Johanna Lukkarila (2003), What Drives Financial Crises in Emerging Markets?, *Emerging Markets Review*, 4:3, 248–272.

Krause, Andreas, K. C. John Wie and Zhishu Yang (2006), Behavioral Bias of Traders: Evidence for the Disposition and Reverse Disposition Effect, *EFM 2006: Symposium Behavioral Finance Discussion Paper* No. 63.

Kroeber, Alfred L. and Clyde Kluckhohn (1952), Culture: A Critical Review of Concepts and Definitions, *Papers of the Peabody Museum of American Archaelogy and Ethnology,* 47:1, Harvard University, Cambridge, Mass.

Kühnen, Ulrich, Bettina Hannover, Ute Roeder, Ashiq Ali Shah, Benjamin Schubert, Arnold Upmeyer and Saliza Zakaria (2001), Cross-Cultural Variations in Identifiying Embedded Figures: Comparisons from the United States, Germany, Russia, and Malaysia, *Journal of Cross-Cultural Psychology*, 32:3, 348-364.

Kumar, Manmohan, Uma Moorthy and William Perraudin (2002), Predicting Emerging Market Currency Crashes, *IMF Working Paper* No. 02/07, Washington D.C.

Lakonishok, Josef, Andrei Shleifer and Robert W. Vishny (1992), The Impact of Institutional Trading on Stock Prices, *Journal of Financial Economics*, 32:1, 23-43.

Lamont, Owen A. (2002), Macroeconomic Forecasts and Microeconomic Forecasters, *Journal of Economic Behavior and Organization*, 48:3, 265-280.

Lenney, Ellen (1977), Women's Self-Confidence in Achievement Settings, *Psychological Bulletin*, 84:1, 1-13.

Lewellen, Wilbur G., Ronald C. Lease and Gary G. Schlarbaum (1977), Patterns of Investment Strategy and Behavior Among Institutional Investors, *The Journal of Business*, 50:3, 296-333.

Li, Wei and Ashish Tiwari (2006), On the Consequences of Mutual Fund Tournaments, *Working Paper*, University of Iowa.

Locke, Peter R. and Steven C. Mann (2001), House Money and Overconfidence on the Trading Floor, *Working Paper*, George Washington University.

Locke, Peter R. and Steven C. Mann (2003), Prior Outcomes and Risky Choices by Professional Traders, *Working Paper*, The George Washington University.

Locke, Peter R. and Steven C. Mann (2005), Professional Trader Discipline and Trade Disposition, *Journal of Financial Economics*, 76:2, 401-444.

Lütje, Torben (2006), To Be Good or To Be Better?, *EFM 2006: Symposium Behavioral Finance Discussion Paper* No. 38.

Lütje, Torben and Lukas Menkhoff (2004), What Drives Home Bias? Evidence from Fund Managers' Views, *Discussion Paper* No 296, Leibniz Universität Hannover.

Lütje, Torben and Lukas Menkhoff (2005), Fund Management in Germany: What do the actors think and do? [Article in German], *Kredit und Kapital*, 38:2, 285-311.

Lundeberg, Mary A., Paul W. Fox and Judith Punccohar (1992), Highly Confident but Wrong, Gender Differences and Similarities in Confidence Judgments, *Journal of Educational Psychology*, 86:1, 114-121.

MacDonald, Ronald (1999), Exchange Rate Behaviour: Are Fundamentals Important?, *Economic Journal*, 109:459, 673–691.

Markowitz, Harry (1952), Portfolio Selection, *The Journal of Finance*, 7:1, 77-91.

Martinez-Peria, Maria S. (2002), A Regime Switching Approach to Studying Speculative Attacks: A Focus on EMS Crises, *Empirical Economics*, 27:2, 299–334.

Masson, Paul (1999), Contagion: Macroeconomic Models with Multiple Equilibria, *Journal of International Money and Finance*, 18:4, 587-602.

Maug, Ernst and Narayan Naik (1996), Herding and Delegated Portfolio Management, *IFA Working Paper* No. 223-1996, London Business School.

Meese, Richard A. and Kenneth S. Rogoff (1983), Empirical Exchange Rate Models of the Seventies: Do They Fit Out of Sample?, *Journal of International Economics*, 14:1-2, 3-24.

Menkhoff, Lukas (1997), Examining the Use of Technical Currency Analysis, *International Journal of Finance and Economics*, 2:4, 307-318.

Menkhoff, Lukas and Ulrich Schmidt (2005), The Use of Trading Strategies by Fund Managers: Some First Survey Evidence, *Applied Economics*, 37, 1719-1730.

Menkhoff, Lukas, Ulrich Schmidt and Torsten Brozynsky (2006), The Impact of Experience on Risk Taking, Overconfidence, and Herding of Fund Managers: Complementary Survey Evidence, *European Economic Review*, 50:7, 1753-1766.

Merritt, Ashleigh (2000), Culture in the Cockpit: Do Hofstede's Dimensions Replicate? *Journal of Cross-Cultural Psychology*, 31:3, 283-301.

Mishkin, Frederic S. (2001), Financial Policies and the Prevention of Financial Crises in Emerging Market Countries, *NBER Working Paper* No. 8087, Cambridge, MA.

Moreno, Ramon and Bharat Trehan (2000), Common Shocks and Currency Crises, *Working Paper Federal Reserve Bank of San Francisco* 00-05.

Moser, Thomas (2003), What is International Financial Contagion?, *International Finance*, 6:2, 157-178.

NCES (2005), *Comparative Indicators of Education in the United States and Other G8 Countries: 2004*, National Center for Education Statistics, Washington.

Nesdale, Drew and Mikako Naito (2005), Individualism-Collectivism and the attitudes to School Bullying of Japanese and Australian Students, *Journal of Cross-Cultural Psychology*, 36:5, 537-556.

Niederle, Muriel and Lise Vesterlund (2007), Do Women Shy Away from Competition? Do Men Comepete Too Much?, *The Quarterly Journal of Economics*, forthcoming.

Niessen, Alexandra and Stefan Ruenzi (2006), Sex Matters: Gender and Mutual Funds, *CFR Working Paper*, No. 06-01.

Oberlechner, Thomas (2001), Importance of Technical and Fundamental Analysis in the European Foreign Exchange Market, *International Journal of Finance and Economics*, 6:1, 81-93.

Oberlechner, Thomas and Carol Osler (2006), Overconfidence in Currency Markets, *Working Paper*, Brandeis University.

Odean, Terence (1998): Are Investors Reluctant to Realize Their Losses?, *The Journal of Finance*, 53:5, 1775–1798.

Odean, Terrance (1998a), Volume, Volatility, Price, and Profit When All Traders Are Above Average, *The Journal of Finance*, 53:6, 1887–1934.

Odean, Terrance (1999), Do Investors Trade Too Much?, *The American Economic Review*, 89:5, 1279–1298.

OECD (2005), *Education at Glance 2005*, Centre for Educational Research and Innovation, Paris.

Olsen, Robert A. and Constance M. Cox (2001), The Influence of Gender on the Perception and Responses to Investment Risk: The Case of Professional Investors, *The Journal of Psychology and Financial Markets*, 2:1, 29-36.

Ong, Li L. and Amadou N. R. Sy (2004), The Role of Mature Market Mutual Funds in Emerging Markets: Myth or Mayhem?, *IMF Working Paper* No. 04/133, Washington D.C.

Osband, Kent and Caroline Van Rijckeghem (2000), Safety from Currency Crashes, *IMF Staff Papers*, 47:2, 238–258.

Otten, Roger and Dennis Bams (2002), European Mutual Fund Performance, *European Financial Management*, 8:1, 75-101.

Otten, Rogér and Mark Schweitzer (2002), Comparison Between the European and the U.S. Mutual Fund Industry, *Managerial Finance*, 28:1, 14-35.

Oysermann, Daphna, Heather M. Coon and Markus Kemmelmeier (2002), Rethinking Individualism and Collectivism: Evaluation of Theoretical Assumptions and Meta-analyses, *Psychological Bulletin*, 128:1, 3-72.

Pasternak, Christoph (2003), The Signals Approach as an Early Warning System for Currency Crises. An Application to Transition Economies – With Special Emphasis on Poland, *International Finance Paper* 0304001.

Pozo, Susan and Catalina Amuedo-Dorantes (2003), Statistical Distributions and the Identification of Currency Crises, *Journal of International Money and Finance*, 22:4, 591–609.

Prendergast, Canince and Lars Stole (1996), Impetuous Youngsters and Jaded Oldtimers: Acquiring a Reputation for Learning, *Journal of Political Economy*, 104:6, 1105-34.

Rayner, Steve and Robin Cantor (1987), How Far is Safe Enough? The Cultural Approach to Societal Technology Choice, *Risk Analysis*, 7:1, 3-13.

Reinhart, Carmen M. (2002), Default, Currency Crises and Sovereign Credit Ratings, *World Bank Economic Review*, 16:2, 151-170.

Renn, Ortwin and Bernd Rohrmann (2000), Cross-Cultural Risk Perception: State and Challenges, Renn, Ortwin and Bernd Rohrmann (Eds.) (2000), *Cross-Cultural Risk Perception – A Survey of Empirical Studies*, Dordrecht, Boston, London, 210-232.

Rohrmann, Bernd and Ortwin Renn (2000), Risk Perception Research: An Introduction, Renn, Ortwin and Bernd Rohrmann (Eds.) (2000), *Cross-Cultural Risk Perception – A Survey of Empirical Studies*, Dordrecht, Boston, London, 11-53.

Rogoff, Kenneth S. (1996), The Purchasing Power Parity Puzzle, *Journal of Economic Literature*, 34:2, 647–668.

Sachs, Jeffrey, Aaron Tornell and Andres Velasco (1996), Financial Crises in Emerging Markets: The Lessons from 1995, *Brookings Papers on Economic Activity*, 27:1, 147–199.

Salvatore, Dominick (1999), Could the Financial# Crisis in East Asia Have Been Predicted?, *Journal of Policy Modeling*, 21:3, 341-347.

Sarno, Lucio and Mark P. Taylor (2002), The Economics of Exchange Rates, Cambridge University Press, Cambridge et al.

Savona, Roberto (2006), Tax-induced Dissimilarities Between Domestic and Foreign Mutual Funds in Italy, *Economic Notes*, 35:2, 173-202.

Savona, Roberto (2006a), Do Mutual Funds Reflect a Country-Specific Investment Philosophy? The Italian Case, *Applied Financial Economics*, 16:4, 303-318.

Scharfstein, David S. und Jeremy C. Stein (1990), Herd Behavior and Investment, *The American Economic Review*, 80:3, 465-479.

Schmidt, Ulrich and Stefan Traub (2002), An Experimental Test of Loss Aversion, *Journal of Risk and Uncertainty*, 25:3, 233-249.

Schmidt, Ulrich and Horst Zank (2005), What is Loss Aversion, *Journal of Risk and Uncertainty*, 30:2, 157-167.

Schubert, Renate, Martin Brown, Matthias Gysler and Hans Wolfgang Brachinger (1999), Financial Decision-Making: Are Women Really More Risk-Averse?, *The American Economic Review*, 89:2, 381-385.

Seasholes, Mark S. (2004), Re-examining Information Asymmetries in Emerging Stock Markets, *Working Paper* University of Berkeley.

Shafiro, Margarita V., Melissa J. Himelein and Deborah L. Best (2003), Differences in Individualism/Collectivism and Gender Attitudes, *Journal of Cross-Cultural Psychology*, 34:3, 297-303.

Shapira, Zur and Itzhak Venezia (2001), Patterns of Behavior of Professionally Managed and Independent Investors, *Journal of Banking and Finance*, 25:8, 1573–1587.

Sharpe, William (1964), Capital Asset Prices: A Theory of Market Equilibrium under Condition of Risk, *The Journal of Finance*, 19:3, 425-442.

Shefrin, Hersh and Meir Statman (1985), The Disposition to Sell Winners Too Early and Ride Losers Too Long: Theory and Evidence, *The Journal of Finance*, 40:3, 777–790.

Shiller, Robert J. (2003), From Efficient Markets Theory to Behavioral Finance, *Journal of Economic Perspectives*, 17:1, 83-104.

Shiller, Robert J. and John Pound (1989), Survey Evidence on Diffusion of Interest and Information Among Investors, *Journal of Economic Behavior and Organization*, 12:1, 47-66.

Shuper, Paul A., Richard M. Sorrentino, Yasunao Otsubo, Gordon Hodson and A. Marie Walker (2004), A Theory of Uncertainty Orientation, *Journal of Cross-Cultural Psychology*, 35:4, 460-480.

Sias, Richard W. (2004), Institutional Herding, *Review of Financial Studies*, 17:1, 165-206.

Sierminska, Eva, Andrea Brandolini and Timothy M. Smeeding (2006), Comparing Wealth Distribution Across Rich Countries: First Results from the Luxembourg Wealth Study, *LWS Working Paper* No. 1.

Sirri, Erik R. and Peter Tufano (1998), Costly Search and Mutual Fund Flows, *The Journal of Finance* 53:5, 1589–1622.

Sjöberg, Lennart, Daniela Kolarova, Alina-Anca Rucai and Marie-Louise Bernström (2000), Risk Perception in Bulgaria and Romania, Renn, Ortwin and Bernd Rohrmann (Eds.) (2000), *Cross-Cultural Risk Perception – A Survey of Empirical Studies*, Dordrecht, Boston, London, 145-183.

Slovic, Paul, James Flynn, C.K. Mertz, Marc Poumadere and Claire Mays (2000), Nuclear Power and the Public: A comparative Study of Risk Perception in France and the United States, Renn, Ortwin and Bernd Rohrmann (Eds.) (2000), *Cross-Cultural Risk Perception – A Survey of Empirical Studies*, Dordrecht, Boston, London, 55-102.

Slovic, Paul, Baruch Fischhoff and Sarah Lichtenstein (2000a), Facts and Fears: Understanding Perceived Risk, in: Slovic, Paul (Ed.), *The Perception of Risk*, Earthscan/James & James, London, 137-153.

Strong, Norman and Xinzhong Xu (2003), Understanding the Equity Home Bias: Evidence from Survey Data, *The Review of Economics and Statistics*, 85:2, 307-312.

Stulz, Rene M. (1981), On the Effects of Barriers to International Investment, *The Journal of Finance*, 36:4, 923-934.

Stulz, René M. and Rohan Williamson (2003), Culture, Openness, and Finance, *Journal of Financial Economics*, 70:3, 313-349.

Sunden, Annika E. and Brian J. Surette (1998), Gender Differences in the Allocation of Assets in Retirement Savings Plans, *The American Economic Review*, 88:2, 207-211.

Svenson, Ola (1981), Are We All Less Risky and More Skillful Than Our Fellow Drivers?, *Acta Psychologica*, 47:2, 143-148.

Sy, Amadou N. R. (2004), Rating the Rating Agencies: Anticipating Currency Crises or Debt Crises?, *Journal of Banking and Finance*, 28:11, 2845-2867.

Tesar, Linda L. and Ingrid M. Werner (1995), Home Bias and High Turnover, *Journal of International Money and Finance*, 14:4, 467-492.

Thompson, Michael, Richard Ellis and Aaron Wildavksy (1990), *Cultural Theory*, Boulder, CO.

Tornell, Aaron (1999), Common Fundamentals in the Tequila and Asian Crises, *NBER Working Paper* No. 7139, Cambridge, MA.

Triadis, Harry C. (1995), *Individualism and Collectivism*, Boulder, CO.

Tversky, Amos and Daniel Kahneman (1991), Loss Aversion in Riskless Choice: A Reference Dependent Model, *The Quarterly Journal of Economics* 107:4, 1039-1061.

Tversky, Amos and Daniel Kahneman (1992), Advances in Prospect Theory: Cumulative Representation, *Journal of Risk and Uncertainty*, 5:4, 297-323.

Van Rijckeghem, Caroline and Beatrice Weder (2001), Sources of Contagion: Is it Finance or Trade? *Journal of International Economics*, 54:2, 293-308.

Walter, Andreas and Friedrich M. Weber (2006), Herding in the German Mutual Fund Industry, *European Financial Management*, 12:3, 375-406.

Walter, Ingo (1999), The Global Asset Management Industry: Competitive Structure and Performance, *Financial Markets, Institutions & Instruments*, 8:1, 1-78.

Weber, Elke U., Niklas Siebenmorgen and Martin Weber (2005), Communicating Asset Risk: How Name Recognition and the Format of Historic Volatility Information Affect Risk Perception and Investment Decisions, *Risk Analysis*, 25:3, 597-609.

Weinstein, Neil D. (1980), Unrealistic Optimism about Future Life Events, *Journal of Personality and Social Psychology*, 39, 806-820.

Wermers, Russ (1999), Mutual Fund Herding and the Impact on Stock Prices, *The Journal of Finance*, 54:2, 58.

World Bank (2001), *Finance for Growth: Policy Choices in a Volatile World*, Oxford et al.

Studien zu Internationalen Wirtschaftsbeziehungen

Herausgegeben von Prof. Dr. Michael Frenkel

Band 1 Christiane Nickel: Insider und Outsider bei der Osterweiterung der Europäischen Währungsunion. 2002.

Band 2 Georg Stadtmann: Noise-Trader auf Devisenmärkten. Viel Lärm um Nichts? 2002.

Band 3 Wolf-Heimo Grieben: Trade and Technology as Competing Explanations for Rising Inequality. An Endogenous Growth Perspective. 2003.

Band 4 Alexander Mende: Order Flow Analyses and Foreign Exchange Dealing. 2005.

Band 5 Torsten Wezel: Determinants of Foreign Direct Investment in Emerging Markets. An Empirical Study of FDI Flows from Germany and its Banking Sector. 2005.

Band 6 Steffen Kern: The Behaviour of Interest Groups in Trade and Industry Towards Monetary Policy and Central Banks. Theory and Evidence on Germany and the Euro Area. 2006.

Band 7 Holger Michaelis: Kapitalbilanzliberalisierung in der Volksrepublik China und ihre Einbettung in den volkswirtschaftlichen Reformprozess. 2006.

Band 8 Ralf Fendel: Monetary Policy, Interest Rate Rules, and the Term Structure of Interest Rates. Theoretical Considerations and Empirical Implications. 2007.

Band 9 Katja Funke: Balance of Payments Issues in Central and Eastern European Countries' Run-Up to Euro Area Accession. 2007.

Band 10 Isabell Koske: Equilibrium Exchange Rate Models, the Euro and the 2004 Expansion of the EU. 2007.

Band 11 Dennis Stremmel: Protektionsmöglichkeiten in der WTO? Geistige Eigentumsrechte im TRIPs-Abkommen und die Forderung nach Sozial- und Umweltstandards. 2007.

Band 12 Daniela Beckmann: From Early Warning Systems to Asset Managers' Behavior: Evidence for Mature and Emerging Markets. 2008.

www.peterlang.de

Robert Schmidt

The Behavioral Economics of Foreign Exchange Markets

A Psychological View on Human Expectation Formation in Foreign Exchange Markets

Frankfurt am Main, Berlin, Bern, Bruxelles, New York, Oxford, Wien, 2006.
XX, 334 pp., num. fig., tab. and graf.
European University Studies: Series 5, Economics and Management. Vol. 3178
ISBN 978-3-631-54814-1 · pb. € 56.50*

This book deals with psychological factors, which may be important for understanding the observable exchange rate movements. Thus, the study belongs to the new research field of behavioral economics, which considers the relevance of psychological factors in economic contexts. The main objective of behavioral economists is to develop a more realistic view of the actual human behavior in the context of economics. Central to the concept of behavioral economics is the assumption that humans' actual behavior deviates from the ideal of economic rationality due to at least two reasons: first, decisions are usually based on an incomplete information basis and, second, the information processing of human beings is limited by their computational capacities. Due to these limitations people are forced to apply simple heuristics in information processing. Our aim is to analyze the relevance of simple heuristics in the context of foreign exchange markets. In our view, the decision situation in foreign exchange markets can serve as a prime example for decision situations in which simple heuristics are especially relevant as the complexity of the decision situation is very high.

Contents: The exchange rate disconnect puzzle · Patterns of exchange rate dynamics and the role of speculation · Behavioral economics as an alternative approach · Experimental and empirical evidence

FSC
www.fsc.org
MIX
Papier | Fördert gute Waldnutzung
FSC® C083411

Kolibri 360 GmbH
Ferdinand-Jühlke-Straße 7
99095 Erfurt, Deutschland
produktsicherheit@kolibri360.de

Druck:
CPI Druckdienstleistungen GmbH
im Auftrag der
Kolibri 360 GmbH
Ferdinand-Jühlke-Str. 7
99095 Erfurt